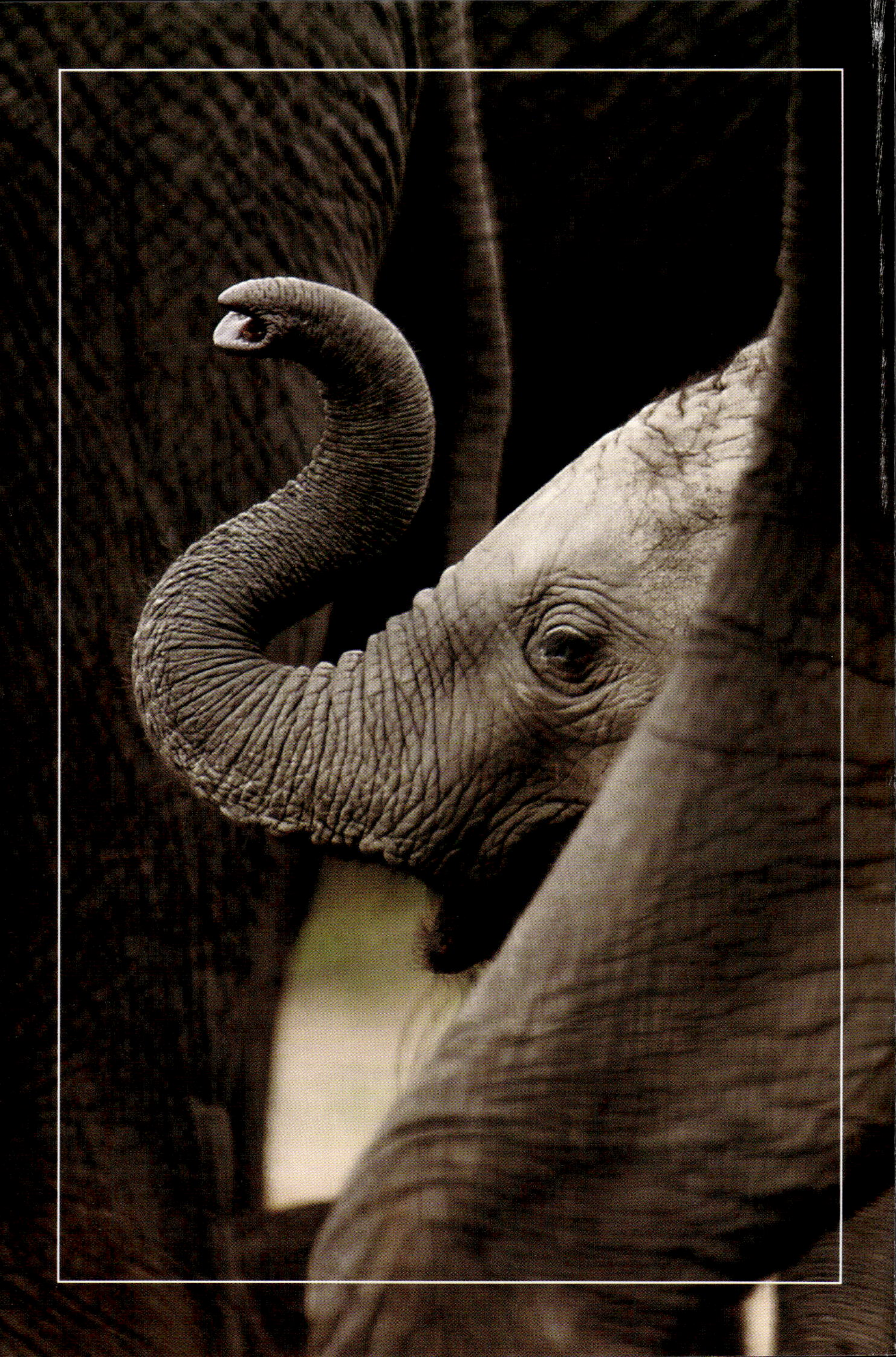

CONTENTS

WILDLIFE PHOTOGRAPHY IN BOTSWANA

A PRACTICAL GUIDE

First print run and Copyright - June 2010

Design and layout by Sarah Kerr
Map courtesy of Sarah Kerr

Part 3

Part 4

Introduction

Botswana is undoubtedly one of the greatest wildlife destinations in Africa. Landlocked and mostly covered by the Kalahari sands, the country supports an impressive diversity of species in vast areas of untouched wilderness. Varying landscapes, habitat and climatic conditions offer both the amateur and professional wildlife photographer remarkable opportunities to capture a huge variety of flora and fauna the whole year round. Over 35 percent of the country is protected through a system of National Parks, Game Reserves, Forest Reserves and private concessions. This, coupled with a spectacular choice of lodges, camps and mobile safari operations, is what makes Botswana truly unique.

This book is designed to improve your photographic skills by sharing our combined experience and intimate knowledge of photographing wildlife in Botswana. We hope that by so doing, you will return home with a better understanding of your equipment, the wildlife, and ultimately with great photographic memories of your safari.

One of photography's appeals is its subjectivity - you have the power to portray a scene as you wish. It requires technical ability but more important is an artistic eye for composition, subject and light. The digital era and technological advances have taken the realm of photography away from a few elite individuals and placed it into the palms of the masses. Once you have grasped the basic technical concepts, passion for your subject and plenty of patience are the most important aspects to creating excellent wildlife photographs. We view the camera as a tool by which we can record the incredible behaviour witnessed in the wilderness, but with a wider goal of helping to create an awareness for the biodiversity that is under such threat across the globe.

James Gifford and Steven Stockhall

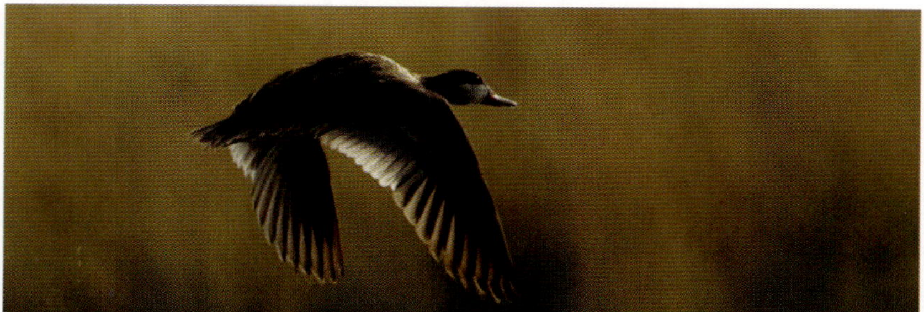

How to Use this Book

The aim of this guidebook is to stimulate you to think about composition and photographic techniques through our images. The 'Technical Elements' chapter is best read chronologically, but if you want to look up a specific term, shooting technique or species, the index will refer you to photographic examples (in bold), relevant tip boxes, as well as the textual explanations. Each photograph includes a caption detailing the camera settings, equipment used and location whilst also explaining how we achieved the desired effect. The glossary should help with any terminology.

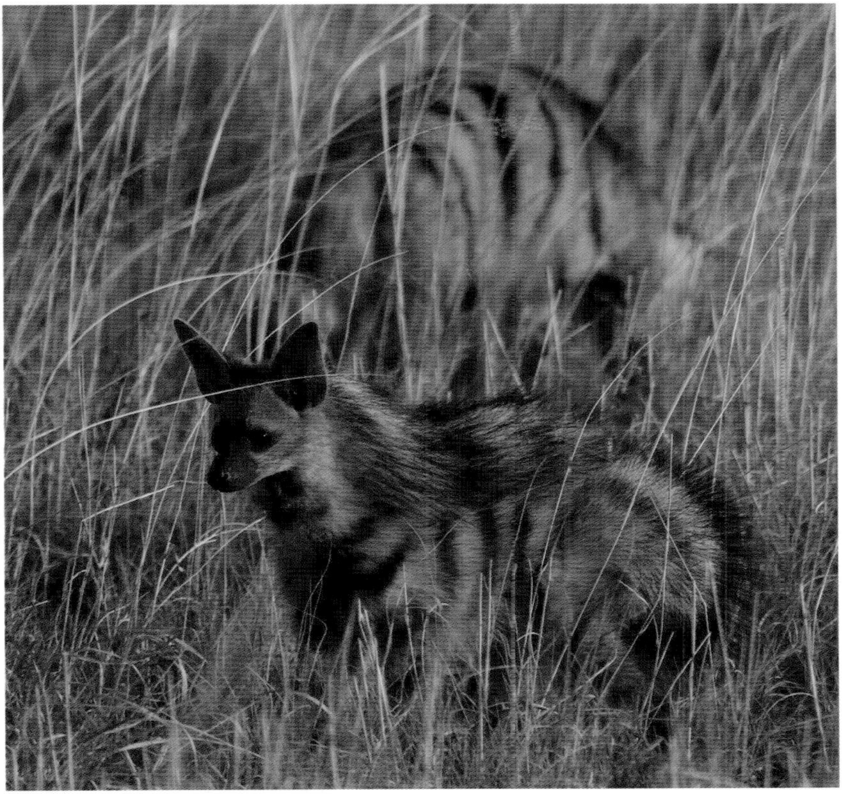

▲ ***Aardwolf Cubs, Makgadikgadi Pans. DSLR, 100-400mm Lens, f/5.6 @ 1/640, ISO 250. JG***

◀ ***Red-billed Teal, Makgadikgadi Pans National Park. DSLR, 100-400mm Lens, f/6.3 @1/2500, ISO 400. JG***

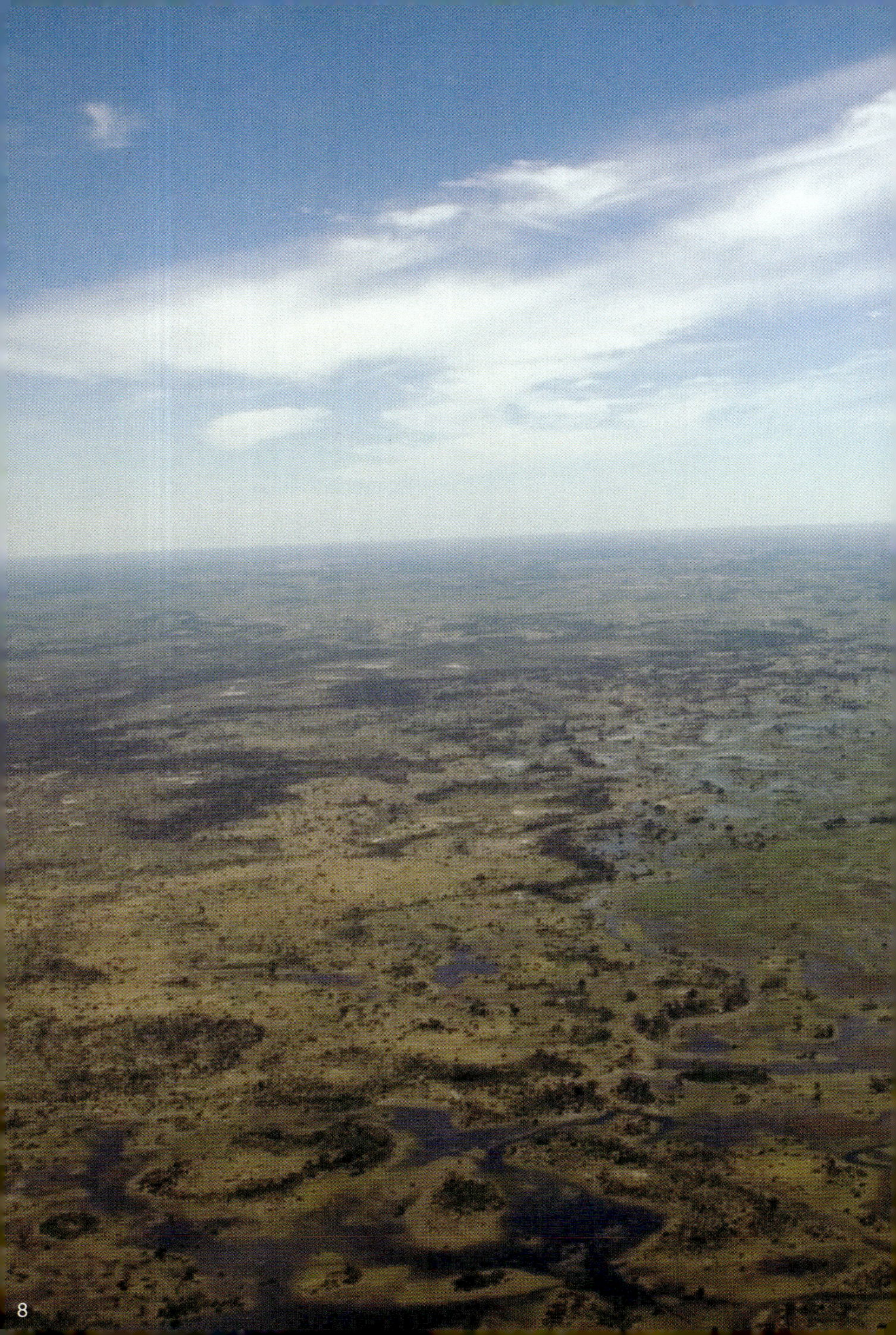

DESTINATION BOTSWANA

THE CALL OF THE WILD

"I just wish the world was twice as big and half of it was still unexplored." *David Attenborough*

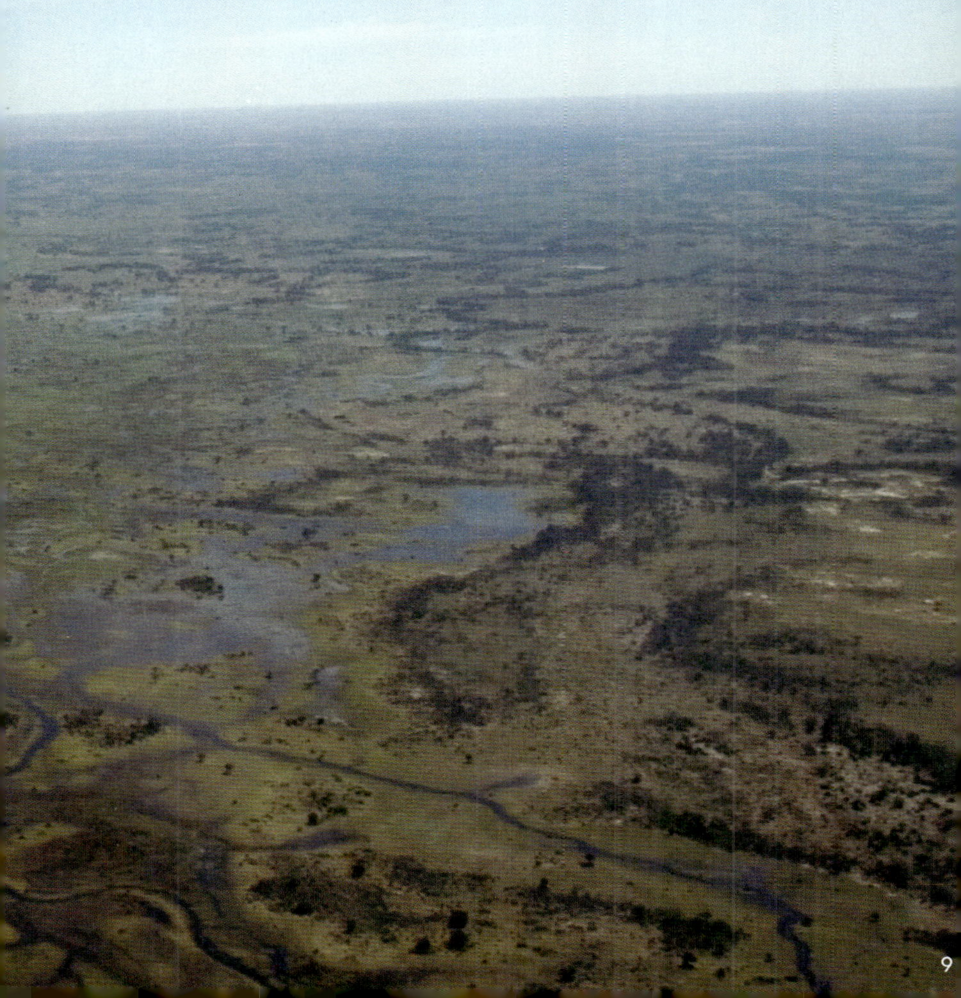

Botswana - A Short History

About 90 million years ago, magma from deep within the Earth's mantle exploded onto the surface creating enormous craters. The solidified fissures of rock, or kimberlite pipes now supply the world with diamonds yet the accumulated crater sediments above them yield jewels more beautiful: thousands of fossilised insects and trees from Botswana's humid, forested past.

Sometime around 60 million years ago, uplift began to cut off the Limpopo River which drained the vast northern region of southern Africa. Inflowing water accumulated behind the rising ridge and the Makgadikgadi depression was formed. Meanwhile, the continents were reorganising themselves in a way that would profoundly affect the climate. Antarctica became isolated, the southern oceans cooled and a high-pressure system cut off the moisture supply from the Atlantic thus reducing rainfall in the interior. In response, grasslands proliferated and the herbivores began to diversify.

About 20 million years ago, the encroaching East African rift began diverting the flow of several rivers into the Lower Zambezi, a process which continues today and might one day reroute the Okavango. For now, the rift faults have turned it into an enormous alluvial fan known as the Okavango Delta. Deprived of inflowing rivers, the Makgadikgadi dried up, but not forever. In the last 2 million years, whilst ice sheets came and went in Europe, huge environmental changes took place. It fluctuated between being wet enough to fill the 60,000km^2 lake to being dry enough to activate its now relict dune fields. Sometime during these colossal shifts of climate, our own ancestors appeared on the scene. Though we know little about who these people were or how they lived, stone tools document a sporadic but long history of human occupation in Botswana stretching back hundreds of thousands of years.

About 2,000 years ago domestic animals appeared and the complex social milieu that characterises Botswana today began to unfold. The Khoesian-speaking hunters and herders saw the influx of a myriad of ethnic groups, the rise and fall of numerous chiefdoms and the coming and going of Europeans.

Enormous social change has ensued but the domestic cattle culture has remained. Fuelled by growing European demand, it is now entirely dependent on groundwater that is thousands of years old. Botswana's cattle, kimberlite diamonds and the grassland-adapted herbivores on which the tourist industry now depends, are thus a product of its long, dynamic and sand-mantled past.

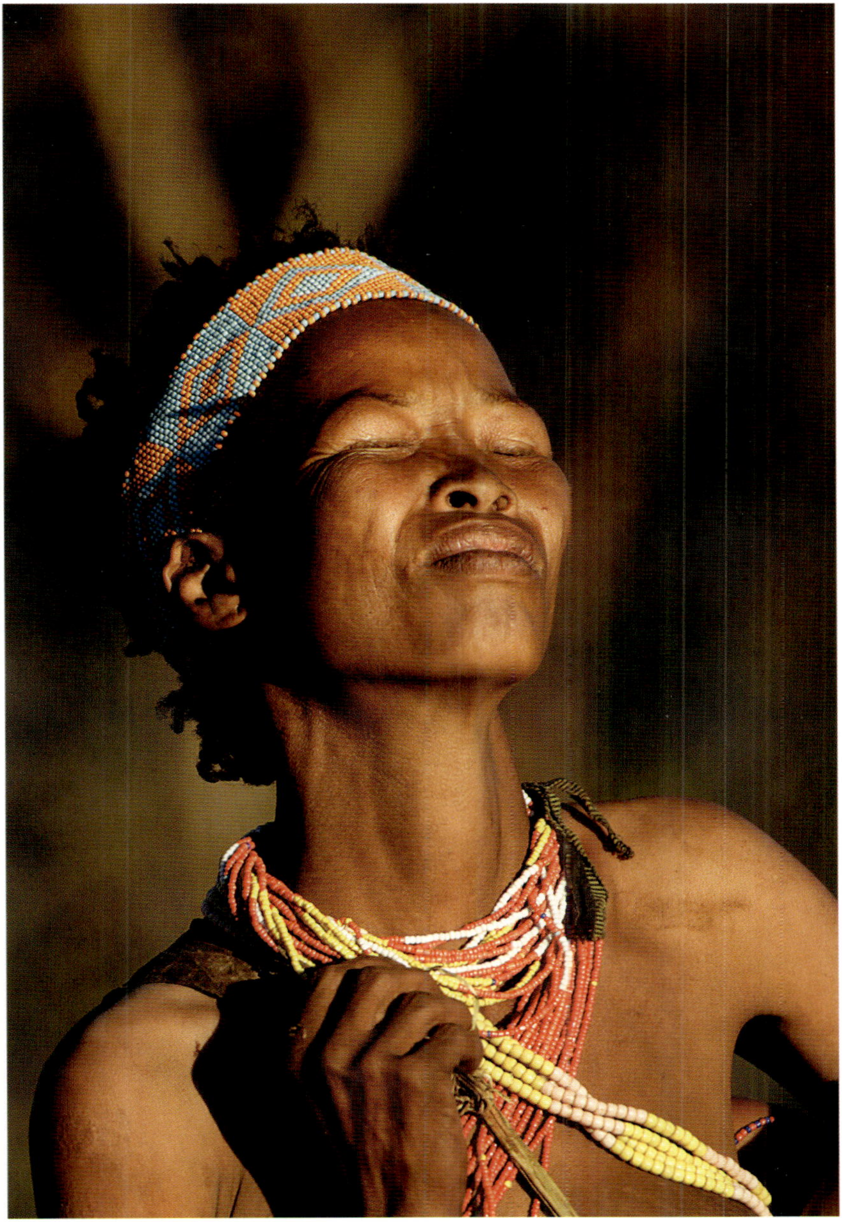

▲ ***Khoesian Woman, Xai Xai Village. DSLR, 100-400mm Lens, f/5.6 @ 1/200, ISO 100. SS***

◀◀ ***Okavango Delta. DSLR, 17-85mm Lens, f/22 @ 1/200, ISO 250. JG***

Maun

This interesting village in northern Botswana is known as the country's safari capital. Situated on the southern edge of the Okavango Delta, many travellers will pass through here on their way to various desert and Delta destinations. The Thamalakane River is ideal for photographing birds, wild flowers and insects. Take an afternoon to wander down the river or hire a motorboat for a sunset cruise. The Maun sanctuary also offers the opportunity to walk through the bush whilst getting close to giraffe, zebra and impala.

Best for: *Birding, Culture*

The Okavango Delta & Moremi Game Reserve

The Moremi Game Reserve protects about a third of the Okavango Delta's wilderness and is completely buffered by private concessions and wildlife management areas. This world famous park is renowned for its stunning game viewing and pristine environment. It is one of Africa's most exciting destinations enticing travellers from around the globe who marvel at this unique inland river delta. The Okavango River, as it is known here, begins life in Angola some 2,000 kilometres north of Maun. Each year when the waters arrive, the ensuing flood spreads out over the Kalahari sands in a 16,000 square kilometre alluvial fan, supporting a myriad of species in a system of channels, lagoons, floodplains and palm islands.

Best for: *Aquatic species, Birding, Predators*

Chobe National Park

In its final stage, the Chobe River is made up of channels and floodplains that support an incredible concentration of wildlife. It is home to large herds of zebra, buffalo, giraffe, antelope and hippo, but its greatest claim to fame is the highest density of elephants left on Earth. After decades of being a protected area, the animals can be very relaxed making it ideal for photography. Situated south of the river is Savuti. The hills here lend great atmosphere to the place and the Savuti Channel, which is now flowing again, attracts large numbers of wildlife.

Best for: *Elephants, Landscapes, Large herds, Predators*

▶ *Elephant, Savuti, Chobe National Park. DSLR, 100-400mm Lens, f/7.1 @ 1/400, ISO 200. SS*

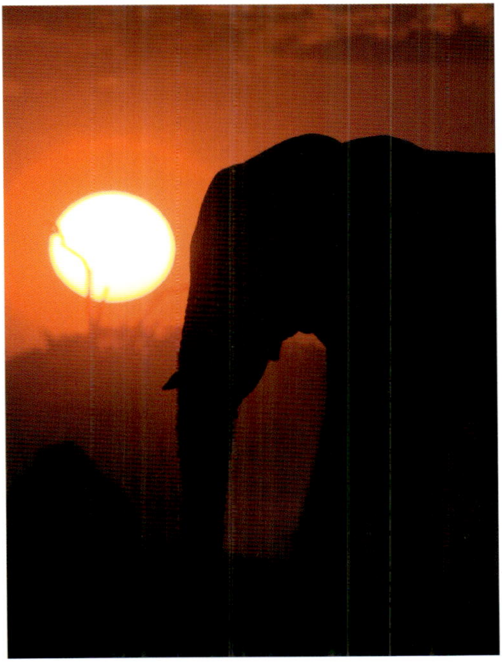

▼ *Mating Lions, Moremi Game Reserve. DSLR, 500mm Lens, f/5 @ 1/800, ISO 1000. JG*

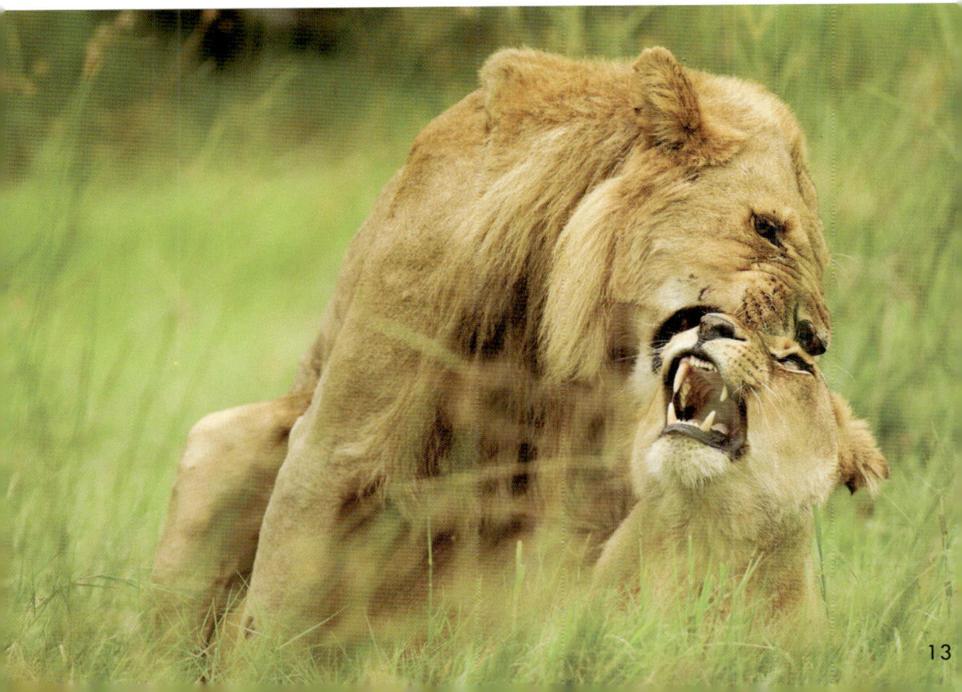

KWANDO, LINYANTI & SELINDA

These areas offer a rich wildlife experience in a variety of habitats. The Linyanti River and marshes are complemented by the contrasting riverine forest, dry woodlands and open grasslands. In the private concessions of Kwando and Selinda, you can also experience the thrill of nocturnal game drives.

Best for: *Elephants, Landscapes, Night photography, Predators*

TSODILO HILLS

Just west of the Delta's panhandle are the four hills that make up Tsodilo Hills. Listed as a world heritage site, it holds the single biggest rock art collection in southern Africa with over 3,500 paintings in roughly 500 sites. Three of the hills represent a male, female and a child respectively while the fourth is unnamed. Most of the paintings are found on the female hill and depict different animals, hunting scenes, abstract patterns, life scenes and events.

Best for: *Birding, Landscapes, Rock art*

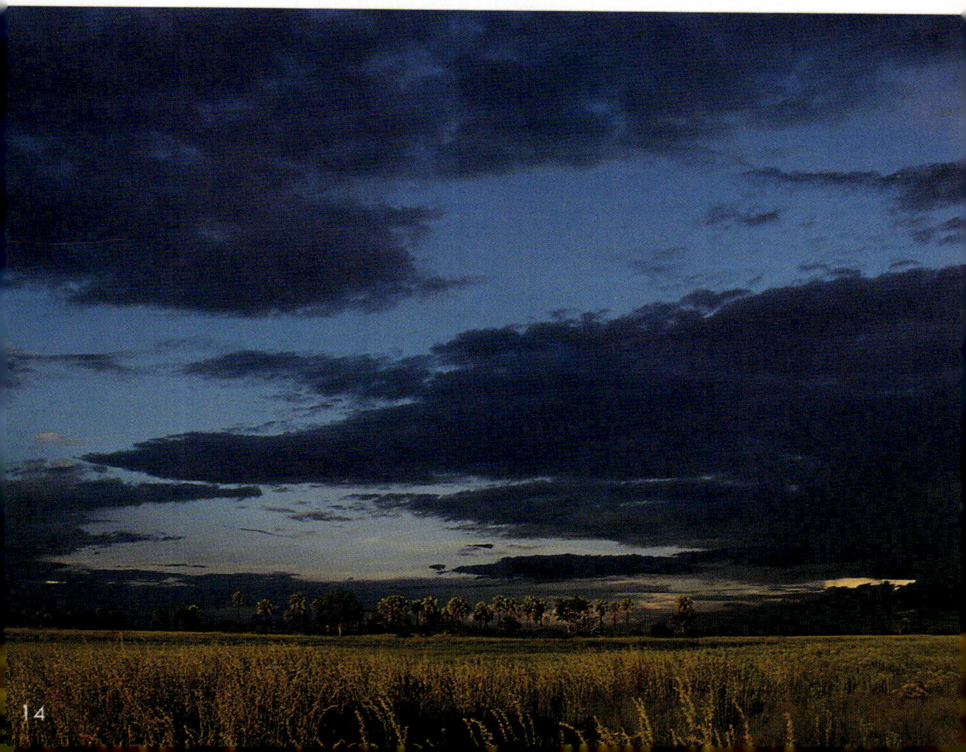

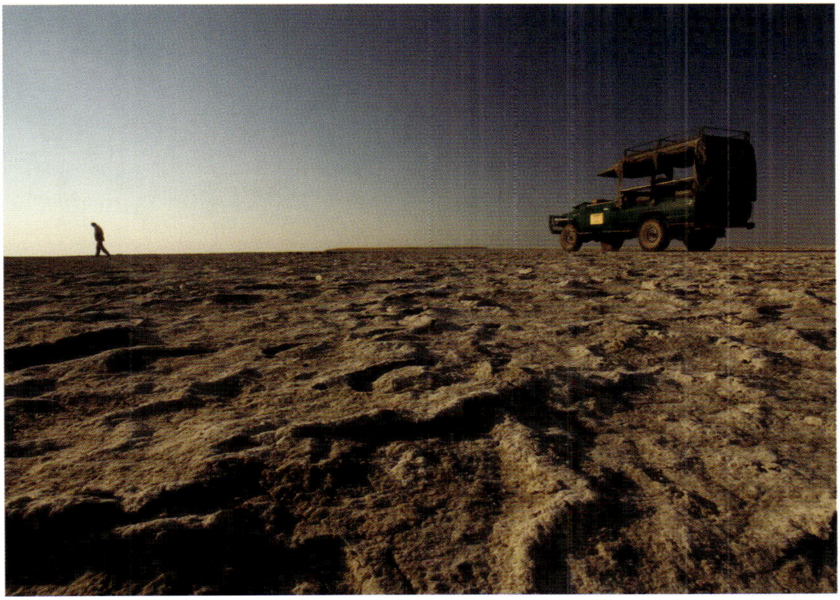

▲ ***Makgadikgadi Pans. DSLR, 11-18mm Lens, f/22 @ 1/50, ISO 250, Polarising Filter. JG***

MAKGADIKGADI SALT PANS & NATIONAL PARK

The Makgadikgadi Salt Pans, formed approximately 10,000 years ago from the remnants of a superlake, have now become a 360° expanse of nothingness the size of Switzerland. Travelling across the pans in the dry season can be a surreal experience: a flat, grey moonscape devoid of landmarks simultaneously both bewildering and awe-inspiring. But the summer rains transform the area as thousands of pink flamingos arrive to create spectacular breeding colonies. The Makgadikgadi Pans National Park to the west of the pans is home to the second largest zebra migration in the world. Attracted by the succulent grass that springs up on the edge of the pans, harems are drawn eastwards with the first onset of the rains.

Best for: *Aerial photography, Landscapes*

◀ ***Linyanti Grasslands. SLR, 18-55mm Lens, Fuji Provia 100F. SS***

Nxai Pan National Park

Separated from the Makgadikgadi Pans National Park by the main Maun-Nata road, this is a little gem of a park whose limited water sparks exciting interaction between springbok herds and resident lion prides, with cheetah sightings also common. In addition, it is home to a number of bull elephants and the impressive Baines' Baobabs - seven arboreal giants perched on an island overlooking the pans.

Best for: *Desert species, Landscapes*

Central Kalahari Game Reserve

As the second largest game reserve in Africa, the Central Kalahari Game Reserve (CKGR) is Botswana at its wildest with just two lodges (both in the more accessible northern section) and various campsites for mobile safari operators and independent travellers. Rains transform the harsh desert environment into lush, emerald meadows supporting large herds of gemsbok and springbok with predators in tow, including the famous black-maned Kalahari lions.

Best for: *Desert species, Landscapes, Predators, Raptors*

▼ *Gemsbok, Central Kalahari Game Reserve. DSLR, 100-400mm Lens, f/11 @ 1/60, ISO 400. JG*

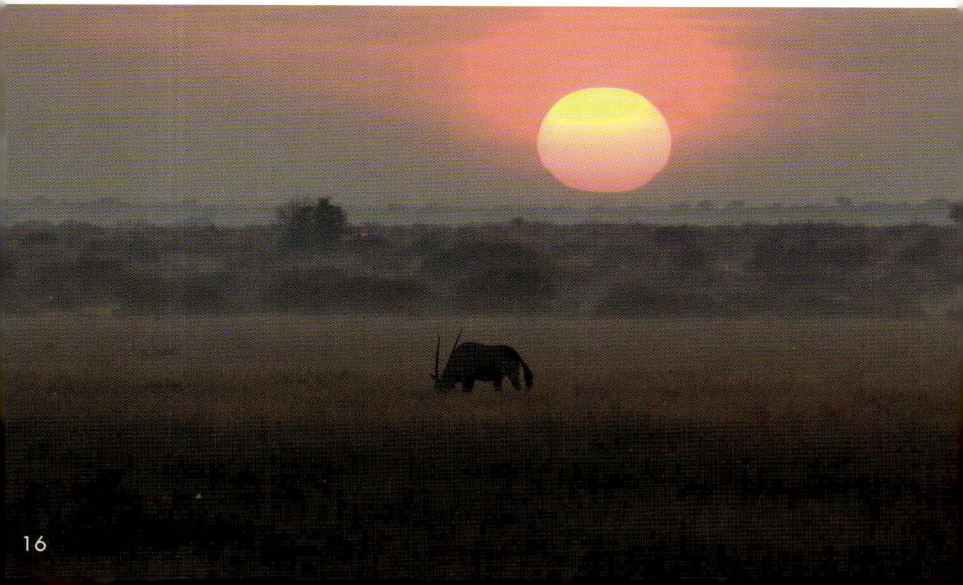

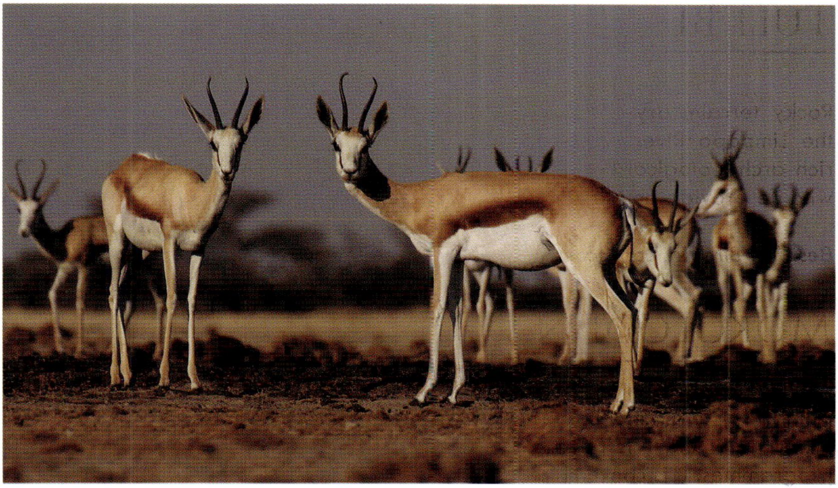

▲ *Springbok, Nxai Pan National Park. DSLR, 100-400mm Lens, f/8 @ 1/500, ISO 100. SS*

KHAMA RHINO SANCTUARY

With both black and white species, Khama Rhino Sanctuary constitutes your best chance to see rhinos in the wild in Botswana. Stemming from a community trust project in 1992, the 4,300 hectares are also home to around 230 bird species, leopard, brown hyena and bat-eared foxes. Situated just outside Serowe, it makes an ideal stopover point if you are travelling between Francistown and Gaborone.

Best for: *Rhinos*

KHUTSE GAME RESERVE

Although from the map Khutse looks like a small appendage adjoining the Central Kalahari Game Reserve (they share a common boundary), its geology makes it very different to its larger cousin. Once part of the ancient river system that flowed up to form Lake Makgadikgadi, the now dry pans provide essential minerals for game, sprouting nutritious grasses during the rains.

Best for: *Desert species, Landscapes*

Tuli Block

Rocky terrain, dry riverbeds and dense riverine forest along the banks of the Limpopo River distinguish this region from the rest of the country. The rich archaeological heritage combined with 350 bird species and abundant wildlife provide ample reason to visit one of the private reserves in this area.

Best for: *Birding, Landscapes*

Mokolodi Nature Reserve

Combining education with conservation, Mokolodi houses a wild animal orphanage and has been instrumental in both rhino and cheetah relocation programmes. It is conveniently located just outside Gaborone.

Best for: *Getting up close, Rhinos*

Kgalagadi Transfrontier Park

This park was the first of its kind in Southern Africa. In 1999, Botswana and South Africa agreed to manage their adjacent parks as one ecological unit. Visitors may move freely across the border within the park in a desert environment similar to that of the Central Kalahari Game Reserve.

Best for: *Desert species, Landscapes*

For more information visit ***www.botswanatourism.co.bw***

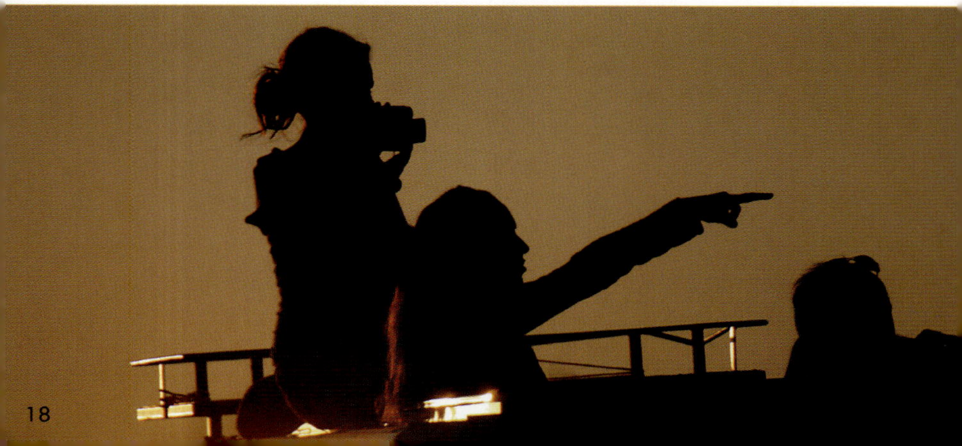

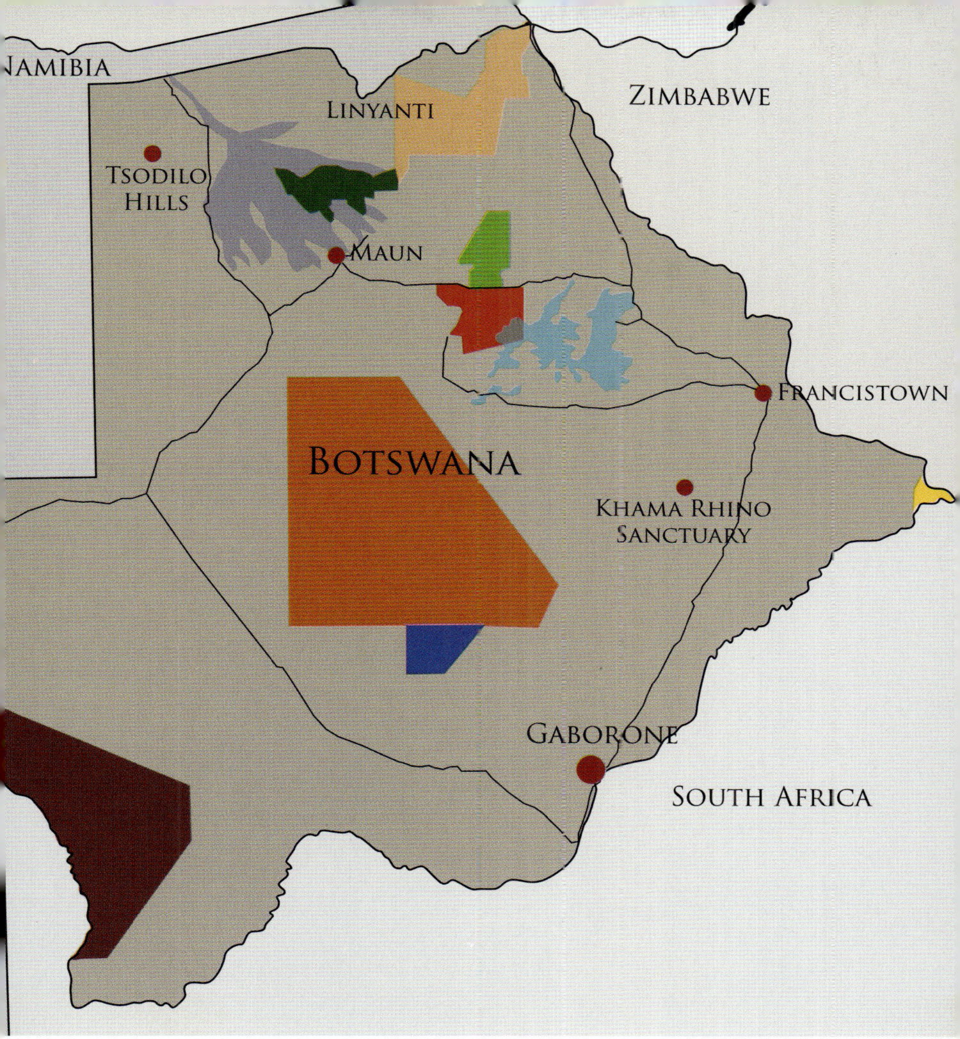

- Central Kalahari Game Reserve
- Chobe National Park
- Kgalagadi Transfrontier Park
- Khutse Game Reserve
- Makgadikgadi Pans National Park
- Makgadikgadi Salt Pans
- Moremi Game Reserve
- Nxai Pan National Park
- Okavango Delta
- Tuli Block

◀ ***Photographers. DSLR, 100-400mm Lens, f/6.3 @ 1/320, ISO 100. SS***

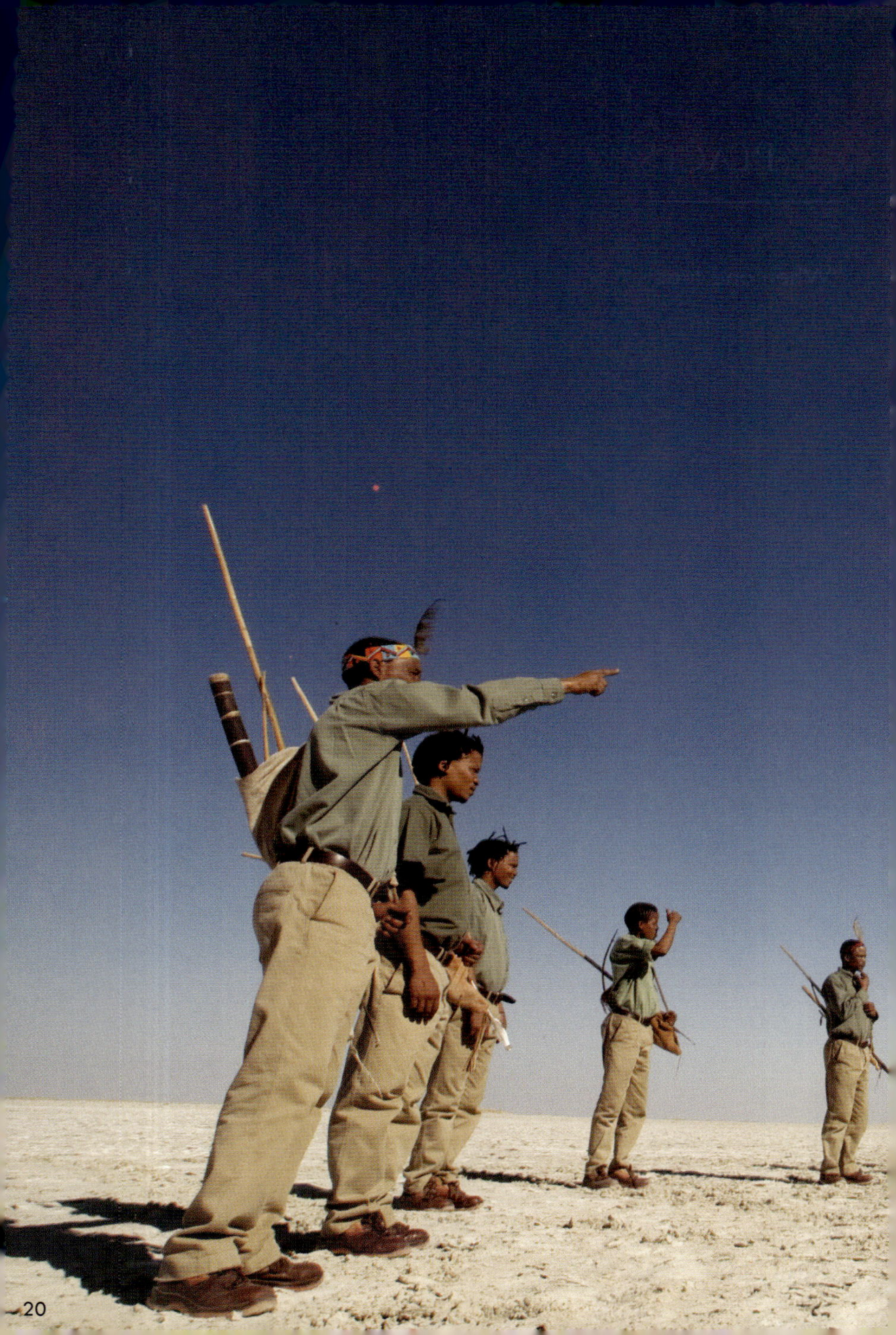

ON SAFARI
PLACES TO STAY, THINGS TO SEE

"When one tugs at a single thing in nature, he finds it attached to the rest of the world." *John Muir*

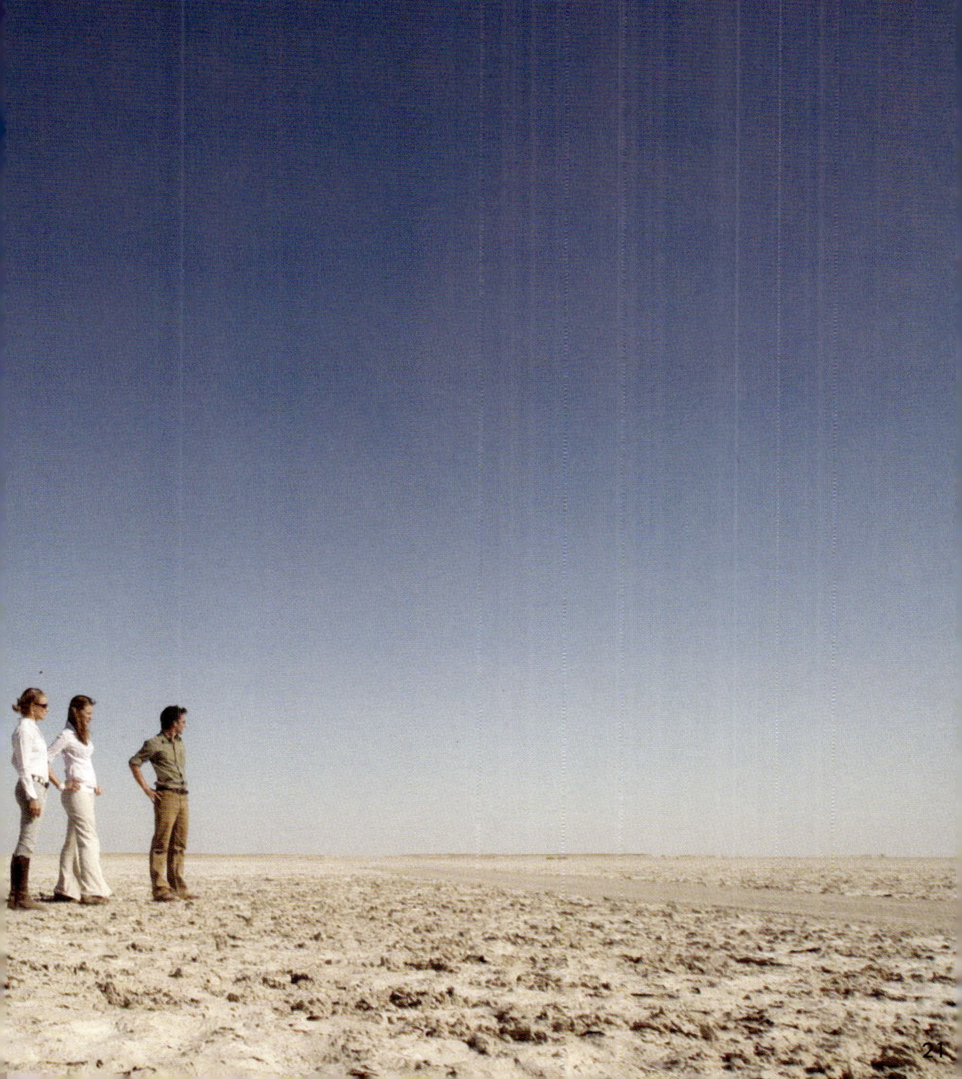

Types of Safari

Botswana offers a great variety of types and styles of safari. The country has a high-cost, low-impact tourism policy and this results in a limited number of available beds, especially in the wilderness areas. The policy seeks to reduce the human footprint on the sensitive ecology of the Kalahari sands as well as to provide you, the traveller, with an unspoilt and private experience.

Luxury Lodges & Camps

There is a large selection of beautifully appointed luxury lodges from which to base yourself. These high-end lodges offer exclusivity, usually in private concessions, with world-class service, stunning architecture and mouth-watering cuisine. The guide teams are both highly skilled and incredibly knowledgeable. There are all sorts of safari options available from the lodges including game viewing by vehicle, night drives, mokoro (dug-out canoe), motorboat and walking safaris. Transport between these lodges is usually by light aircraft.

Game Drive Tips

◊ Try to sit in a different place in the vehicle on each game drive to give you an alternative angle and perspective.

◊ Mention to your guide that you have a special interest in photography so that he or she can bear you in mind at a sighting when it comes to positioning and light.

◊ Avoid sudden movements at a sighting and keep noise to a minimum.

◊ Listen to your guide when it comes to safety.

◊ Have your camera at the ready at all times as things can happen quickly.

▶ Elephant, Okavango Delta. DSLR, 100-400mm Lens, f/5.6 @ 1/800, ISO 250. JG

◀ Makgadikgadi Pans. DSLR, 11-18mm Lens, f/8 @ 1/800, ISO 400, Polarising Filter. JG

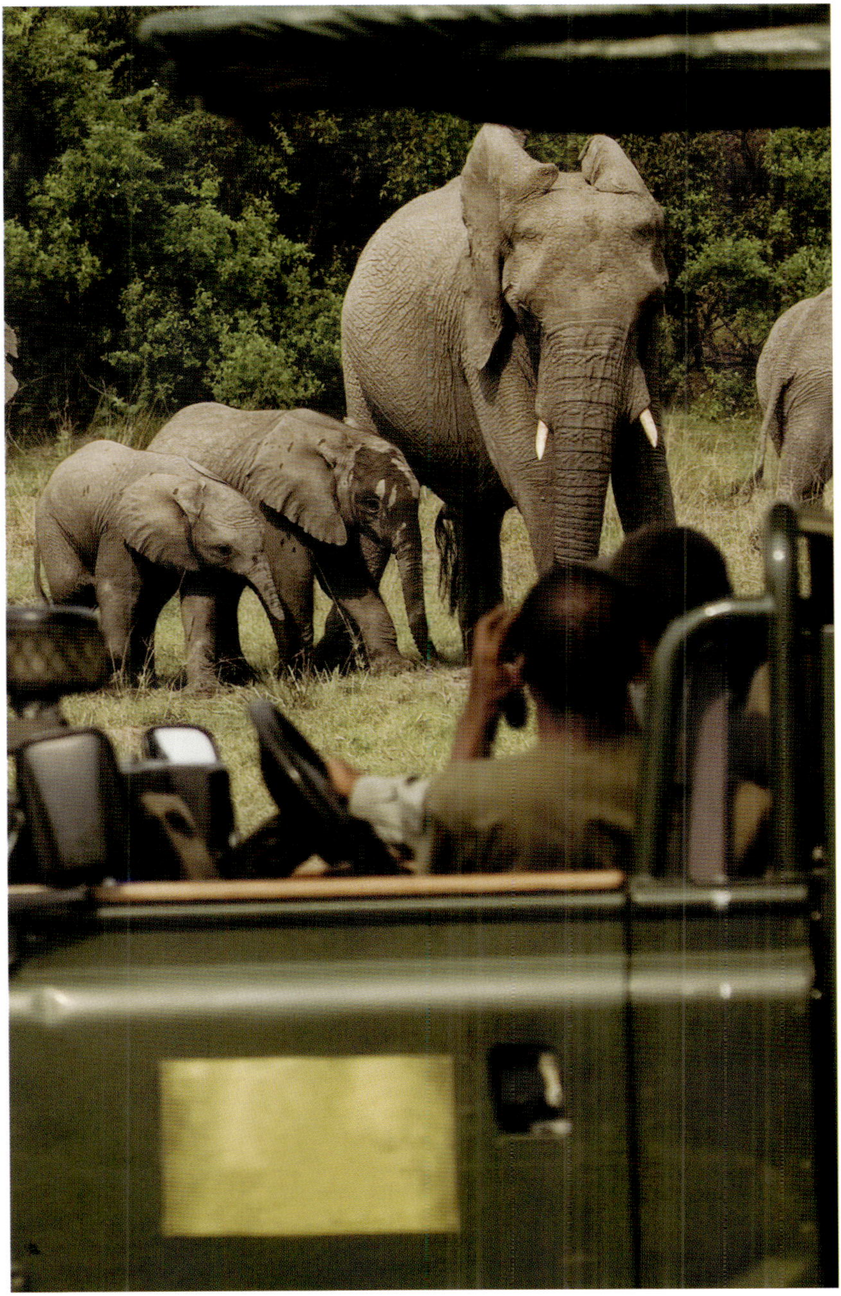

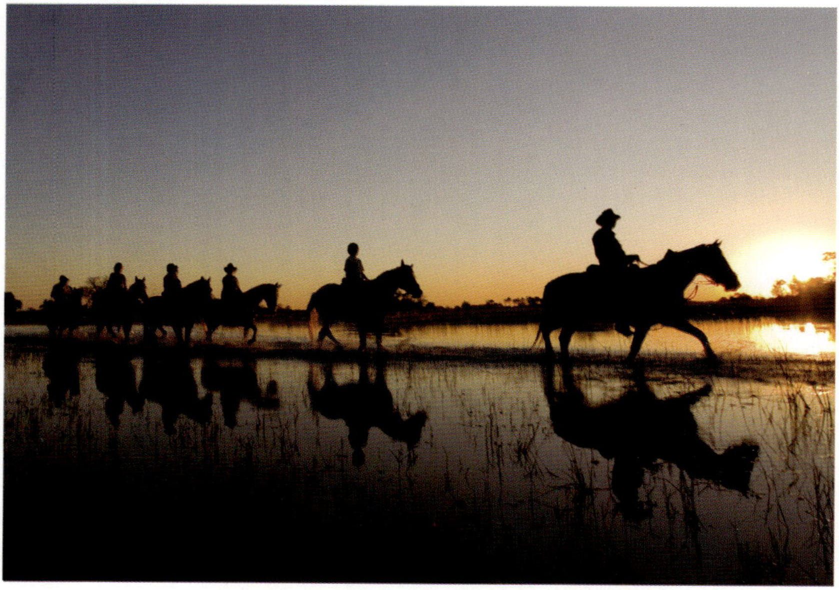

▲ ***Horseback Safari, Okavango Delta. DSLR, 11-18mm Lens, f/5.6 @ 1/800, ISO 400. JG***

Specialist Safaris

There are a handful of camps that offer a unique safari experience. These include safaris on horseback, elephant back, on foot and even on 4x4 quad bikes on the salt pans. There are also several companies running specialist safaris which focus on specific interests. These can range from birding, reptiles, stars and trees to photography and filming. For the more adventurous folk, you can embark upon a "Trans Okavango" travelling from the northern panhandle to Maun by mokoro, kayak or motorboat.

Mobile Safaris

With a more classic feel, mobiles involve travelling through a variety of destinations while the camp moves with you. Most nights are spent in private campsites in the Game Reserves and National Parks. Having a single guide for the whole safari can be hugely rewarding and the flexible nature of these trips is excellent for photography. Options vary from luxury and mid-range to participation safaris and they can last from a few days to 3 weeks or more.

Independent Safaris

For the more intrepid, travelling independently or self-driving allows you to conduct your safari at your own pace. It is very important that you have knowledge of the bush coupled with both 4x4 driving experience and basic mechanical skills. Breaking down, getting lost or stuck could easily wreck your trip, especially in remote areas. Since you are in charge, you are responsible for exercising respect and sensitivity towards the environment, so please adhere to the rules of the park at all times.

Children on Safari

Children are most welcome on safari and are the key to protecting the future of the world's natural heritage. Each company has varying policies so it is worth checking in advance with your operator which activities they can and cannot do. Whilst you are on safari, never forget that you are in a wild environment.

Food on Safari

The safari industry has high food standards and the hospitality staff are well-trained. Most companies can cater for any dietary requirements given advanced notice, so notify your operator prior to travel.

▼ ***Bush Dinner, Okavango Delta. DSLR, 11-18mm Lens, f/13 @ 6, ISO 100, Tripod. JG***

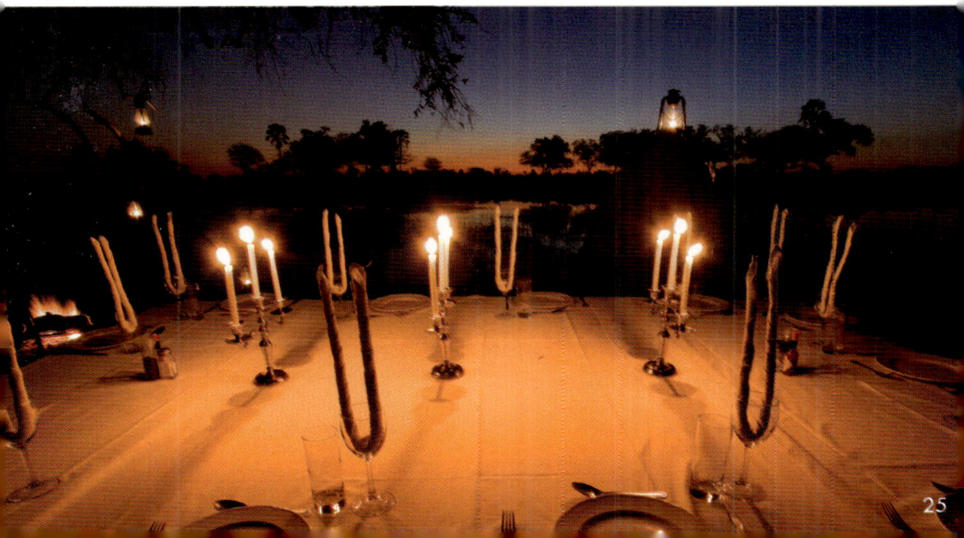

When to Visit

Botswana is an all-year-round destination for photographers. The seasons vary considerably but each has something special to offer. The rainy season (our summer) is from November through to April. During this time the colour saturations are intense with a backdrop of clouds that add character to the sky in your images. Sunsets are dramatic and these are the months for the migrant bird species. The drier and cooler winter months (May to September) often offer easier game viewing conditions when the grasses have died back.

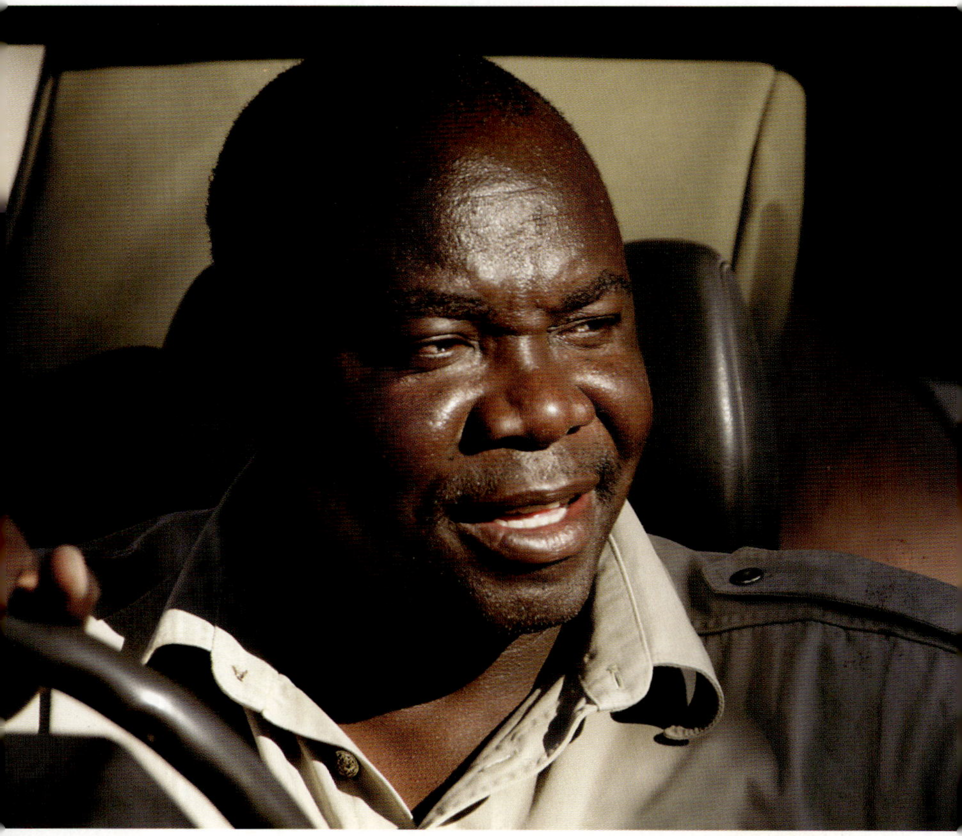

▲ ***Safari Guide, Savuti, Chobe National Park. DSLR, 100-400mm Lens, f/5.6 @ 1/400, ISO 100. SS***

▶ ***A Surprising Sign, Makgadikgadi Pans. DSLR, 17-85mm Lens, f/6.3 @ 1/1600, ISO 100. JG***

Power to the People

Check in advance whether you will have access to appropriate charging facilities and always carry spare batteries. Mobile safari companies usually supply power inverters and if you are self-driving, make sure that you purchase one beforehand.

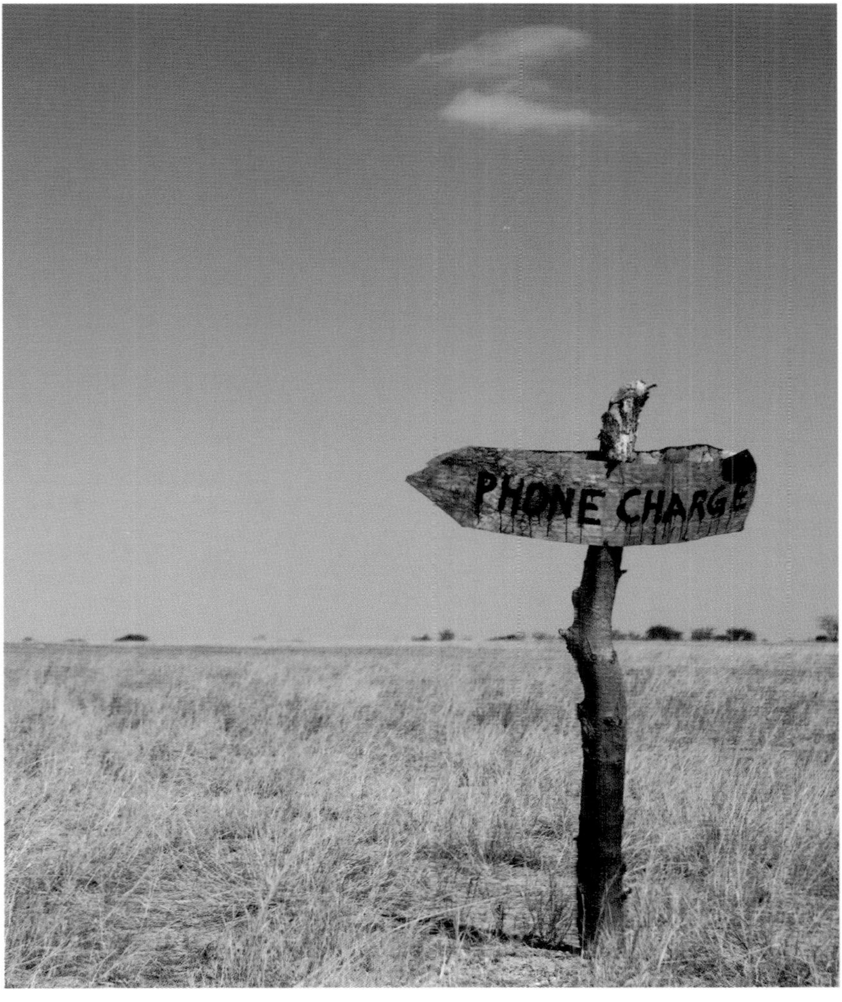

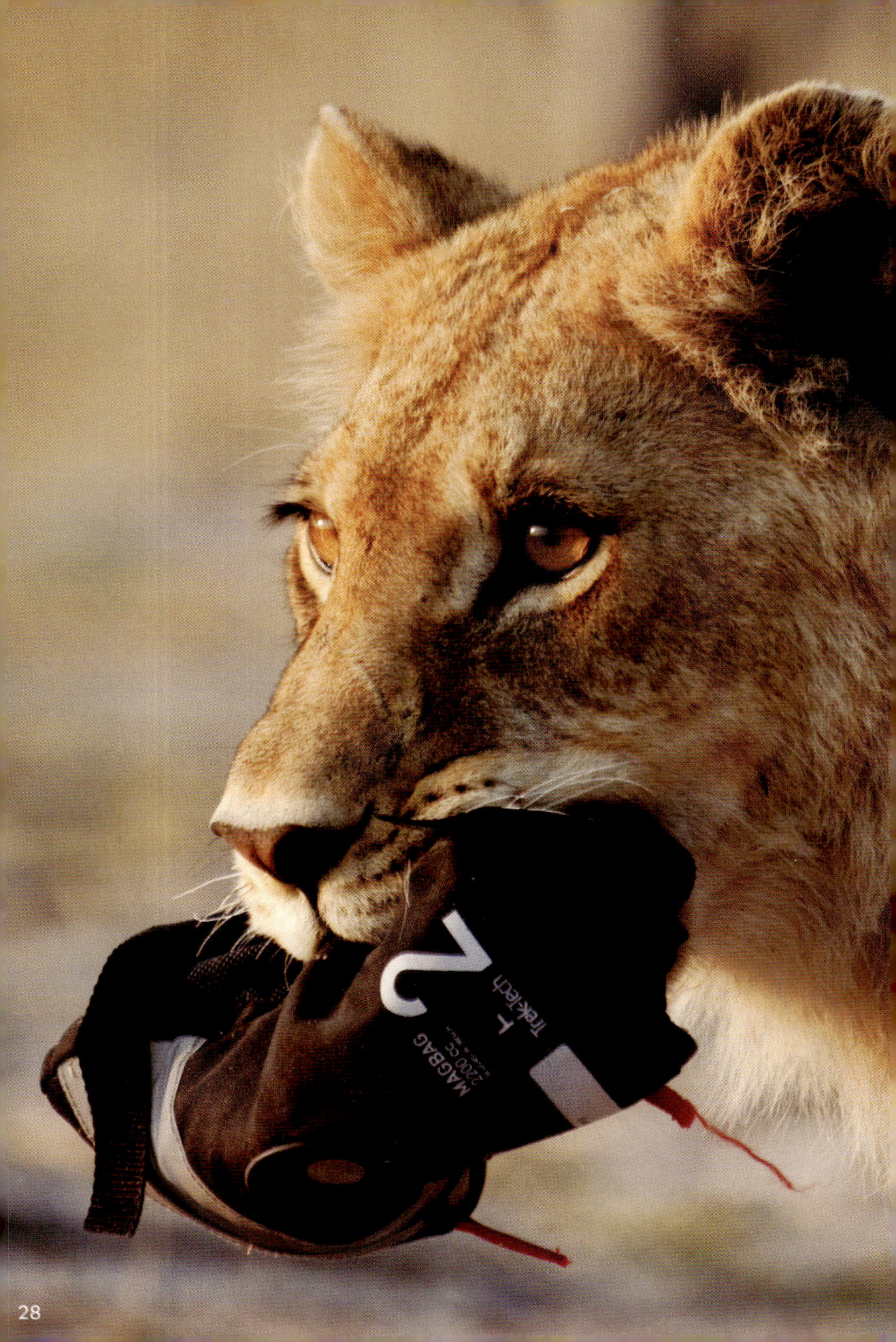
2
Trek-Tech
MAGBAG
2200 cc

Equipment
Tools of the Trade

"A camera didn't make a great picture any more than a typewriter wrote a great novel." *Peter Adams*

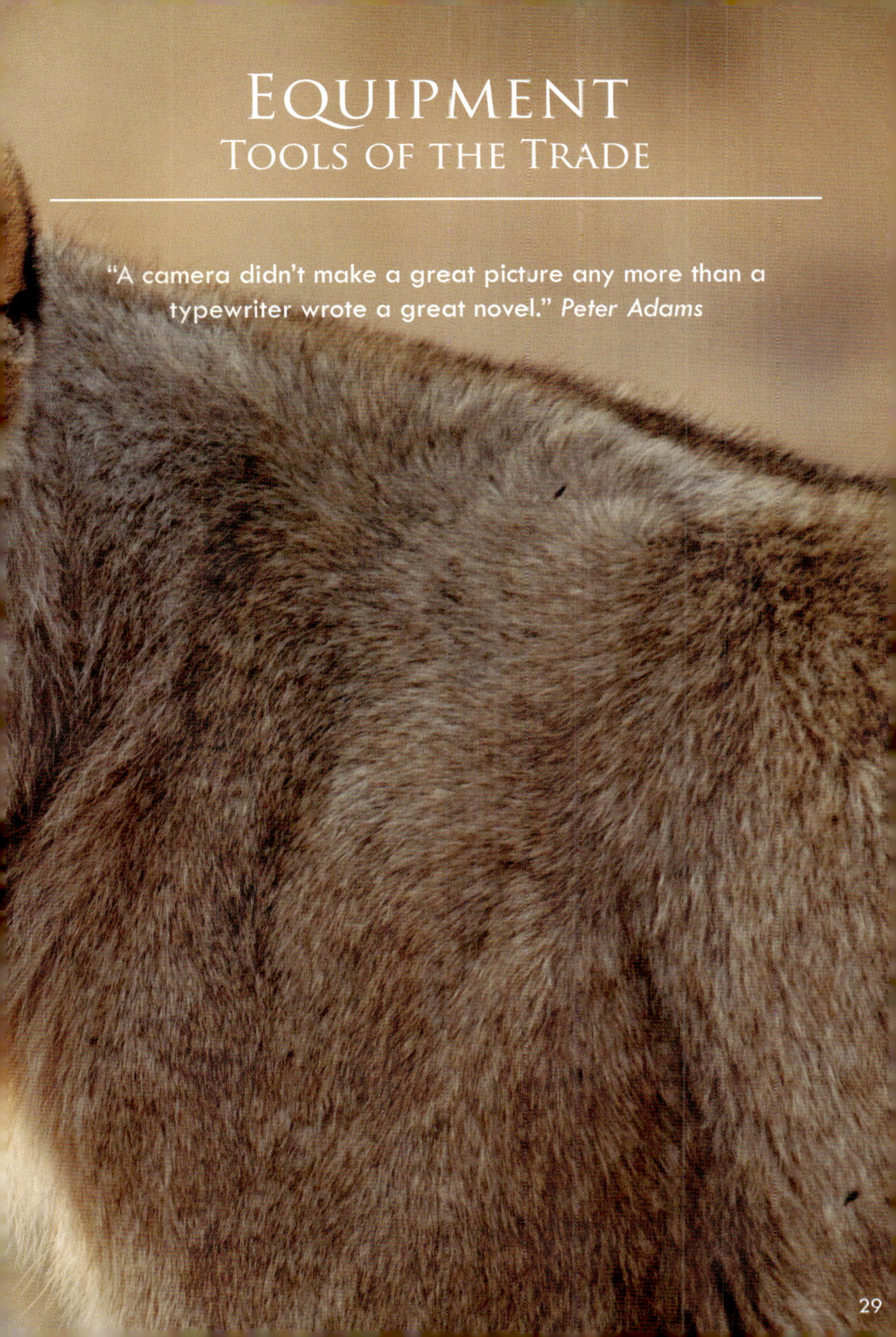

Digital Single Lens Reflex Camera Bodies (DSLR)

The pace of change of today's technology means choosing a DSLR camera may seem daunting, but it need not be. Here is a list of features to consider:

Pixels: A pixel is the smallest unit of a digital image (the tiny square you see if you zoom in as far as possible on a picture) so a 10 mega-pixel (mp) camera produces images with 10,000,000 pixels. The greater the number of pixels, the larger you can print the images without loss in quality, but 10 mega-pixels is adequate for print and for entering wildlife photography competitions so don't get too hung up on pixel-envy!

Sensor: This is the most valuable and complex part of your camera, so look after it well (see p.36). With over 200 metres of circuitry on a miniscule circuit board, it is essentially a microchip with an array of photoreceptors and records the light values necessary to produce an image. These days, even point-and-shoot cameras have upwards of 10mp but produce inferior images to a DSLR due to the quality of the sensor. DSLR models sport different sensors - the main distinction being size. Entry-level and mid-range DSLRs have a cropped (smaller) sensor. This is cheaper to manufacture but has an impact on the range of your lenses. Shooting with a 100mm lens on a sensor with a 1.6x crop factor is equivalent to shooting with a 160mm lens on a full-frame sensor. Upgrading from a cropped to a full-frame sensor will therefore widen your wide-angle lens and conversely shorten the effective magnification of your telephoto lens.

Make: Historically, the primary DSLR manufacturers have been Nikon and Canon, with little to choose between the two. Recently more companies have entered into the fray, but they have yet to build up the same range of lenses and so for now we would still recommend either Nikon or Canon.

Cost: Apart from a better quality sensor, the top of the range bodies are more durable and have extra functions like improved focusing systems with more focal points, higher frames per second and greater ISO ranges. Although these are beneficial, an entry-level model can still produce good images.

▶ ***Leopard & Springbok Kill, Nxai Pan National Park. DSLR, 100-400mm Lens, f/6.3 @ 1/320, ISO 100.*** I only spotted this leopard when I saw a herd of springbok through my binoculars all looking in the same direction, suggesting a predator was nearby. **JG**

◀ ***Lion with Beanbag, Okavango Delta. DSLR, 100-400mm Lens, f/5.6 @ 1/640, ISO 400.*** On a safari in the Delta a visitor accidently dropped her beanbag off the vehicle. The young lion we were watching took great delight in playing with it for a while. **SS**

LOOKING FURTHER

A good pair of binoculars is essential for finding wildlife, observing behaviour and studying detail. 10x42 is an ideal specification - '10' refers to magnification and '42' to the aperture of the front lens. A wide aperture lets in more light so you can use them after dusk and even for star-gazing.

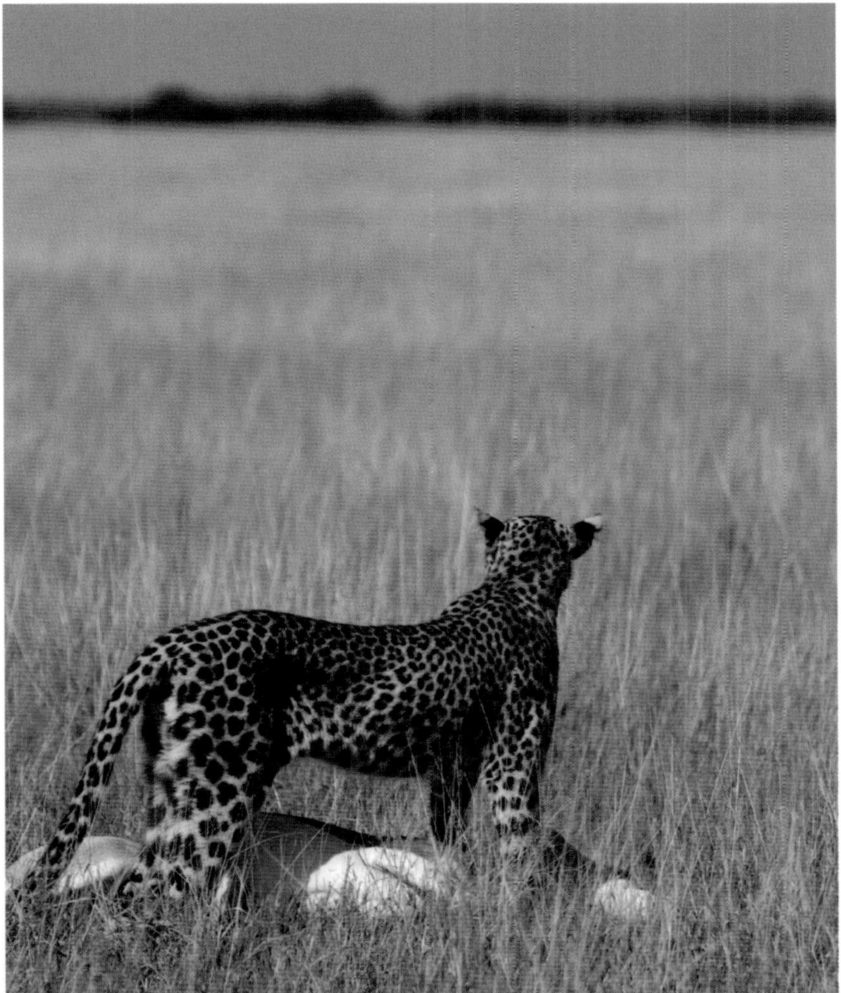

LENSES

Everyone will tell you that you should spend as much as you can afford on a lens: "There's no substitute for good glass" is an oft-quoted line and to an extent this is correct as it has the biggest impact on image quality (after the photographer). The advice we would add is that having a range of different lenses builds skills and encourages experimentation. Lenses are defined by their **Focal Length**. This is literally the distance between the optical centre of the lens and the focal point. It is measured in millimetres and refers to the magnification of the lens - 50mm is standard, 100mm is 2x zoom, 200mm is 4x, etc..

Wide-Angle Lenses (e.g. 14mm) have smaller focal lengths, a wider angle of view and increase the space between objects in the image.

Telephoto Lenses (e.g. 400mm) have greater focal lengths, increased magnification and compress the distance between objects in the image.

Zoom Lenses (e.g. 17-85mm) have a range of focal lengths. More convenient than a fixed **Prime Lens,** they reduce the need to change lenses but you often compromise on quality, especially if the range is large (e.g. 24-300mm).

Macro Lenses are specifically designed for close-up photos, projecting a life-size or larger image of the subject onto the film or digital sensor. They are particularly useful for magnifying insects or flowers.

▼ ***Photographers, Savuti, Chobe National Park. DSLR, 100-400mm Lens, f/6.3 @ 1/320, ISO 100. SS***

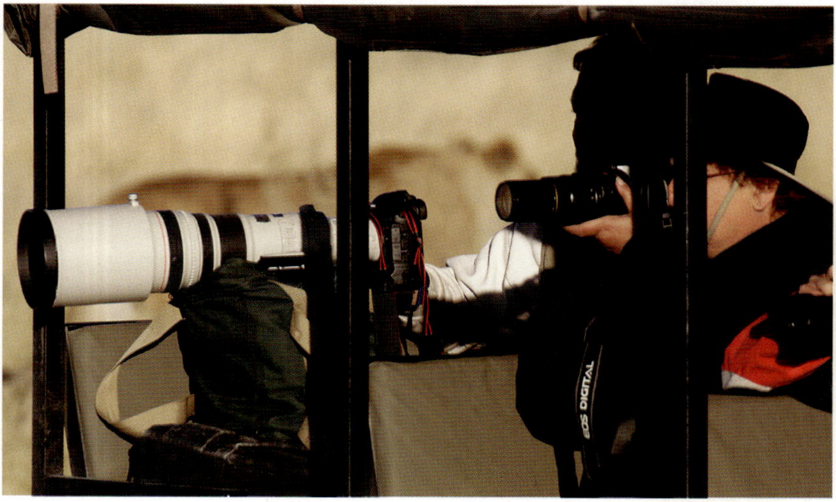

The second key lens characteristic is its maximum aperture denoted by its f-number eg f/4. The lower the number, the wider the aperture. Since a wider aperture lets in more light (see p.42), the result will be a faster shutter speed. Hence this number is also used to describe the speed of the lens - a lower number equates to a faster lens.

Extenders (Converters): Rather than investing in an expensive telephoto lens, extenders offer a cheaper way of increasing the focal length of your lenses. However, they will reduce the maximum aperture of the lens and you may experience a small loss in image quality.

Brands: Importantly, the lenses from one manufacturer will only work on the same make of DSLR (i.e. a Canon lens will not work with a Nikon body), so when you start buying lenses you could effectively be tying yourself into that manufacturer forever. Some independent manufacturers make lenses compatible with both Canon and Nikon bodies: Sigma and Tamron are the more popular makes. They can provide a more affordable alternative but make sure you buy the correct version for your make of camera.

▼ ***Kubu Island, Makgadikgadi Pans. DSLR, 11-18mm Lens, f/16 @ 1/250, ISO 250.***
A wide-angle lens can create interesting landscapes. ***JG***

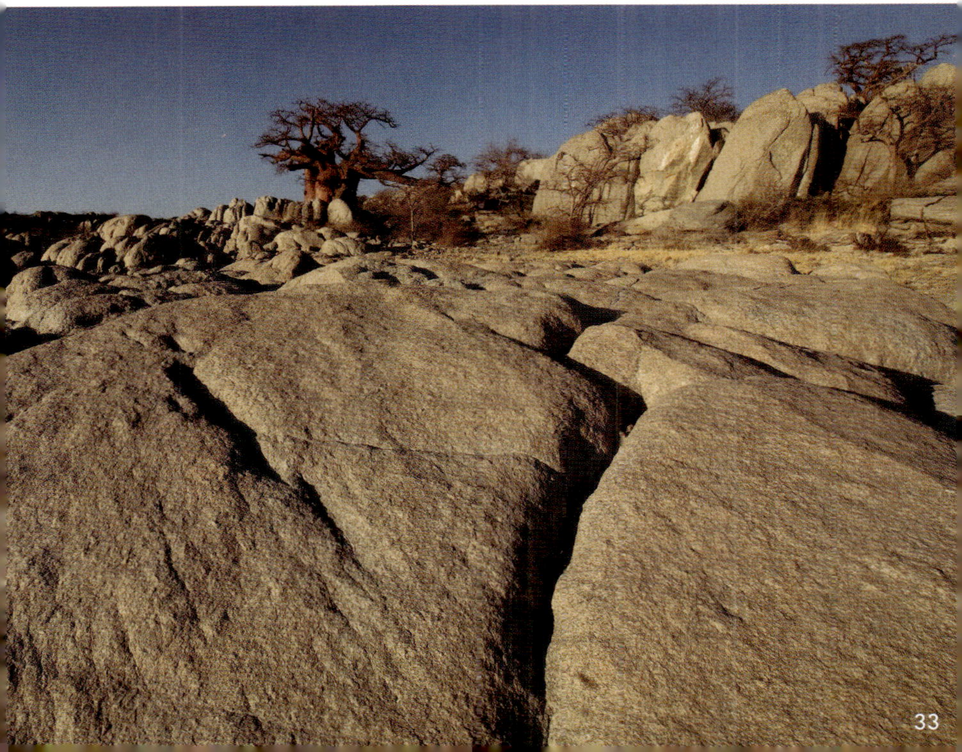

STABILISING EQUIPMENT

Most wildlife photographers make use of a telephoto lens to get close to the action. Unfortunately long lenses tend to be quite heavy and this makes it difficult to hold them still enough to get a sharp image. An image stabiliser, built into most telephoto lenses, is vital to combat camera shake but for those golden morning or afternoon low light shots, additional stabilisation is necessary.

Tripods: This is one of the best solutions if you have the space and time to use it. You will need a good tripod that is sturdy enough to carry the weight of your heaviest lens but light enough to be easily transportable. Do not make the mistake of buying an inexpensive tripod only to have to replace it when it breaks: it is cheaper in the long run to invest in good quality. Some models have a hook underneath the centre plate to hang a camera bag or weights to increase stability. Avoid extending the middle column if possible as this can make the camera susceptible to vibrations and/or movement during exposure. Tripod heads come in two guises: ball-and-socket and pan-and-tilt. Generally the former is slightly easier to master but both can be equally effective.

Monopods: As the name suggests, this is a tripod with one leg meaning it takes up less space and is particularly useful if you are in a game-viewing vehicle.

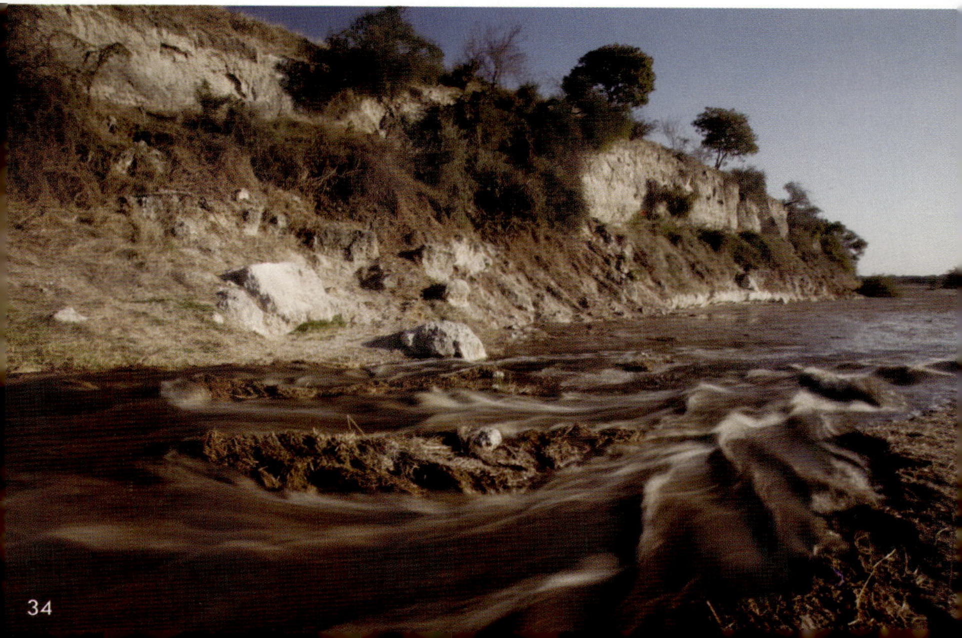

Beanbags: These are a very versatile way of stabilising your camera and fit easily onto ledges and windows in vehicles. They take up limited space and can be quickly moved when the need to recompose suddenly arises. When travelling between destinations, empty the beanbag to save space and weight and refill it with rice or something similar when you arrive on the other side.

Brackets: These can be fixed to the side of a car door to allow tripod-like stability with similar movement characteristics. Given the cost (and the installation process), they are only worth investing in if you are a professional shooting in the bush on a regular basis.

Remote switch: When using a tripod for long exposures such as sunsets or night shots, a remote switch will counteract camera shake caused by pressing the shutter button. It is also vital for star shots and this is one of the most useful pieces of kit. If you do not have one, use the self-timer on your camera body.

Camera Bags & Storage

The choice of camera bag will depend on the type of travelling you are doing. A shoulder bag is great for easy access but less comfortable for carrying long distances, while a camera backpack is the best carrying option and some can even fit in a laptop. A sling bag is a hybrid between the two allowing you to swing the bag to one side to remove items. The final option is a hard Pelican case - this is the ultimate choice to protect your gear but it can be difficult to get through as hand luggage on airlines. Some backpacks now come with rolling wheels which is great for transporting but it does add extra weight when flying. Look for durability, padding and water or moisture resistant materials to protect your equipment.

◀ ***Boteti River, Makgadikgadi Pans National Park. DSLR, 11-18mm Lens, f/22 @ 0.4, ISO 100, Neutral Density Graduated Filter, Tripod. JG***

Wear in the World

Choose lightweight, durable, neutral-coloured clothing that dries quickly. This will help keep the weight down in your main luggage. Your shirts should have a pocket for storing lens caps, spare memory cards and a notepad and pen. If you wear glasses, bring a second pair in case one breaks.

Note: Light aircraft travel restricts you to a total luggage allowance of 12kg in a soft bag so pack lightly if you will be flying from camp to camp.

Cleaning

Dust is the bane of every wildlife photographer. Even with the latest cameras' anti-dust technology, there is nothing you can do to stop it getting onto your lenses and camera sensor, especially if you want to be ready to capture that split-second shot. The solution is to learn how to get rid of the pesky spots. Lenses are relatively simple: first use a Gitzo bulb blower to get rid of light dust particles. Then, if there are more stubborn spots there are several lens solutions and associated cloths on the market which are effective. Make sure you buy something specifically for camera lenses and do not use more than 1 or 2 drops of solution on the cloth to avoid smears. Also, do not forget to clean both sides of your filters.

The Gitzo blower can also work well on the sensor. Turn on sensor cleaning via the menu and press the shutter button. The mirror will lock up enabling you to access the sensor. Remember this also grants access to all the dust particles that might be in the vicinity so do not try this when you are driving at 30km/h in the Kalahari! Ensure the nozzle of the blower does not go beyond the lens mount as if you touch or scratch the sensor itself, it could turn out to be a very expensive repair job. Try holding the camera upside down to get gravity on your side. If the Gitzo blower does not do the job, then your choice is either to risk cleaning the sensor yourself with a dedicated sensor swab (a delicate process), or waiting to get back home to have it cleaned by a professional. Fortunately, there is now an alternative option in the form of the Arctic Butterfly (made by Visible Dust) - a very fine, soft, motorised brush which will pick up 90% of dust particles with no risk to the sensor.

The more you change lenses, the greater the chance that dust will make its way onto your sensor so beware of being too meticulous. For each time you lock up the mirror to clean your sensor you risk more dust. Wherever possible clean your equipment in a dust-free environment.

Sands of Time

The best way to check the sensor for dust is to take a test shot of a clear sky or white wall. A narrow aperture (see p.42) with the subject out of focus will highlight any dust. Ideally view the image on a laptop or, if that is not possible, zoom in on your camera LCD screen to all parts of the image. Repeat the process with a different lens and if the spots disappear you know that the dust was on the lens and not on the sensor.

MEMORY CARDS & MEMORY BANKS

Working out how much memory you bring is up to you. If you shoot in RAW you will get fewer images per card as it is the highest file size on the camera. Consider getting a memory bank or multimedia photo viewer to download your images onto and make sure you bring a bare minimum of two cards so that when one is downloading, you can continue to shoot with the other. Cards also come with faster reading capabilities - try to get the fastest you can.

FILTERS

From the wide range of filters available the following are worth considering. **UV filters** help to protect your front lens but avoid cheap ones as they can affect the quality of your image. One option is to remove them when shooting and replace them when storing your equipment. **Polarising filters** will saturate blues and greens and reduce reflections, making them particularly useful for landscapes. **Neutral density filters** are handy if one half of the image is much brighter than the other. They can be used to darken a bright sky resulting in a uniform exposure. Beware that filters will also increase the risk of lens flare.

▼ ***Meerkat, Makgadikgadi Pans. DSLR, 11-18mm Lens, f/5.6 @ 1/500, ISO 200, Polarising Filter. JG***

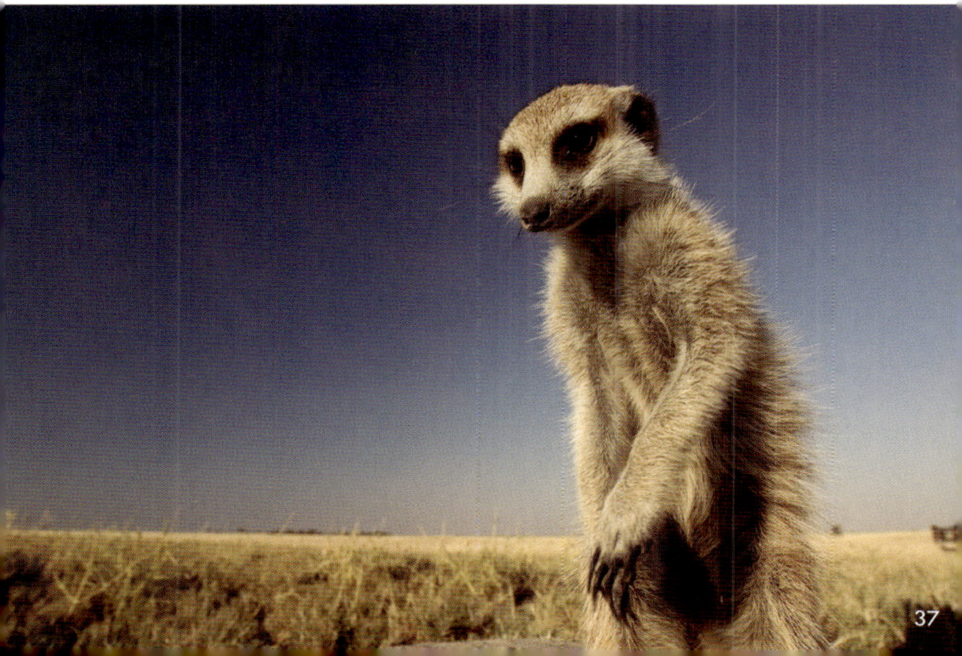

What's in the Bag?

You do not need to spend a fortune to take good wildlife photographs. Although a decent lens will help, improving your photography skills will have a greater impact on the quality of your images. Once your techniques improve, you can then gradually start to invest in equipment. Based on our experience, the following list should act as a guide:

Essential kit list:

◊ DSLR: preferably a minimum of 10 million pixels with a high frames per second burst rate.
◊ Lenses: Wide-angle: e.g. 14mm f/2.8
Standard: e.g. 24-70mm f/2.8
Telephoto zoom: e.g. 100-400mm f/4.5-5.6
◊ Beanbag
◊ Gitzo bulb blower, cleaning cloth and solution
◊ Spare battery and sufficient memory cards
◊ UV filters
◊ Camera manual
◊ 10x42 binoculars
◊ Strong and sturdy camera rucksack
◊ (This book!)

If money is no object:

◊ Spare DSLR body
◊ Dedicated macro lens
◊ 70-200mm f/2.8 lens
◊ 500mm f/4 lens
◊ 1.4x extender (converter)
◊ Top mounted flash unit
◊ Lightweight sturdy tripod
◊ Arctic Butterfly sensor cleaning brush
◊ Remote switch, preferably wireless
◊ Memory bank/photo viewer
◊ Polarising and neutral density filters
◊ (Someone to carry it all!)

Hiring and Firing

If you are not ready to invest in buying expensive equipment then consider hiring from reputable companies that offer this service. It will also allow you to test drive equipment before you clean out your bank account.

Careless Memory

Change cards sooner rather than later. If you only have 20 or so images left on the card then swap it for new one rather than risk having to change cards in the middle of an exciting shoot. Keep a spare card in your pocket to allow for a quick change.

▼ ***Bush Dinner, Makgadikgadi Pans. DSLR, 16-55mm Lens, f/5 @ 1/60, ISO 200. SS***

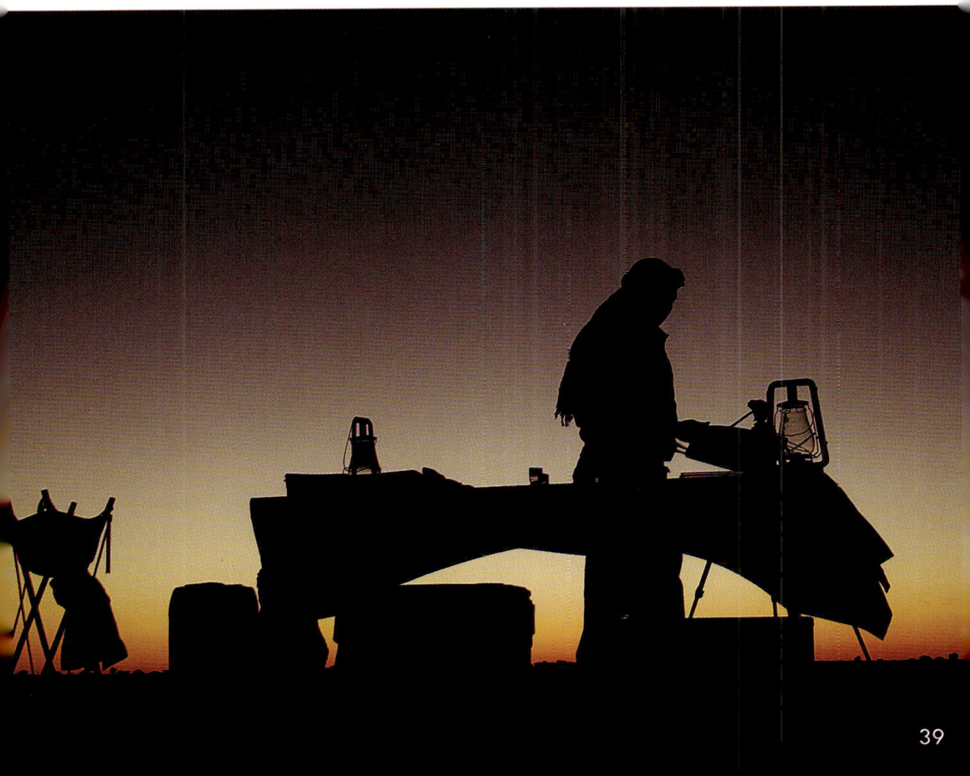

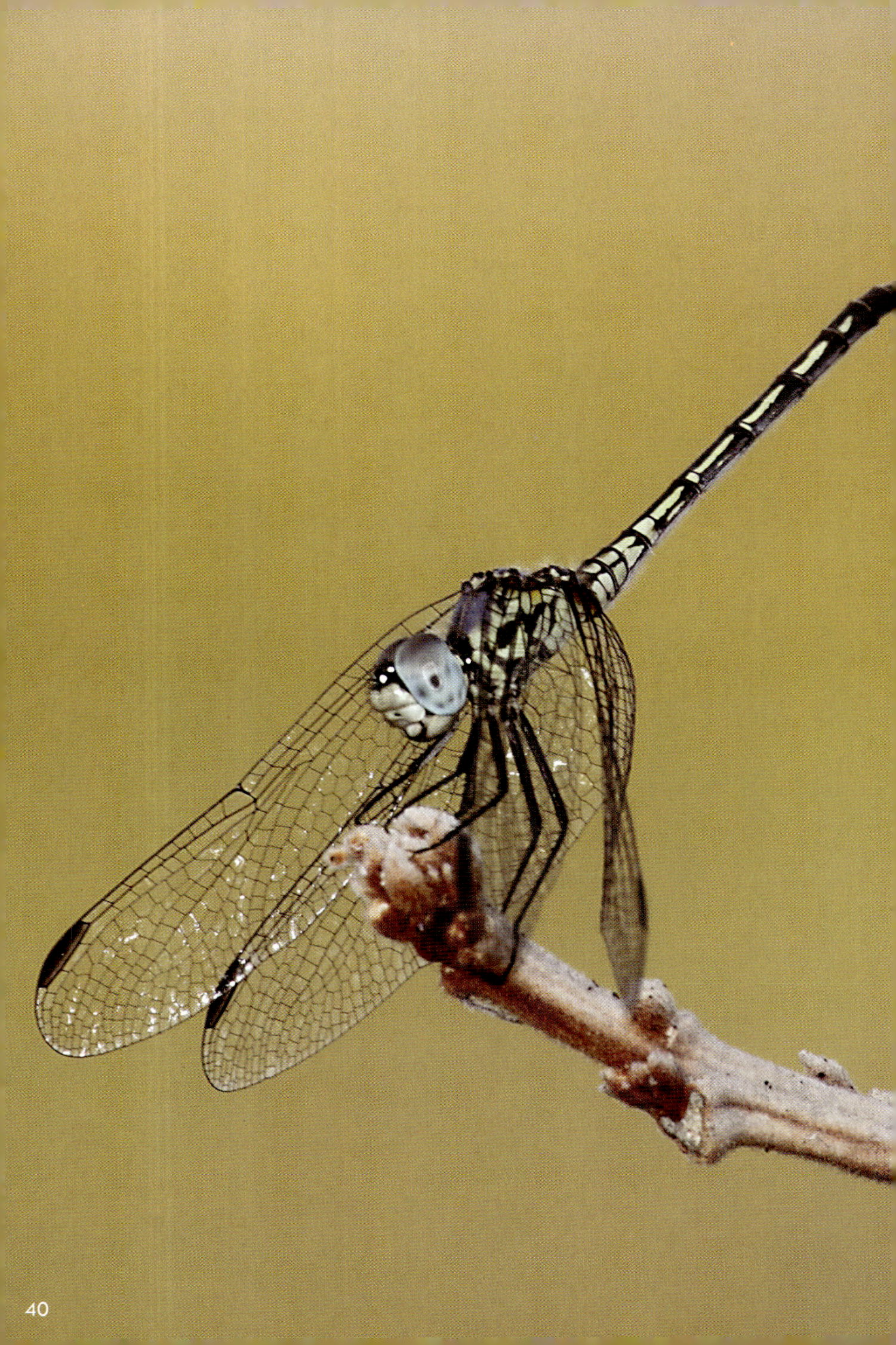

TECHNICAL ELEMENTS
SOUTHERN EXPOSURE

"There are no rules for good photogrcphs only good photographs." *Ansel Adams*

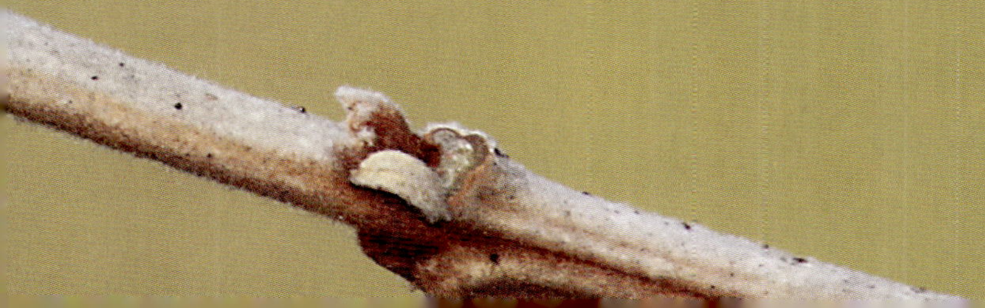

Technical Elements

Grasping the basic technical elements of aperture and shutter speed will give you the control to create the image and effect that you desire. The more you practice, the easier this will become until it is almost second nature. Getting familiar with your equipment prior to travelling will give you a huge advantage in the field, as when it comes to wildlife photography, there is often very little time to change your settings. Make sure you bring your manual to refer to if necessary.

Aperture

The lens aperture is the hole in the lens through which the light passes before it hits the camera sensor. By adjusting the aperture (signified by the f-number on your camera), you can change the size of this hole. The lower the f-number, the wider the hole and the more light that is let into the camera.

In addition, the aperture controls the **Depth of Field** (i.e. how much of the picture is in focus). A wide aperture (e.g. f/2.8) causes a shallow depth of field and is ideal for portraits as the blurred background emphasises the subject. A narrow aperture (e.g. f/16) has a greater depth of field and is useful for landscapes when you want both foreground and background in focus. Your choice of aperture will be restricted by the range available on your lens. Note that a lot of non-professional lenses tend to lose sharpness at extreme apertures, particularly at the narrow end of the scale. As a rough guide, we would not recommend reducing the aperture beyond f/18 or maybe f/22 at a stretch.

▶ ***Pretty Lady, Okavango Delta. DSLR, 100-400mm Lens, f/5.6 @ 1/320, ISO 100.*** A wide aperture blurs the background making the subject stand out. ***SS***

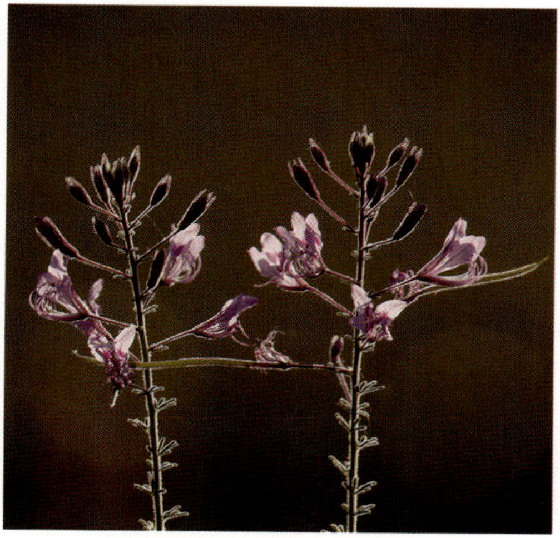

◀ ***Okavango Dropwing Dragonfly, Okavango Delta. DSLR, 100-400mm Lens, f/11 @ 1/200, ISO 200. If the background is some distance away, you can still create a shallow depth of field with a mid-range aperture. SS***

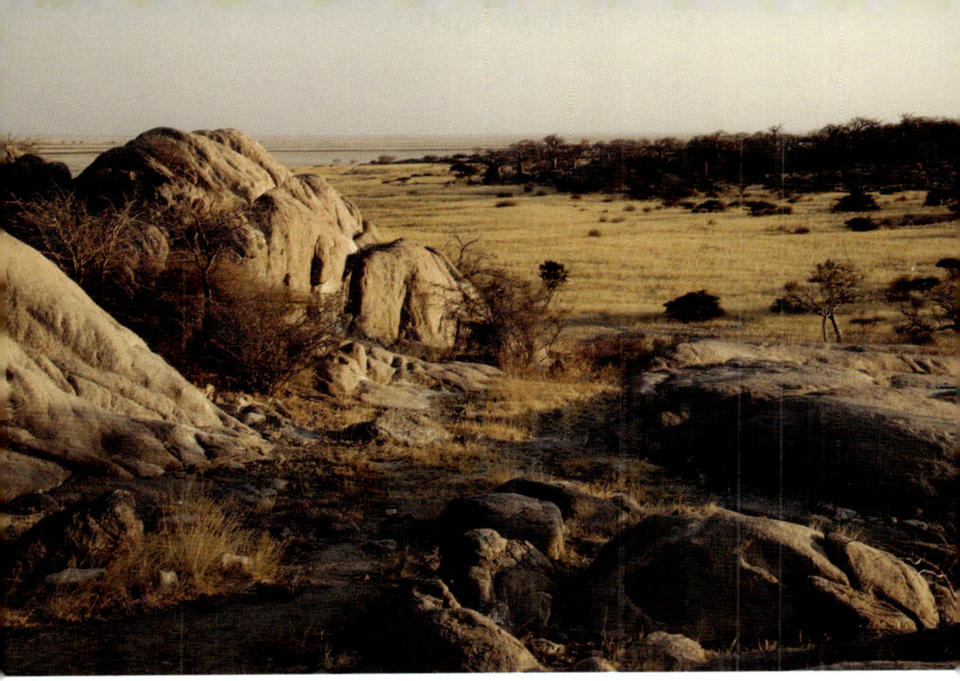

▲ ***Kubu Island, Makgadikgadi Pans. DSLR, 17-85mm Lens, f/16 @ 1/250, ISO 400.*** A narrow aperture creates a large depth of field, emphasising detail in a landscape. ***JG***

SHUTTER SPEED

The shutter speed refers to the length of time the shutter is open while the photo is being taken and on most models can range from 1/8000 to 30 seconds. It is normally measured in fractions of seconds thus 100 really means 1/100 of a second. When photographing a moving subject, setting the shutter speed to a high value like 1/500 will freeze the action and will also result in a crisper, sharper image when hand-holding the camera as it negates the effect of camera shake. The longer the lens (i.e. the greater the focal length), the faster the shutter speed needs to be.

The conventional rule when hand-holding is to shoot at a shutter speed no slower than 1/focal length i.e. a 400mm lens requires a minimum shutter speed of 1/400. However, with improving image stabilisers and the use of beanbags, it is now possible to obtain sharpness with slower speeds (although remember that movement of your subject will be a limiting factor). Alternatively, a slower shutter speed can be used to create impressionistic panning images to illustrate motion in a contrasting style (see p.44-45).

▶ ***Elephant, Makgadikgadi Pans National Park. DSLR, 100-400mm Lens, f/5.6 @ 1/3200, ISO 250.*** A fast shutter speed is vital to freeze the movement of water into individual droplets. **JG**

▶▶ ***Impala, Okavango Delta. DSLR, 100-400mm Lens, f/18 @ 1/25, ISO 800.*** Selecting continuous focus is an important element to creating a panning image. **SS**

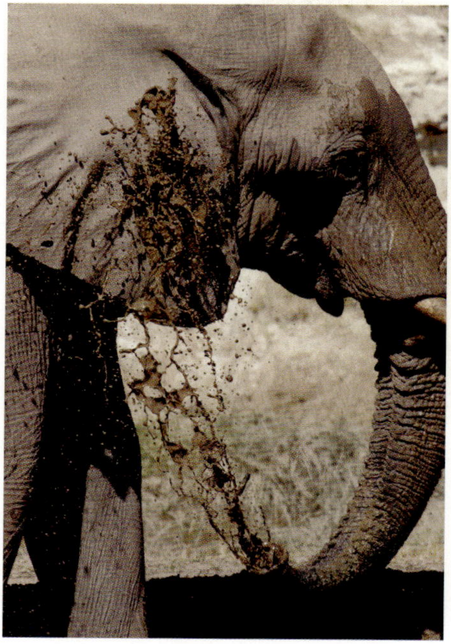

PANNING FOR GOLD

If an animal is moving parallel to you, you can create a striking, panning effect by tracking it with your camera using a slow shutter speed. This will streak the background into a blur whilst maintaining a sharp subject. It will take a lot of practice and many deleted files but if captured successfully, the exaggerated movement generates an impressive, artistic image. Use continuous focus mode (AI Servo) and try to pan at the same speed as the animal so it stays in exactly the same part of the viewfinder during the exposure. If you are using a telephoto lens with two stabiliser modes, you should switch to mode 2. The slower an animal is moving, the easier it will be to track accurately but you will also require a slower shutter speed to create the effect. This makes it harder to capture a sharp subject since any vertical movement, such as a nod of the animal's head, will blur that part of the image. Panning is particularly useful when low light prohibits the faster shutter speed needed for a normal shot. Leaving the shutter speed set to around 1/20 of a second in shutter priority mode allows you to quickly change modes for a panning shot without having to change any settings.

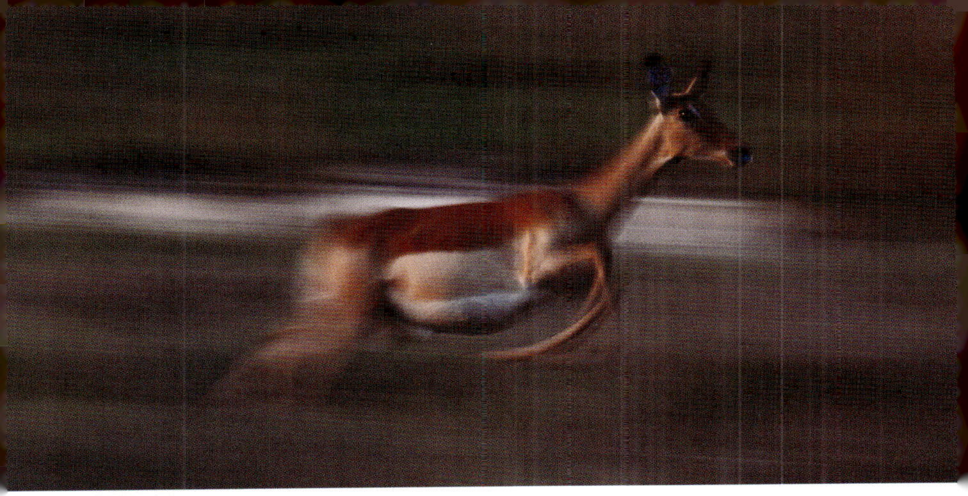

EXPOSURE - THE BASICS

The first step to taking a good photograph is to expose it correctly. This means allowing the precise amount of light onto the sensor so that the final image is neither too light nor too dark. The primary tools to do this are the aperture and shutter speed which work in conjunction so that in a given situation, raising one requires you to reduce the other for the image to be correctly exposed. Imagine you are filling a bucket from a tap: the more you turn on the tap (the wider the aperture), the shorter the time it will take to fill the bucket (the quicker the shutter speed). Adjustments to aperture and shutter speed are measured in stops: widening the aperture by 1 stop, say from f/8 to f/5.6, lets in twice the amount of light. To maintain the correct exposure you must therefore halve the amount of time the sensor is exposed by increasing the shutter speed by one stop, say from 1/250 to 1/500. There are therefore a number of different combinations of aperture and shutter speed which result in a perfectly exposed image: let's say you set an aperture of f/8 and a shutter speed of 1/250 which correctly exposes the scene. The following combinations would also be possible:

Exposure	Shutter Speed
f/4	1/1000
f/5.6	1/500
f/8	**1/250**
f/11	1/125
f/16	1/60

▶ ***N.B.*** *Many cameras will offer increments of 1/3 of a stop to allow more control. For example, between f/4 and f/5.6 you could also choose f/4.5 or f/5.0.*

The decision as to which of these pairs you choose to shoot with depends on the effect you are trying to portray. Specifically, do you want to emphasise movement by using a slower shutter speed or freeze fast-moving action using a higher shutter speed? Do you want to blur the background using a wide aperture or create a greater depth of field using a narrow aperture?

Shooting Modes

This may seem like a lot to think about, but fortunately your DSLR camera has two modes to make things easier once you have chosen your desired effect. If you want to freeze the action by using a fast shutter speed, then set the camera to **Shutter Priority Automatic Exposure (Tv/S)**, select the desired shutter speed and the camera will automatically match it with the aperture that will result in a correct exposure. If, however, it is more important that you have a greater depth of field, select **Aperture Priority Automatic Exposure (Av/A)**, choose a narrow aperture (high f-number) and your camera will select the appropriate shutter speed.

▼ ***Lion Cubs, Savuti, Chobe National Park. DSLR, 100-400mm, f/5.6 @ 1/400, ISO 400.***
High-speed continuous mode (see p.56) lets you capture the best shot in a sequence. ***JG***

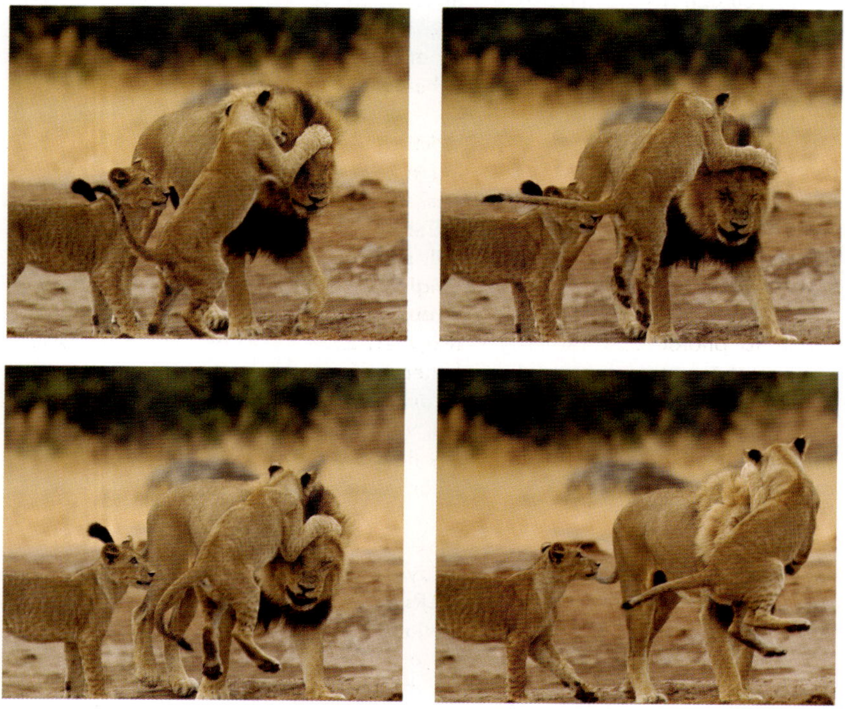

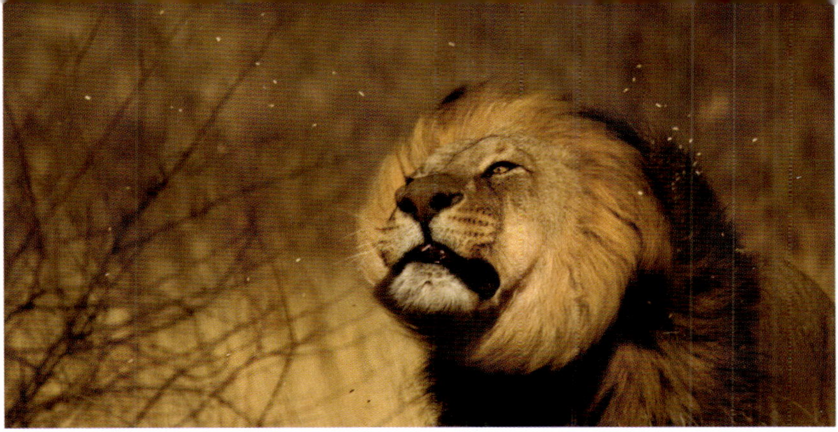

▲ ***Lion, Central Kalahari Game Reserve. DSLR, 100-400mm Lens, f/5.6 @ 1/1250, ISO 100.*** Selecting the widest aperture on Av/A ensures the fastest shutter speed. **JG**

In contrast, the **Manual Exposure (M)** mode allows you to adjust both aperture and shutter speed independently (see p.49 for more detail). The final creative mode is **Program Automatic Exposure (P)** where the camera selects both aperture and shutter speed as in **Automatic** mode, the difference being you can also change the other settings (ISO, focal points, metering etc). Program shift enables you to alter the aperture/shutter speed combination. It is therefore akin to a halfway house between Automatic and Aperture/Shutter Priority, but is probably most useful when shooting with a flash (see p.55).

Under Shutter Priority, the one restriction on your choice of shutter speeds is the brightness of the scene. If shooting in low light for example, you may select too fast a shutter speed for your lens: if your camera selected the maximum aperture the image would still be underexposed. In this situation the aperture number will flash and the camera will not allow you to take the picture. You can reduce the shutter speed accordingly until you attain the aperture needed to expose correctly but, by the time you have done this, the leopard you were trying to photograph may have disappeared. Conversely, in bright light if you select too slow a shutter speed then there may not be an aperture small enough to stop the scene from being overexposed. The equivalent dilemma in Aperture Priority is most common with very narrow apertures. In low light the appropriate shutter speed selected by the camera will be very slow which may blur the image through camera shake or subject movement.

Consequently, it always pays to have the camera set up so you can take a shot instantly. When in the field, always leave your camera switched on (an automatic sleep function on most DSLRs will save your batteries) and, under Aperture Priority mode, choose the widest aperture. This is the quickest way of obtaining the highest possible shutter speed given the available light and offers you the best chance of catching that split-second award winning shot!

More on Exposure

The camera measures the exposure of a particular scene using its built-in light meter to assess the tones of the image. Given the camera "sees" in tones rather than colours, in order to expose the image correctly, it will assume the subject is a mid-tone grey. So, to achieve a correctly exposed image, you need to point the camera at a mid-tone object. Unfortunately, often your subject is not so conveniently coloured, in which case you need to compensate accordingly. If, for example, your subject is a white egret, the camera will automatically underexpose (because it assumes the subject is grey) so you must "dial in" 1-2 stops of **Exposure Compensation** to portray the egret as white - i.e. overexpose by 1-2 stops. Conversely, if you are photographing a dark honey badger, the camera will automatically overexpose so you must underexpose by 1-2 stops to bring out the black of his fur. If you are unsure about the amount of compensation required, then reviewing your histogram will help (see p.56).

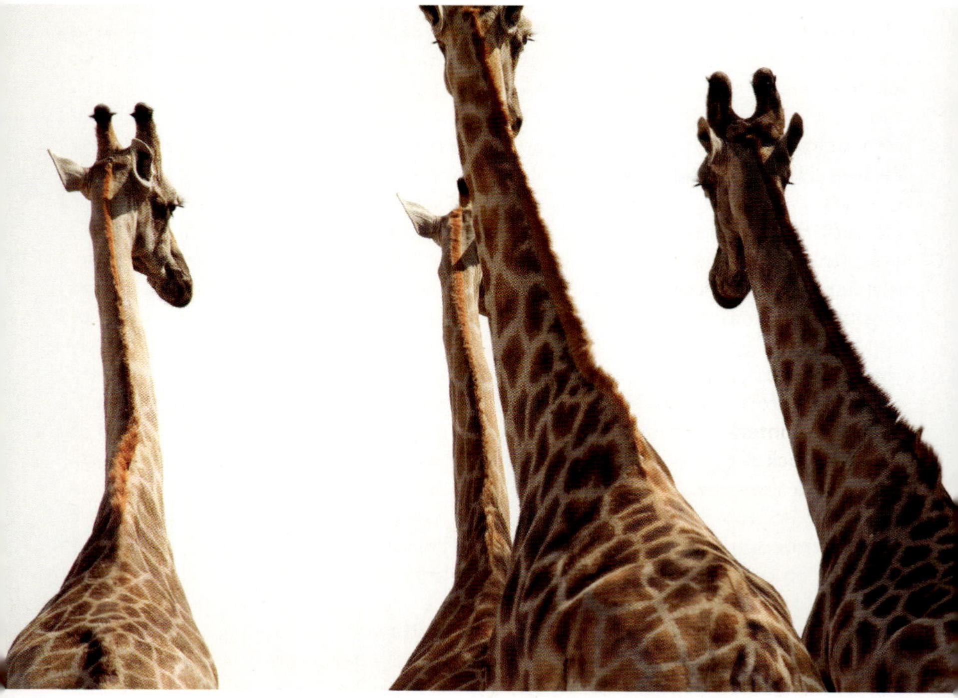

▲ ***Southern Giraffe, Central Kalahari Game Reserve. DSLR, 100-400mm Lens, f/5.6 @ 1/640, ISO 250.*** Metering on the giraffe ensured they were correctly exposed but necessitated blowing out the sky. ***JG***

Check Please

Get into the habit of checking your settings in the viewfinder before each shot. It is all too easy to accidentally adjust everything from the shooting mode dial to the eye-piece calibration, or to forget to reset exposure compensation which might ruin your subsequent photos. This is especially important first thing in the morning as often you will have raised your ISO the previous evening. Ultra-high shutter speeds will act as a pointer if you have forgotten.

Also, make sure the brightness of your LCD screen is on a mid-range setting. If it is too bright, dark images can look correctly exposed and you may only discover your mistake during processing when it is too late.

Exposure compensation only works in Aperture, Shutter Priority and Program modes. The camera calculates the appropriate shutter speed or aperture and you can then tell it to over or underexpose by a certain amount.

An alternative to using the exposure compensation function is to switch to **Manual Exposure (M)** mode. This allows you to adjust the shutter speed and aperture independently using the built-in light meter to gauge the exposure (see p.50). Consequently, you can select a combination which, according to the meter, is over or underexposing by the desired amount. The resultant aperture and shutter speed settings will be the same as if you had used the exposure compensation function under Shutter or Aperture Priority.

Exposure Lock (AE-L) allows you to lock the exposure at a different place to the point of focus before then recomposing the image. It is particularly useful when spot metering (see p.50) as you can point the centre of the camera to a mid-tone, lock the exposure, then take the picture as normal thereby obviating the need to use exposure compensation.

Auto Exposure Bracketing (AEB) can be useful if you are concerned you are not going to achieve a correctly exposed image. After setting the AEB amount (normally up to 2 stops), you take three shots of the same scene. The result is a bracketed sequence whereby the first shot will be of standard exposure, the second will underexpose by the AEB amount, and the third will overexpose by the AEB amount. Given the time taken to set AEB up and the extra memory space used, we normally prefer to check the exposure of the image using the histogram (see p.56) then retake the shot using exposure compensation if necessary.

METERING METHODS

There are several different methods that control how the camera evaluates the brightness of, or meters, a scene.

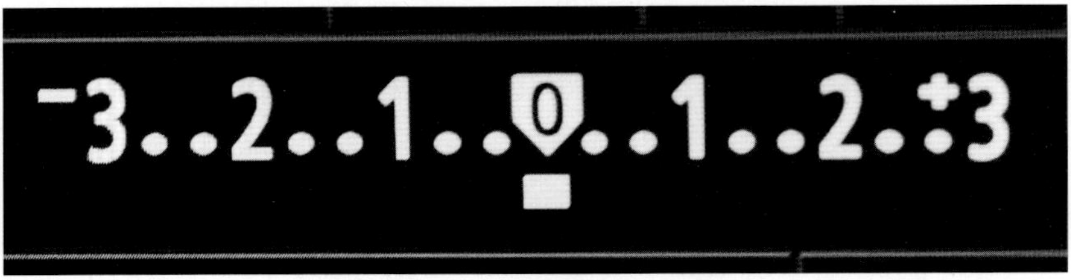

▲ ***Light Meter.*** When the bar lines up with 0 it indicates correct exposure. The numbers to the left of 0 represent stops of underexposure and, to the right, overexposure. Under Av(A), Tv(S) or P modes you can move the bar to dial-in exposure compensation.

Evaluative metering (also known as **Pattern** or **Matrix**) is the default system which divides the frame into segments then uses a database of shots to determine the correct exposure. For example, if the top of the image is brighter than the rest, it may assume that that is the sky and therefore less important and will expose for the rest of the image. This will often yield effective results, unless a tricky lighting situation "fools" the light meter. Ever tried to take a picture of a giraffe in the shade only for it to come out as a black silhouette?

If the subject is very dark or bright or, more importantly, much darker or brighter than the background (e.g. if you are shooting into the sun), then you should switch to **Spot Metering** which takes a meter reading from a small area at the centre of the viewfinder. You will probably want to use this in conjunction with the exposure-lock function (see p.49). In this way you can ensure your subject is correctly exposed without it being affected by the relative brightness of other parts of the image. If the difference in brightness between the subject and background is too great, then you must choose whether you want to expose for the whole scene (and risk underexposing your subject) or to expose for the subject (and overexpose the sky, as on p.48)

Partial or **Centre-Circle Metering** is similar to spot, but uses a slightly larger area at the centre of the viewfinder. By increasing the area, this avoids the risk of accidentally metering on a non-mid-tone, for example if your subject area contains bright spots of reflected light.

Centre-Weighted Metering assumes your subject is in the centre of the image and therefore the metering is weighted towards the centre and then averaged for the rest of the frame. Although occasionally useful, this system has largely been superseded by evaluative metering.

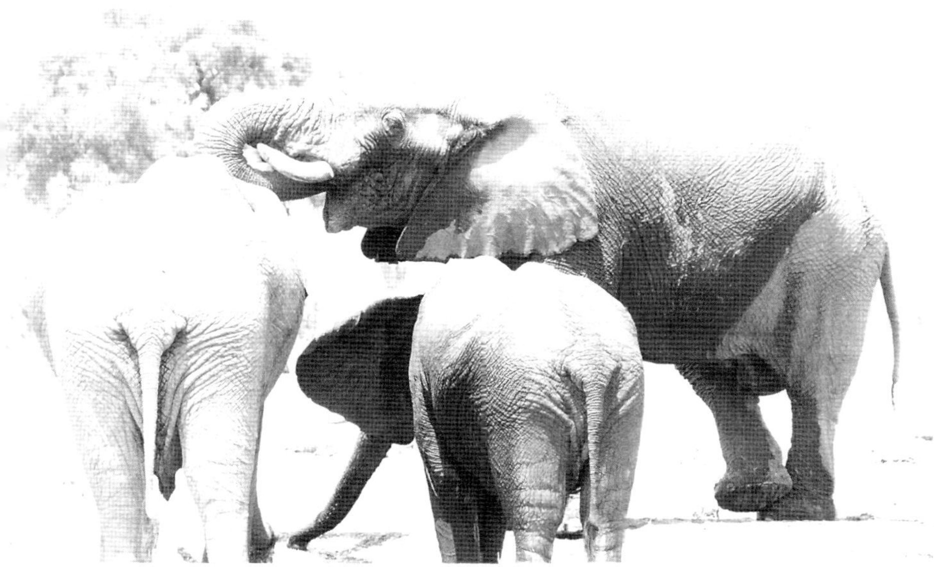

▲ ***Elephant, Savuti, Chobe National Park. DSLR, 100-400mm Lens, f/5.6 @ 1/4000, ISO 12800.*** I purposefully overrode the camera's metering to illustrate the effect of overexposing. ***SS***

FOCUS

It does not matter how amazing the subject matter, an out of focus picture will always look amateurish. Fortunately, with today's auto-focus technology, sharp focus is not that difficult to achieve - all that is needed is concentration and, well... focus!

The first question is where you want to be focusing and that depends on your choice of aperture. When shooting with a wide aperture you will have a shallow depth of field. It is therefore vital that your point of focus is the most important part of the image as this is what the viewer will immediately be drawn to. For wildlife portraits, most often this will be the eyes of the animal or bird unless you are deliberately trying to emphasise an alternative characteristic. Being the most expressive feature, sharp eyes will boost the photograph's power and appeal.

If there is more than one animal in the picture however, you must choose which one to focus on. Experiment with different focal subjects in the same scene and you will be surprised by the effect it makes on the impact of the photograph. The larger the distance between the animals and the closer you are to the subject, the greater the effect will be.

Shooting with a narrow aperture requires an alternative approach. The aim of a narrow aperture is to have as much of the image in focus as possible - so where do you focus? The principle is that at minimum aperture, the maximum depth of field (i.e. the range of focus) is achieved by focusing on a point one third of the way into the image. So, if the furthest subject in the frame is 120m away from you, then your focal point should be one third of that distance, i.e. 40m away from the camera. Obviously, you are not going to get your tape measure out in the middle of the Okavango Delta, but it is a useful guideline. The **Depth of Field Preview** button can also be used to check the focus before you take the picture.

The next step is telling the camera where you want it to focus. By setting the **Auto-Focus (AF)** mode to **One Shot (Single)** and looking through the viewfinder, you will see various tiny boxes, any of which you can choose to be your **Focal Point.** Alternatively, you can let the camera choose the correct focal point automatically, but despite all its impressive attributes, a DSLR is not a mind-reader so this should only be used in unusual situations (examples on next page). Of course, the points do not cover every part of the image, so most of the time you will be using **Focus Lock.** By pressing the shutter button down halfway, you can lock the focus, recompose the shot then take the picture. In difficult lighting situations or if your subject is partially hidden by vegetation, the camera may fail to achieve auto-focus (signified by the lens continually "searching" in and out). In this case it is best to switch the lens to **Manual Focus** and do it the old-fashioned way.

▼ ***Trithemis Dragonfly, Makgadikgadi Pans National Park. DSLR, 100-400mm Lens, f/5.6 @ 1/640, ISO 160.*** The choice of focal point can change the impact of your image dramatically. Always look for the opportunity to create an original perspective. ***JG***

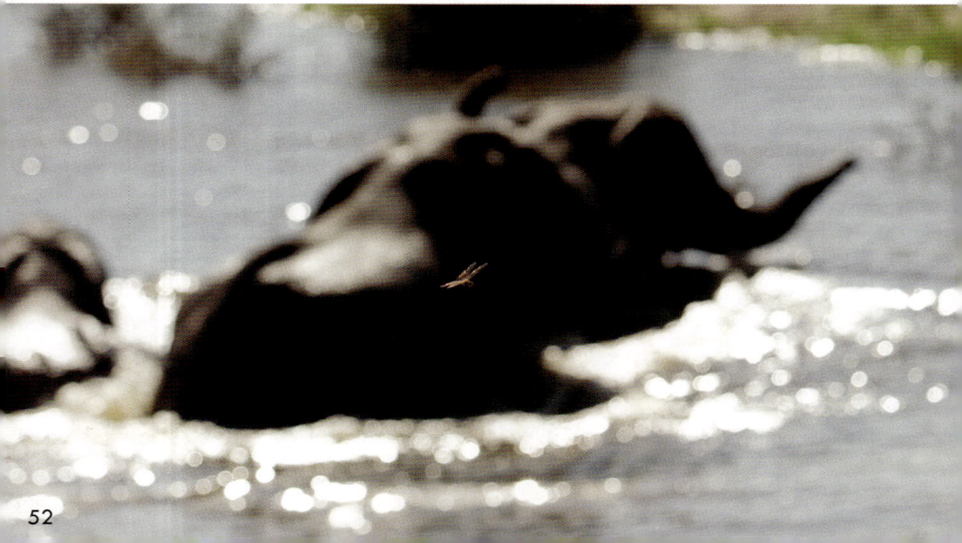

If your subject is moving quickly, for example a bird in flight, it may be difficult to keep a single focal point on the bird. This is one of the few situations that you might switch to **Automatic Focal Point Selection.** Given the background is clear, the camera can easily identify the subject and choose the appropriate focal point thus allowing you to concentrate on composing the shot and keeping the bird in your viewfinder.

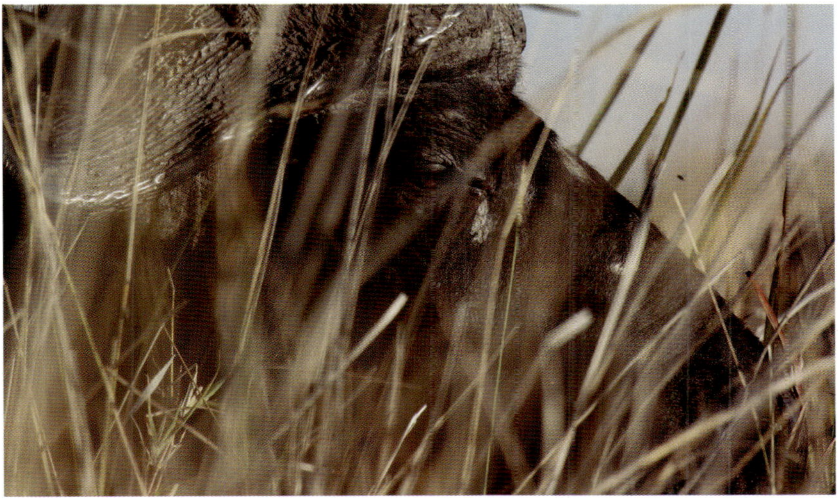

▲ ***Cape Buffalo, Okavango Delta. DSLR, 100–400mm Lens, f/10 @ 1/400, ISO 320.*** Switching to manual focus allowed me to focus on the buffalo's eye instead of the grass in front of him. ***SS***

The other problem with moving animals is that the distance between the subject and the camera may change in the second or two between locking the focus and actually taking the picture. Since the focus is locked on the place where the subject was, this means the final image will be slightly out of focus. In this case, you should switch the Auto-Focus mode from single shot to **Continuous (AI Servo)** focus. Instead of locking the focus, the camera will now continually refocus on the moving subject thereby ensuring a sharp final picture. Under continuous focus, you can either select the focal point yourself (for example if a lion is approaching you slowly and you want to ensure the focal point is on his eyes). Alternatively, you can switch to automatic focal point selection if the animal is moving more quickly, when using a single focal point may inadvertently risk focusing on the background instead of the subject.

Several cameras also have a hybrid auto-focus mode sometimes called **AF-A** or **AI Focus.** The idea is that the camera automatically switches from single to continuous if the subject starts moving. However, this often yields imperfect results and we would advise against using it.

▶ ***Small-spotted Genet, Okavango Delta. SLR, 100-400mm Lens, Fuji Provia 100F, Flash.*** A flash will illuminate your subject but be mindful of upsetting their night vision. **SS**

▼ ***Lion, Okavango Delta. DSLR, 100-400mm Lens, f/5.6 @ 640, ISO 3200.*** A high ISO rating will add grain to your image. ***SS***

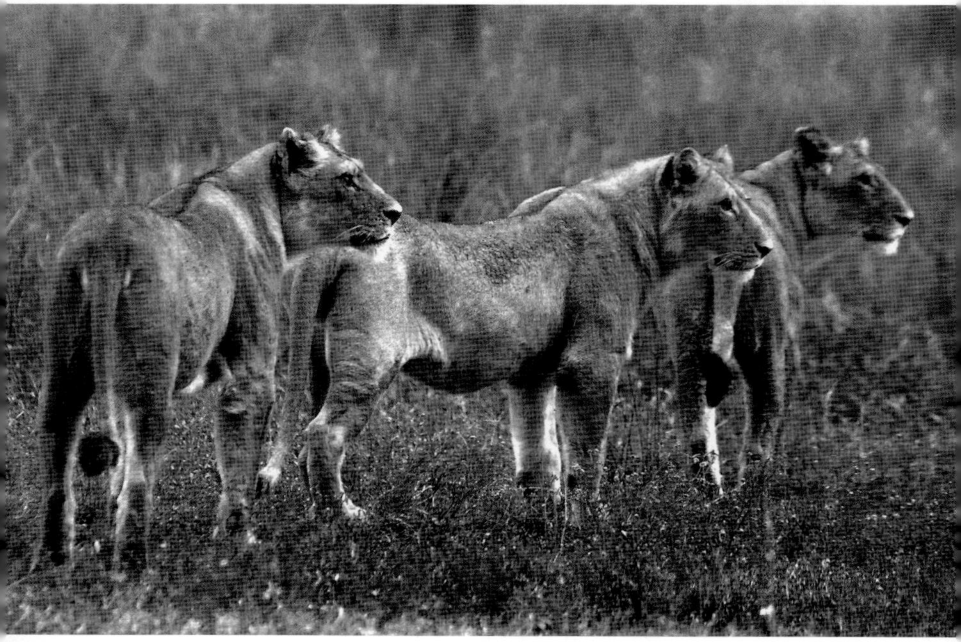

ISO

The ISO refers to the sensitivity of your sensor in the case of digital, and to film sensitivity in the case of a film camera. The effect of raising the ISO is to permit a faster shutter speed with the same aperture, so it is particularly useful in low light scenarios where even the maximum aperture does not give you a quick enough shutter speed to capture sharp, correctly exposed images. There is a cost to this however, which is reflected in the quality of the image as higher ISOs will result in more grain or noise. Generally, shooting on an ISO of 400 or less, this impact will be negligible and technical advancements are constantly pushing this boundary further. If the light is poor and your shutter speed is too slow on your widest aperture, then your immediate reaction should be to increase the ISO. Top end DSLRs are capable of ISOs of 12,800 or more, allowing photography in almost no light, albeit with an element of noise. Occasionally however, this grainy effect is desirable, particularly if you are shooting in black and white or sepia.

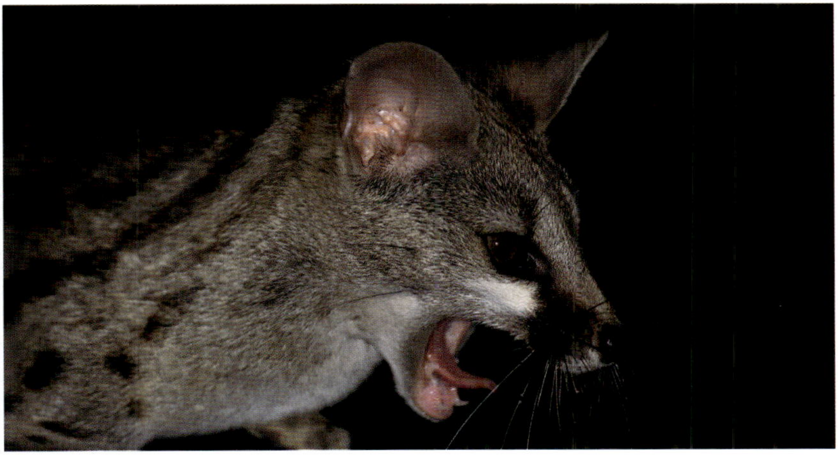

Using Flash

Flash photography brings its own set of technicalities that could take up an entire chapter. Luckily we have plenty of light in Botswana but there are still occasions during the day where a flash can be useful, such as when photographing a leopard in the shady canopy of a tree as well as the more obvious nocturnal situations. A sharp light can disturb your subject so it is best to check with your guide if using a flash is appropriate.

Although most cameras have built-in flashes, using an external unit will provide much more power and therefore cover a greater distance. Unless you are experienced with flash, you are best off setting a dedicated flash unit to **TTL (Through-The-Lens)** which automatically calculates the strength of beam to emit. For dark scenes, Program (P) mode is the easiest way to ensure correct exposure. Adding a **Flash Extender** will increase its range further while conversely, a **Diffuser** will soften the light but reduce its reach.

In harsh midday light the overhead sun can cast unsightly shadows on an animal's face, an instance where **Fill-in Flash** can be useful. Shooting on aperture priority with evaluative metering will expose correctly for the rest of the scene, while the burst of light will 'fill in' the shadows on your foreground subject. If you are relatively close to the animal, you may have to dial in minus **Flash Exposure Compensation** of 1-2 stops to avoid overexposing (this can be done on the camera or on the flash itself).

When low lighting forces a slower shutter speed, a burst of flash can also help to freeze movement thus improving sharpness while the infra-red beam emitted before firing will simultaneously assist with auto-focus.

Drive Modes

For normal photography, your drive mode should be set to **Single Shooting** which (unsurprisingly) means that pressing the shutter button results in a single photo being taken. With fast action sequences, such as a sprinting cheetah or a yawning lion, it is worth switching to **Continuous** drive mode. The camera will fire off a burst of shots as long as the shutter button is depressed thus improving your chances of capturing the best image of the sequence. Some cameras give you the choice of high-speed or low-speed continuous, the difference being the number of frames shot per second (fps), which will be capped by your camera model. The final drive mode, **Self-timer,** is worth using on long tripod exposures to avoid camera vibration if you do not have a remote switch.

Histograms

Most cameras can display two histograms of each image: a RGB (colour) graph and a brightness chart, but the latter is the most useful. The x-axis indicates the brightness level (dark on the left progressing to light on the right), while the y-axis measures the number of pixels recorded for each tone. Theoretically, the histogram should peak in the centre for a correctly exposed photograph. If there are too many pixels on the far left of the graph, the image is underexposed while too much on the right indicates overexposure. By checking the histogram in the field, you can retake the shot with exposure compensation if necessary. In difficult lighting situations, such as when capturing silhouettes, creating the desired effect may require an underexposed image.

▶ ***Blue Wildebeest, Makgadikgadi Pans National Park. DSLR, 100-400mm Lens, f/18 @ 1/15, ISO 100.*** A narrow aperture and low ISO enabled a slow shutter speed for this panning effect. ***JG***

Buffer Zone

When shooting in high-speed continuous drive mode, it is not just the camera that determines how fast you can shoot. The number of fps will certainly be a limiting factor but the photos are stored on a buffer while you are still shooting. When you release the shutter button (or the buffer gets full - whichever is first), the images get written onto your memory card. So if you have a really fast camera with a slow memory card, once the buffer is full, you will have to wait several seconds before you can shoot again.
Consequently, it pays to be selective over when you start and stop high-speed shooting as otherwise the card may still be recording the images when the real action begins.

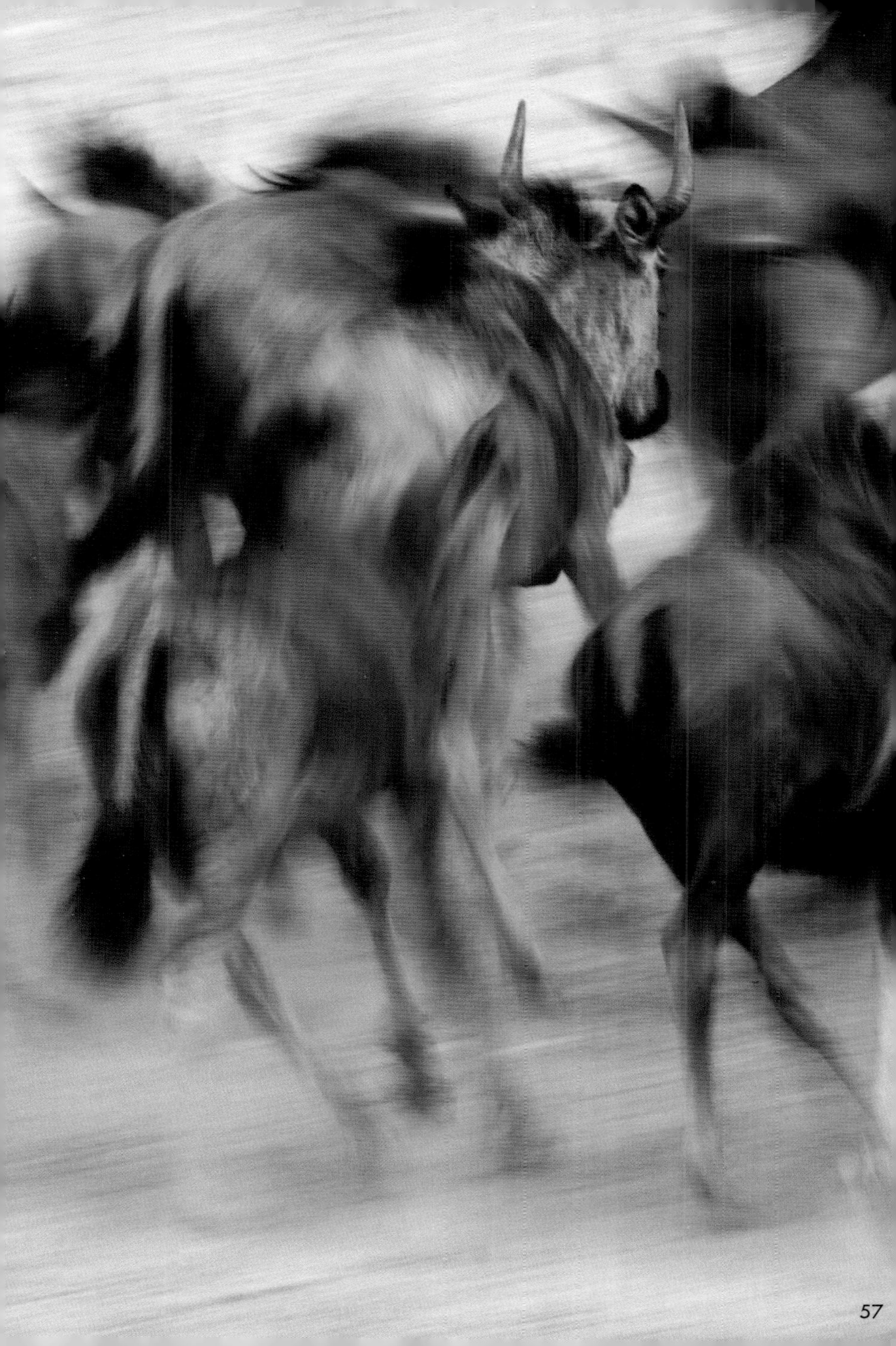

White Balance

The colour of light varies according to its source and is calibrated by its temperature. Adjusting the white balance on your camera will help it to identify the lighting situation and ensure the colours of your image are recorded accurately.

In most conditions, leaving your white balance on **Automatic (AWB)** will be adequate so you will usually only need to adjust this under artificial lighting, such as fluorescent, tungsten or if using a flash. On overcast days, setting the white balance to Cloudy will help to warm up your photographs. By shooting in RAW, you can easily adjust the white balance when processing the image in case your camera has misread the lighting circumstances.

▶ ***Brown Hyena, Makgadikgadi Pans. DSLR, 100-400mm Lens, f/5.6 @ 1/500, ISO 160.***
By shooting in RAW, I could add extra punch to this hyena with minor post-production adjustments without impacting the quality of the image. **JG**

Why Aren't My Images Sharp?

◊ Shutter speed is too slow causing camera shake. Use a beanbag/tripod, widen the aperture or raise the ISO.

◊ Shutter speed is too slow for a moving subject. Widen the aperture, raise the ISO or try panning instead.

◊ Lens image stabiliser has been switched off or is on the wrong mode.

◊ Lens is on manual focus instead of auto-focus.

◊ Telephoto lens focusing range is set to the wrong distance.

◊ Focal point selection is set to automatic instead of manual.

◊ Auto-focus is set to continuous mode instead of one/single shot.

◊ Vegetation is obscuring the subject confusing the auto-focus.

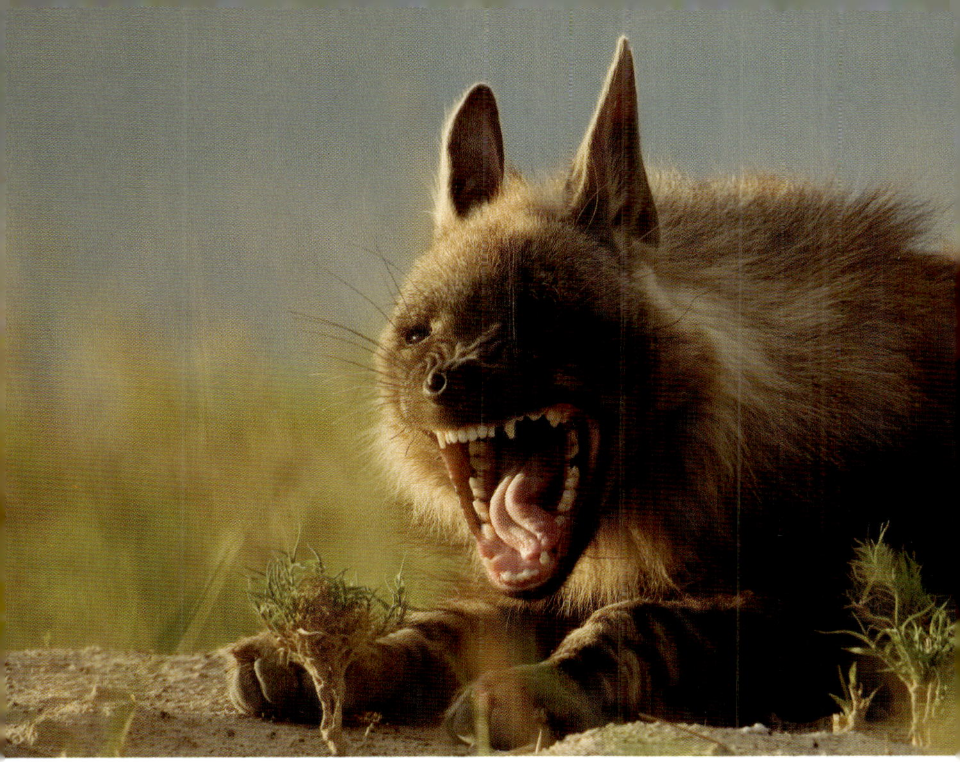

RAW vs. JPEG

RAW files record all the settings used in the shot and store them separately which allows you to alter them later during computer processing without any loss in image quality. **JPEG** files compress the image information, taking up less memory space. However, it is a "lossy" format so editing the file (and even resaving) can result in a loss in image quality.

If you shoot in RAW, you will have to process the photos when you get home, but this format produces the highest quality files and is the choice of the professionals. If you have no plans to edit the photos afterwards, then you are better off shooting in JPEG - the quality will still be sufficient to produce decent prints, although not to the same scale as in RAW format.

Once you have finished processing the RAW file, you can choose to save it as either a JPEG or a **TIFF** file. TIFFs are 'lossless" meaning they do not discard any data and you can make subsequent changes to the file without any loss in quality. They are therefore much bigger than the equivalent JPEG (requiring more hard drive space) but will produce better quality prints - the difference becoming more apparent the larger the print.

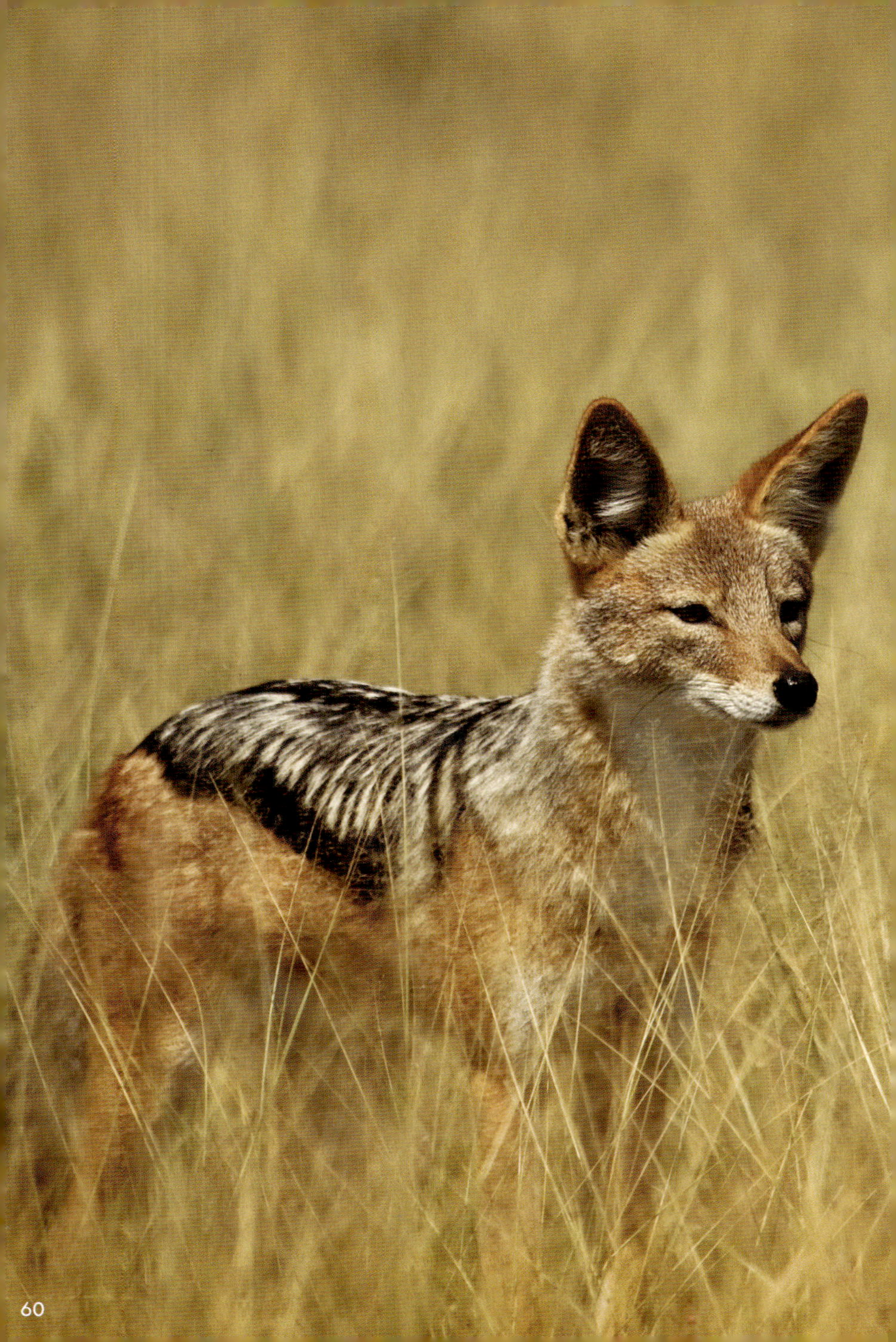

Composition
In the Eye of the Beholder

"Before a camera is even touched much of the hard work of photography is done." *David Noton*

Composition

Understanding the technical elements of photography is vital for taking good pictures, but these are only the tools which allow you to create the image. More important is the composition of the photograph itself and this is where you can let your creative side take over. An almost infinite combination of the type of lens, filters, apertures, shutter speeds and shooting angles mean there are thousands of possible pictures you could create from an identical scene. As the photographer, you have the ability to choose to portray a male lion as a powerful predator or as a beautiful and affectionate father. This chapter will provide a few guidelines for achieving better compositions but the best way to learn is to look at images you like and to ask yourself why you like them. Originality is key so experiment whenever you have the chance and by analysing your photos, you will slowly build a unique style.

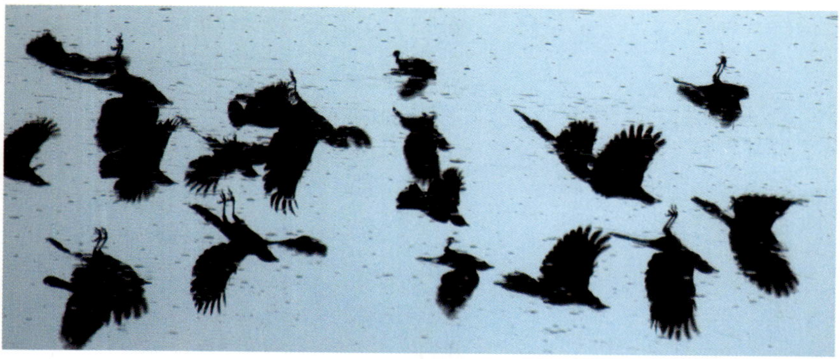

▲ ***Reflected Burchell's Starlings, Makgadikgadi Pans National Park. DSLR, 100-400mm Lens, f/5.6 @ 1/800, ISO 400***

Having heard lions all night, I arrived at this waterhole before dawn hoping to see a feline visitor. Despite their notable absence, the time spent waiting gave me the opportunity to capture this more creative shot of starlings coming to drink. **JG**

▶ ***Burchell's Zebra, Makgadikgadi Pans National Park. DSLR, 100-400mm Lens, f/9 @ 1/160, ISO 400***

A popular compositional tool is the use of lines which can transform a good photograph into an excellent one. Often these lines are more subtle than in this example so keep your eye out for anything which can be used to draw the viewer into the picture. **JG**

◀ ***Black-backed Jackal, Central Kalahari Game Reserve. DSLR, 100-400mm Lens, f/5.6 @ 1/1250, ISO 100***

When thinking about where to place your subject in the picture, it is worth considering how to use empty space. The eye will naturally follow the direction in which an animal is looking and so, if it is facing slightly away from the camera, give space to his directional gaze. This adds impact to the image. **JG**

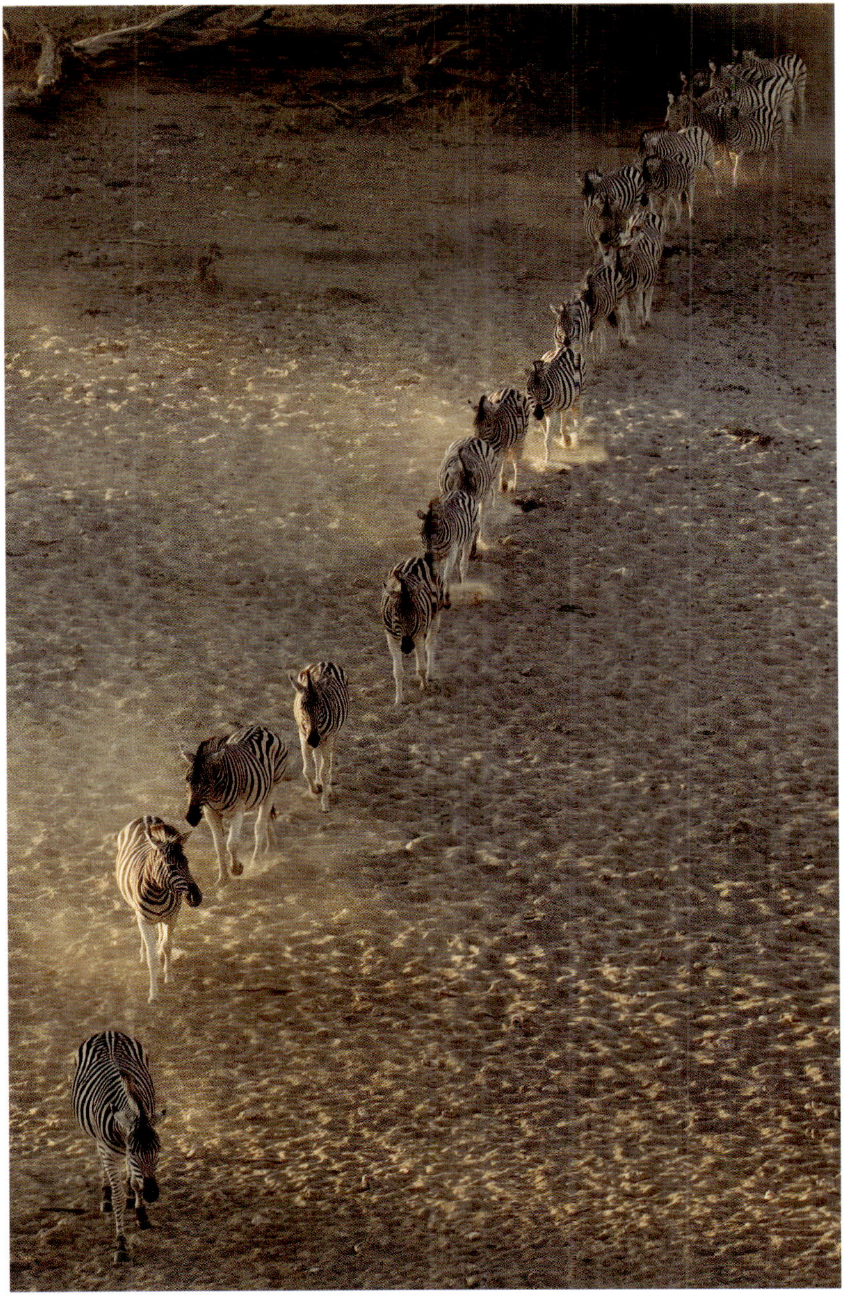

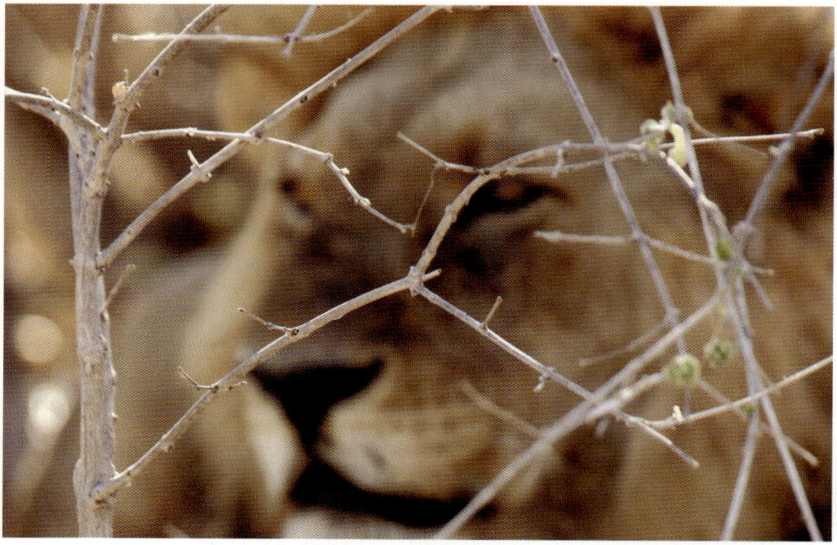

▲ ***Lion, Savuti, Chobe National Park. DSLR, 100-400mm Lens, f/5.6 @ 1/125, ISO 200***

We came across a Savuti pride male one morning and, as is so often the case, branches obstructed our view. I switched the lens to manual focus and instead focused on the branches in front of him. This creates a very interesting perspective and makes use of a situation that would otherwise seem unlikely to produce a decent image. **SS**

The Rule of Thirds

The rule of thirds is probably the most discussed aspect of composition. Essentially, if you imagine your viewfinder divided into thirds, both horizontally and vertically, then the most important parts of the picture should lie as close as possible to one of those four lines. It will often work well for landscapes and can also be a useful guide for portraits, especially when starting out. You will quickly learn not to place the subject in the centre of the frame which generally leads to a less interesting composition. However, rules are there to be broken and it is just as important to think outside the box and to experiment - sometimes the results can be even more arresting.

▶ ***Impala with Young, Okavango Delta. DSLR, 100-400mm Lens, f/8 @ 1/320, ISO 200***

Framing is an all-important aspect of photography. Look for different angles and ways to capture your subject. This image offers an unusual height perspective of the young impala under its mother's belly. **SS**

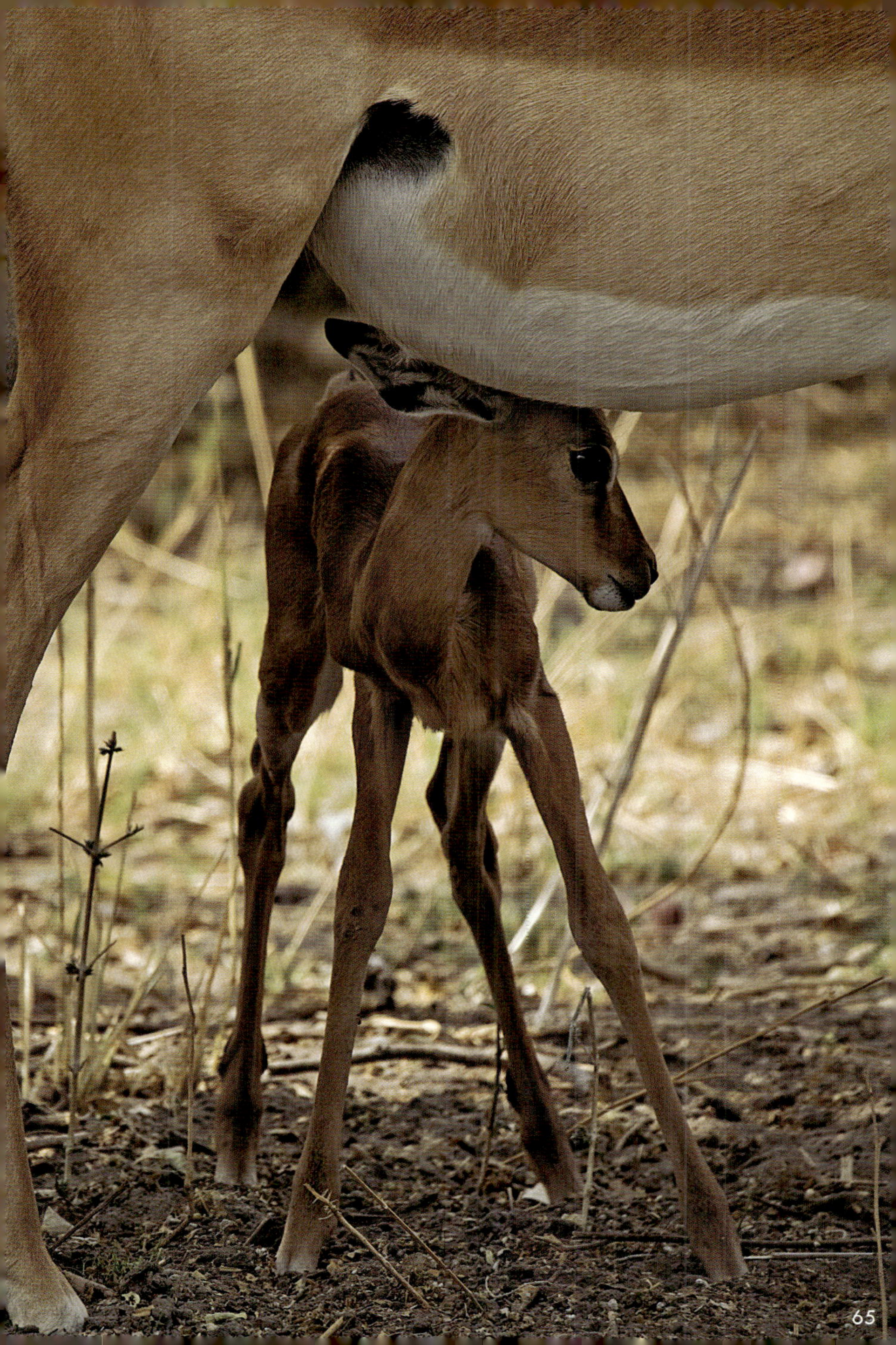

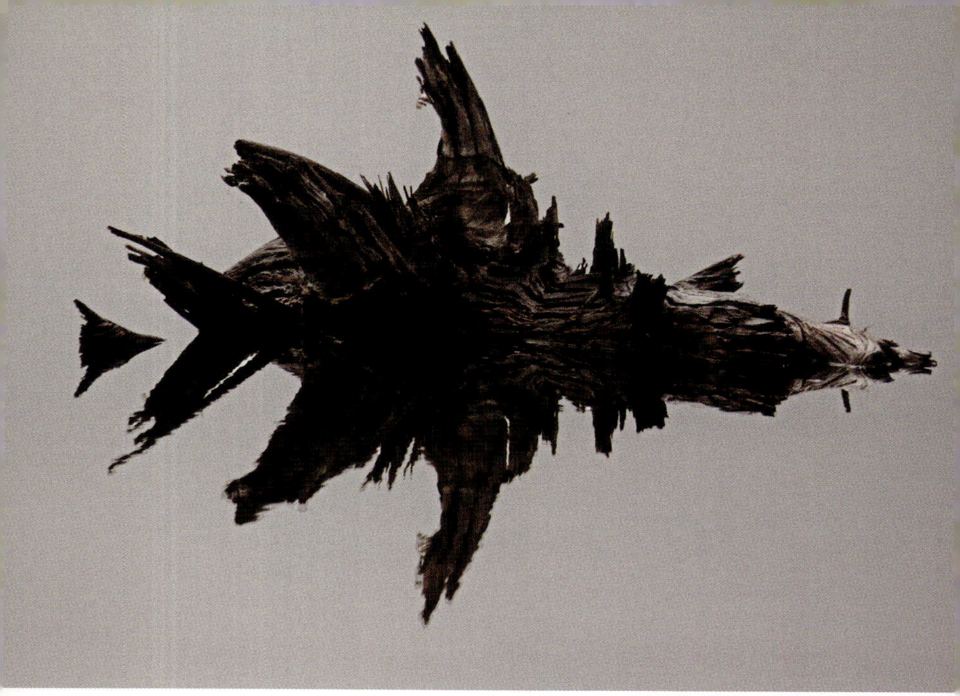

▲ ***Log Reflection, Okavango Delta. DSLR, 100-400mm Lens, f/5.6 @ 1/3200, ISO 3200***

There is always something to photograph when you are on safari. Travelling along the Khwai River, I noticed this clear reflection of a log surrounded by the recently arrived flood waters. **SS**

▶ ***Flamingo Colony, Makgadikgadi Pans. DSLR, 100-400mm Lens, f/5.6 @ 1/1600, ISO 100***

A classic example of the rule of thirds, this was taken on the edge of Sowa Pan where flamingos form a giant nesting colony during the rains. A spectacle to behold, it is worth stopping off at Sowa when travelling between Francistown and Nata if the flamingos are around. **JG**

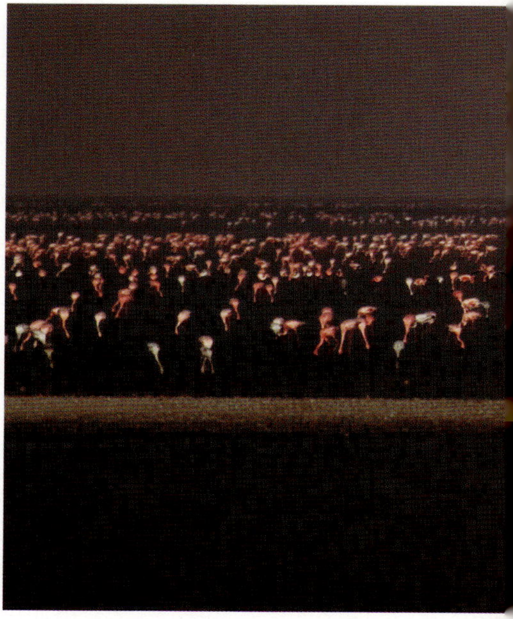

▶ ***Southern Giraffe, Chobe River. DSLR, 18-55mm Lens, f/11 @ 1/250, ISO 200***

Getting down low in the vehicle gave these giraffes a beautiful silhouette against the golden skyline of the Chobe River. Low angle images emphasise the height of your subjects, especially with larger mammals. **SS**

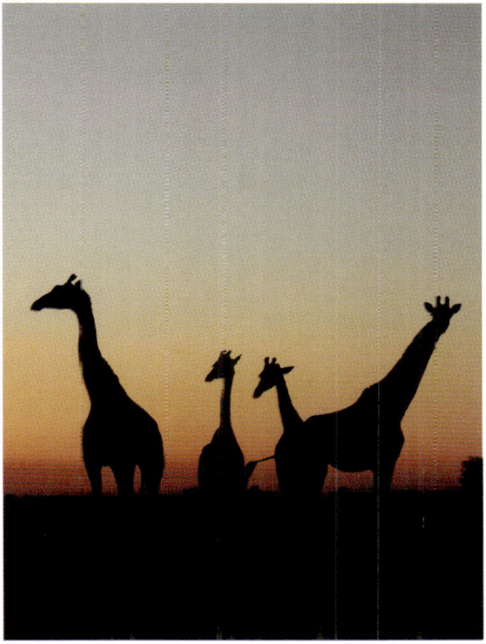

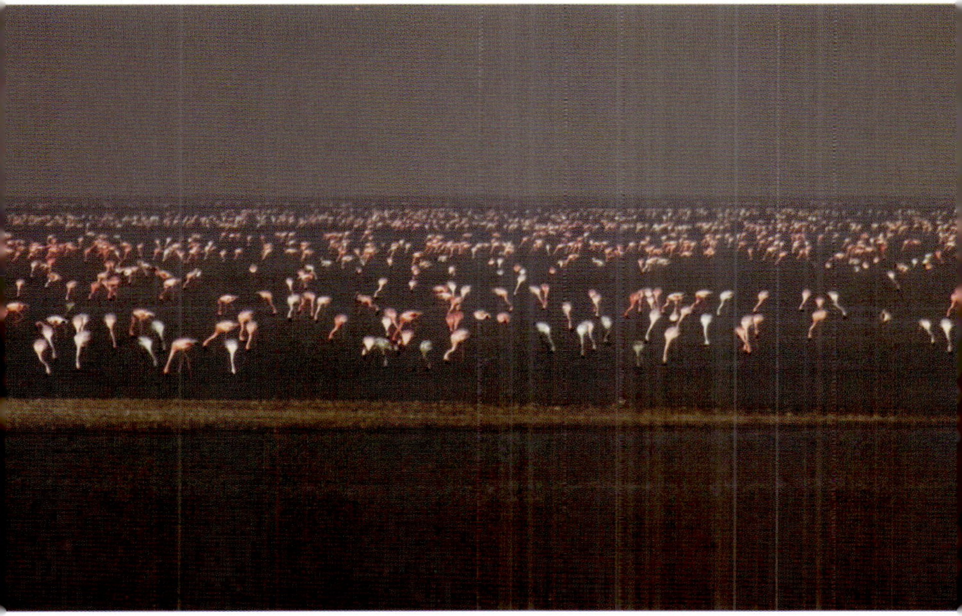

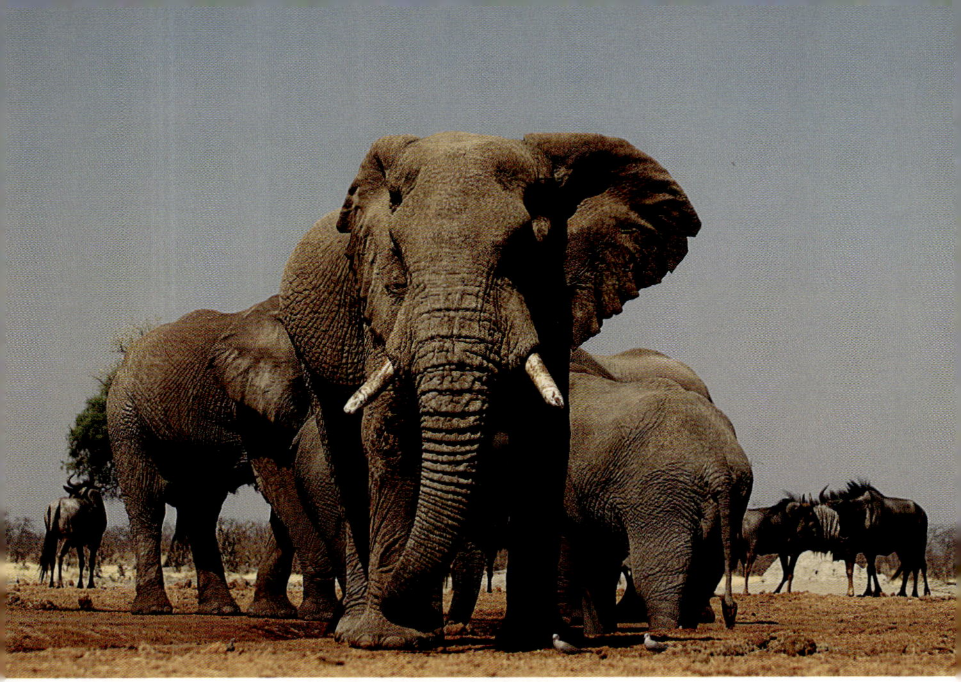

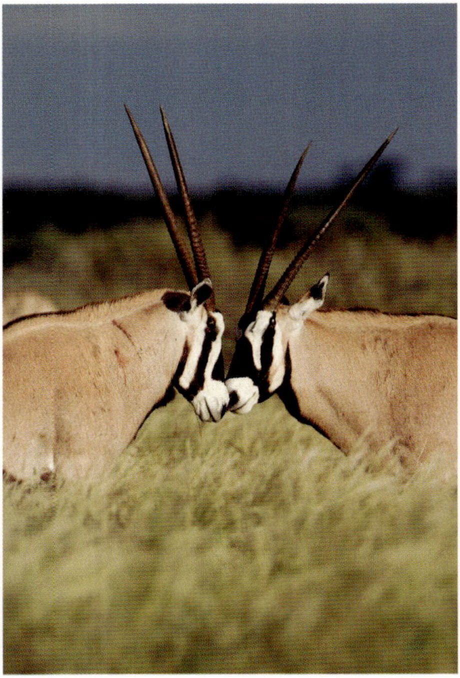

▲ *Elephant & Blue Wildebeest, Savuti, Chobe National Park. DSLR, 100-400mm Lens, f/5.6 @ 1/200, ISO 100*

The triangular composition of this image is a classic and a much sought after way of presenting your subject. Shooting below eye-level magnifies the size of this pachyderm in contrast to the blue wildebeest in the background. ***SS***

◀ *Gemsbok, Central Kalahari Game Reserve. DSLR, 500mm Lens, f/5 @ 1/1250, ISO 200*

Symmetry is another compositional trick that can yield effective results. Interestingly, it does not necessarily comply with the rule of thirds guideline - remember that some rules are there to be broken. Experimentation is the best way to learn how to construct the best composition. ***JG***

▼ *Southern Yellow-billed Hornbill, Okavango Delta. DSLR, 100-400mm Lens, f/5.6 @ 1/500, ISO 250*

Using an alternative angle can create a dramatic image from a relatively ordinary subject. Often this will mean being at eye-level with the animal but looking down at, or directly up at the subject as in this photograph, can be equally arresting. **JG**

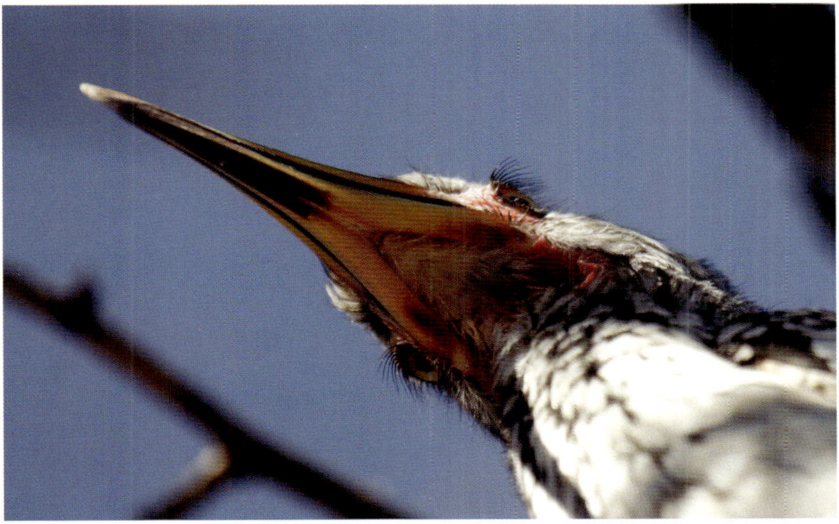

▼ *Brown Hyena Cubs, Makgadikgadi Pans. DSLR, 100-400mm Lens, f/5.6 @ 1/1000, ISO 400*

A combination of having a central figure to focus on, together with the natural symmetry, means that odd numbers of subjects tend to create bolder and more balanced compositions. Note that it is still possible to create an interesting image without seeing an animal's face and sometimes this unusual perspective adds even more character to the photograph. **JG**

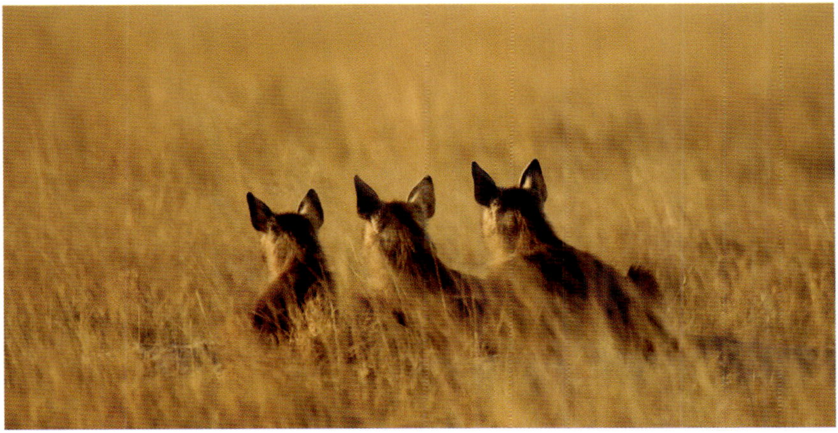

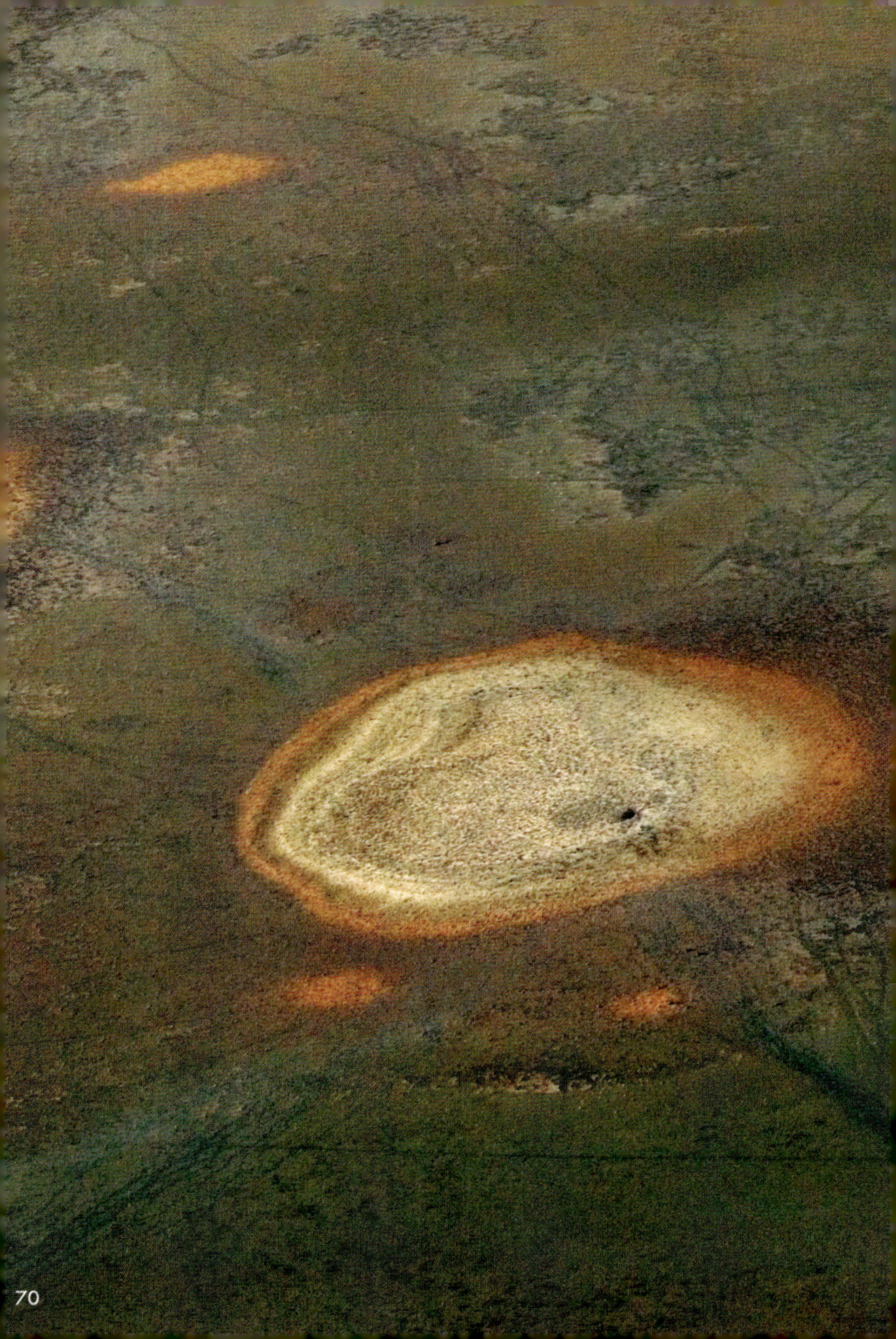

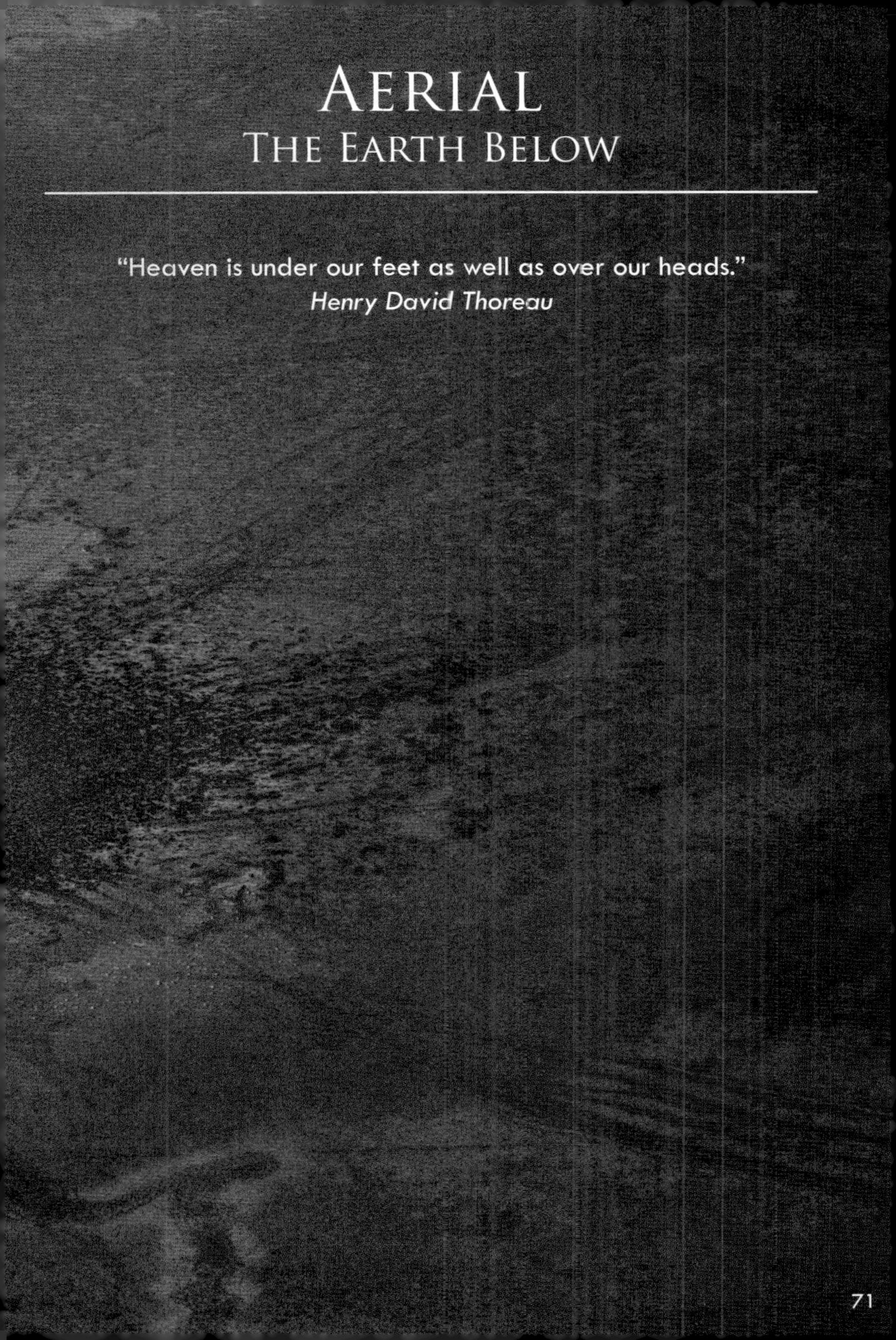

Aerial
The Earth Below

"Heaven is under our feet as well as over our heads."
Henry David Thoreau

Aerial

Though aerial photography is a genre best left to specialist photographers, make the most of any opportunity you get to take images from the air. Indeed, many visitors to Botswana will travel by light aircraft at some point on their safari. Unless you are chartering a helicopter or plane, you will have to shoot through perspex windows but even then it is still possible to create pleasing photographs.

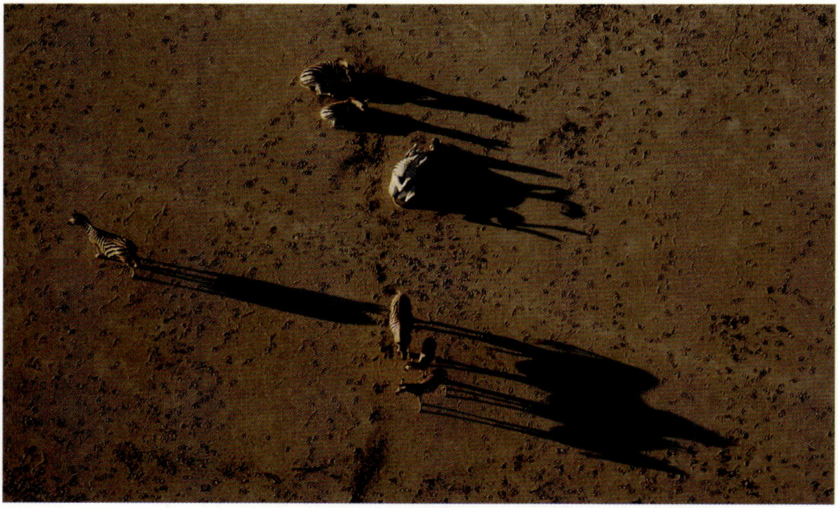

▲ ***Burchell's Zebra, Makgadikgadi Pans. DSLR, 100-400mm Lens, f/5.6 @ 1/1600, ISO 400***

If you are lucky enough to be flying either early or late in the day and see animals from the air, make use of the long shadows. This was taken early one morning flying over the Makgadikgadi when fortunately, every zebra appeared to be striking a different pose. **JG**

▶ ***Dry Season, Makgadikgadi Pans. DSLR, 17-85mm Lens, f/13 @ 1/10, ISO 400***

A combination of a short focal length of 17mm and tilting the camera at an angle to suit the shape of the abstract pan below, helped to create the illusion of the earth's curvature - almost the equivalent of using a fish-eye lens. I find it amazing to compare this shot of the pans with the one taken in the wet season on the previous page. ***JG***

◀ ***Wet Season, Makgadikgadi Pans. DSLR, 100-400mm Lens, f/5.6 @ 1/1250, ISO 400***

Flying over the Makgadikgadi in the wet season gives you a completely different perspective as the orange colours of the mineral deposits form rings around the white pans. The tiny white dots just below and to the right of the pan are zebras that migrate eastwards each year with the first onset of the rains. ***JG***

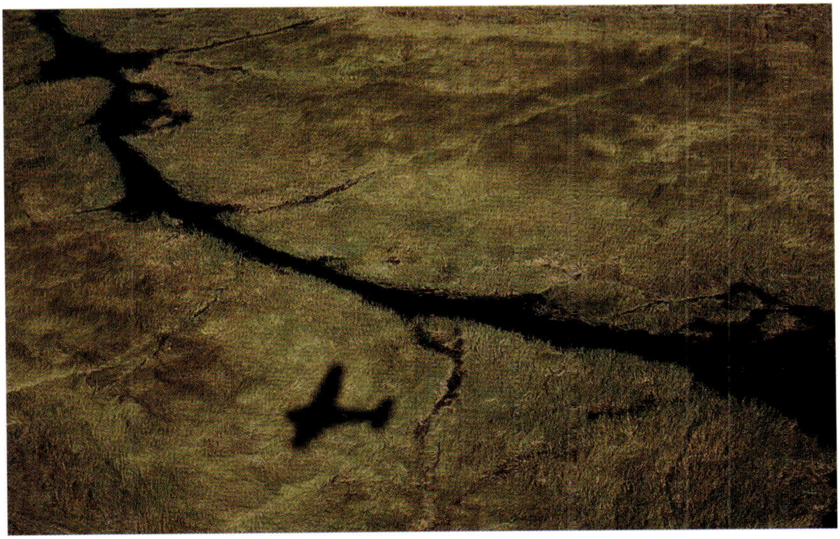

▲ ***Light Aircraft Shadow, Okavango Delta. DSLR, 18-55mm Lens, f/5 @ 1/1600, ISO 200***

This image was taken whilst flying to Khwai River on the eastern side of the Okavango Delta. As we came down for landing, the plane's shadow was noticeable on the ground below us. Although I took several shots, I was ideally waiting until I could capture the river and the plane in the same frame. **SS**

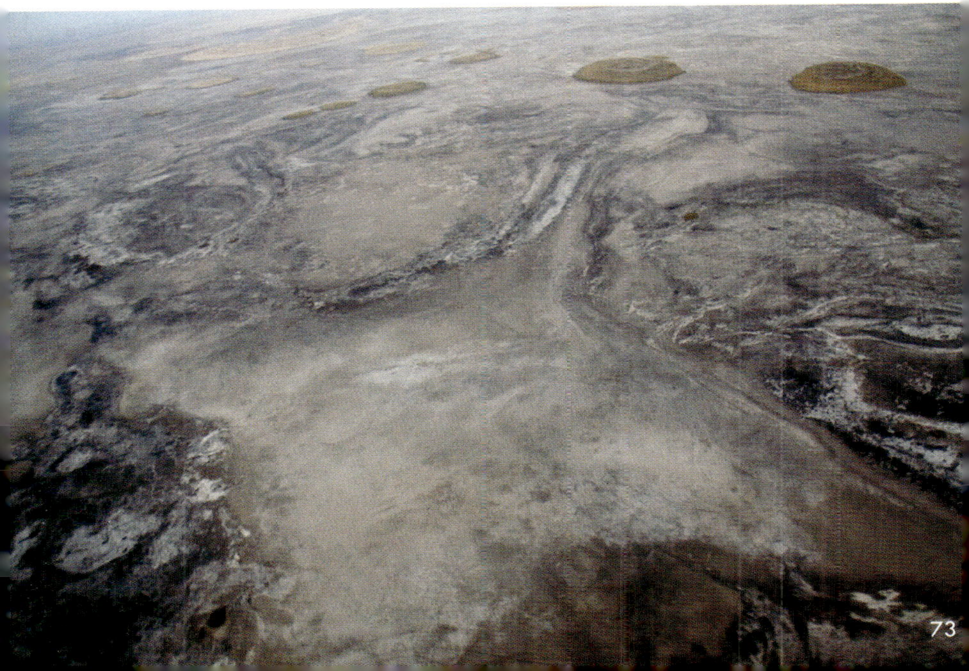

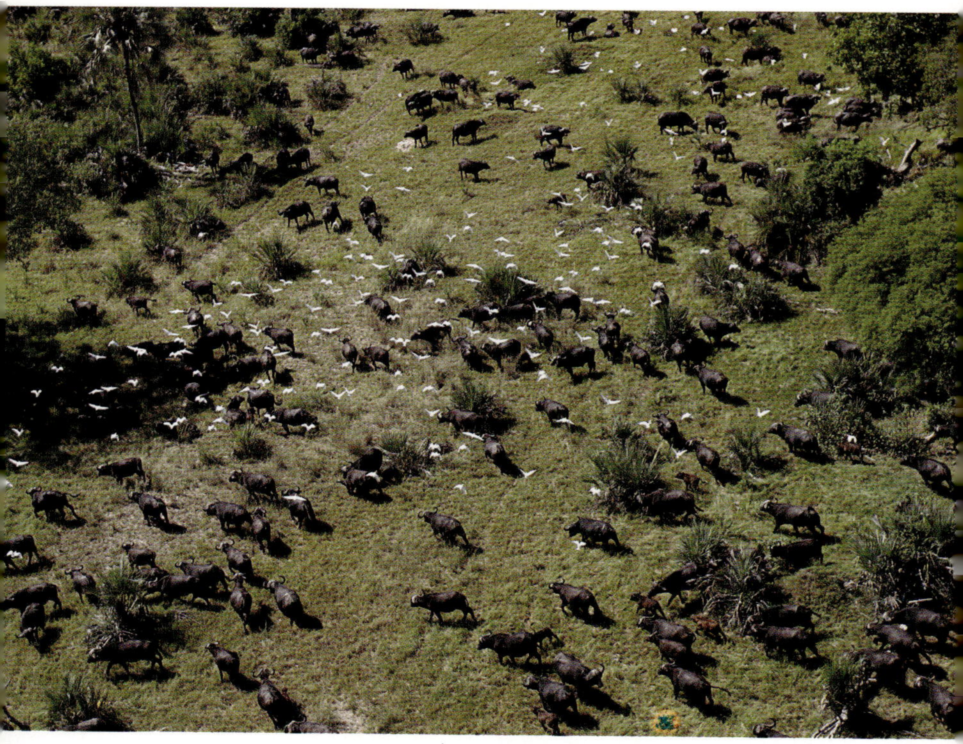

▲ ***Cape Buffalo, Okavango Delta. DSLR, 18-55mm Lens, f/6.7 @ 1/750, ISO 400***

This image was taken from a Tiger Moth biplane. The airspeed of that particular craft is only 65mph - nice and slow for photographing from the air. The image is strengthened by the flock of cattle egrets which contrast well with the darker buffalo. **SS**

Shooting from the Air

Generally a shorter lens is most effective. Set your camera to a higher ISO as you will need the highest shutter speed available to help compensate for the movement of the plane. This will also allow you to shoot with a narrower aperture to give a greater depth of field if desired. Always have a tissue handy in case you need to wipe the window before shooting. The most impressive aerial animal photographs are often taken from directly above the subject, emphasising their shadows. The speed of the plane may mean that you will have to start tracking the animal in advance so that you are ready to capture the image as you reach the optimum shooting angle.

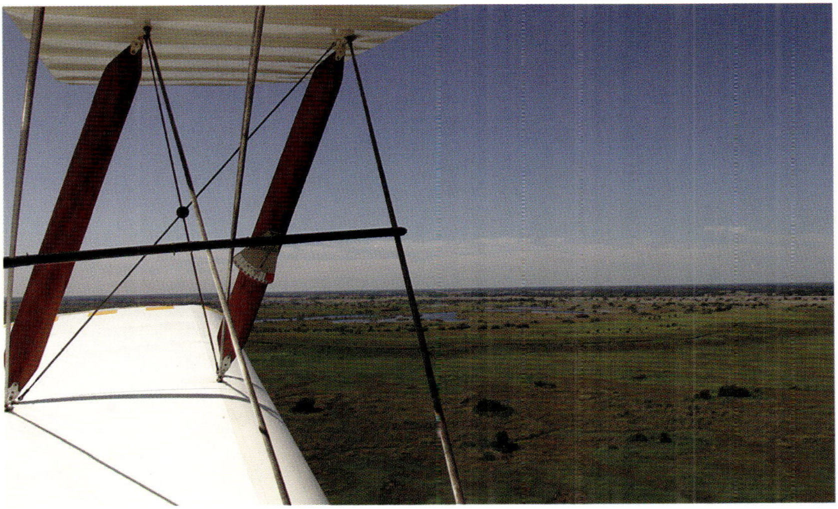

▲ *Biplane over the Okavango Delta. DSLR, 18-55mm Lens, f/9.5 @ 1/750, ISO 400*

The open cockpit and passenger seat gave us a very clear view all around. Using a short lens allowed me to take a wide-angle shot that included the wings of the plane with the Okavango Delta in the background. **SS**

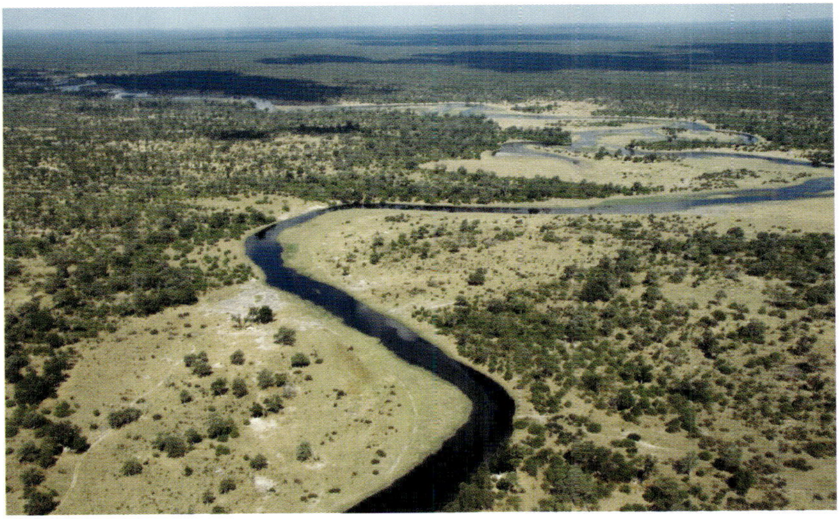

▲ *View over the Okavango Delta. DSLR, 17-85mm Lens, f/16 @ 1/500, ISO 500*

I took this through a plane window whilst on my way out to one of the camps in the Delta. The composition encourages the viewer to follow the meandering path of the river into the heart of the picture. **JG**

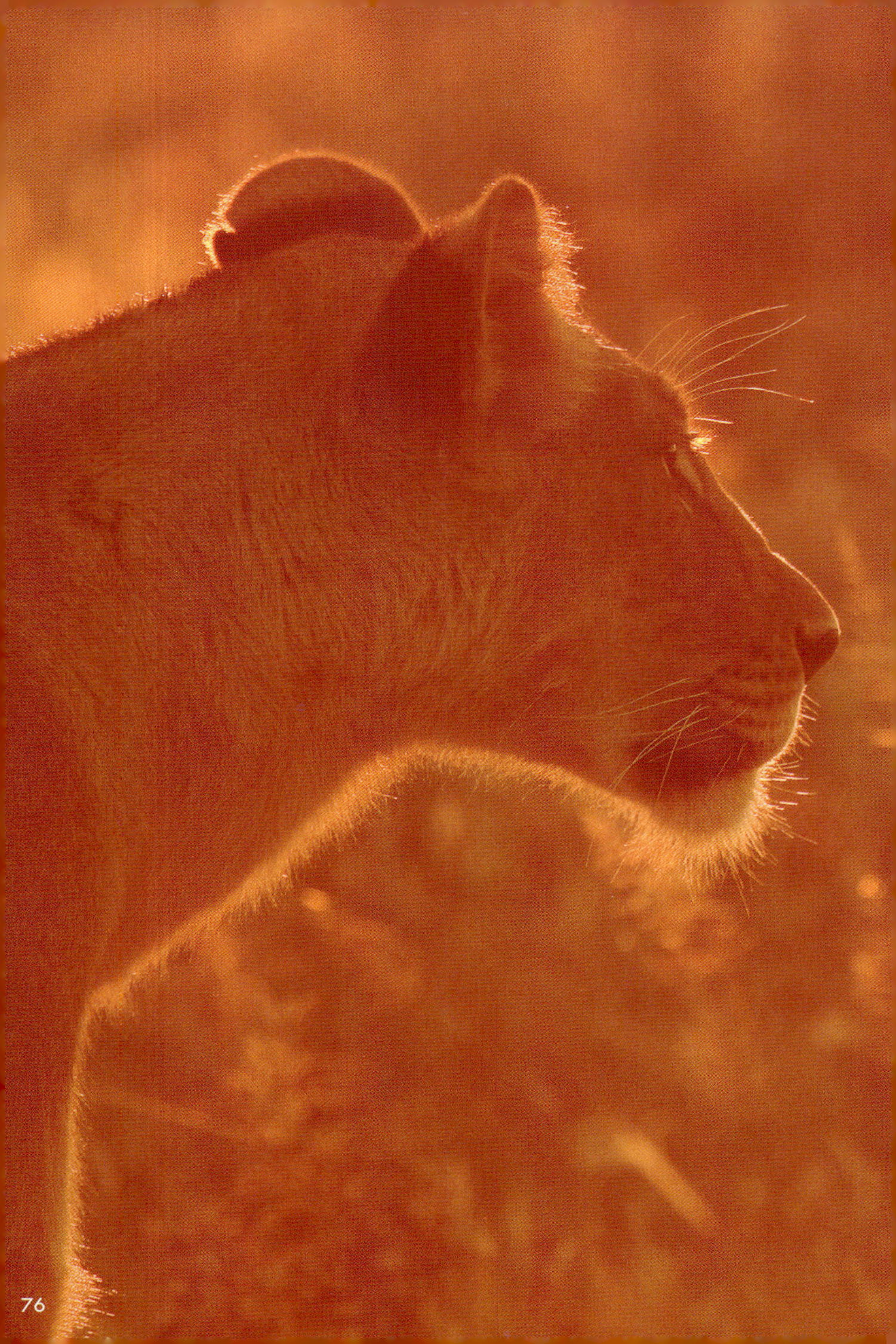

Mammals
Life in Warm Blood

"Adopt the pace of nature: her secret is patience."
Ralph Waldo Emerson

Mammals

Unless you are on a specialist birding safari, mammals will probably be your primary photographic subject matter in Botswana and the huge diversity of species is a photographer's paradise. Given the plethora of existing stunning wildlife images, the real challenge is the quest for originality which requires both compositional creativity as well as an astute application of all your camera techniques. The subsections of this chapter: Portraits, Behaviour, Expressions, Lighting, Groups, and Environment should give you an insight into the vast range of possible interpretations of the same scene outside of conventional portraits.

Portraits

▶ ***Lion, Central Kalahari Game Reserve. DSLR, 100-400mm Lens, f/5.6 @ 1/200, ISO 200***

If you get the chance to get close enough, you can take an unusual and arresting portrait by zooming in on a certain aspect of the animal. This is a striking illustration of the rule of thirds (see p.64). **JG**

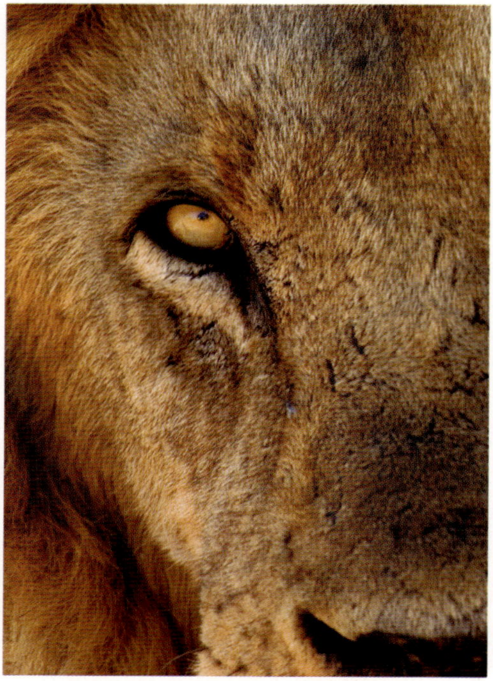

▶ ▶ ***Warthog, Okavango Delta. DSLR, 100-400mm Lens, f/6.3 @ 1/500, ISO 200***

Up close, a male warthog really shows off his skin texture and sparse hair. These endearing and shy little animals can be seen quite frequently but getting close to them is not always easy. **SS**

◀ ***Lioness, Central Kalahari Game Reserve. DSLR, 100-400mm Lens, f/5.6 @ 1/400, ISO 640***

Given the choice, most wildlife photographers will attempt to position themselves with the sun behind them. Although shooting into the sun may make exposure trickier, backlit shots can sometimes yield dramatic results. A lens hood is vital to avoid flare from the sun. If you can still see sunspots, adjust your shooting angle accordingly. **JG**

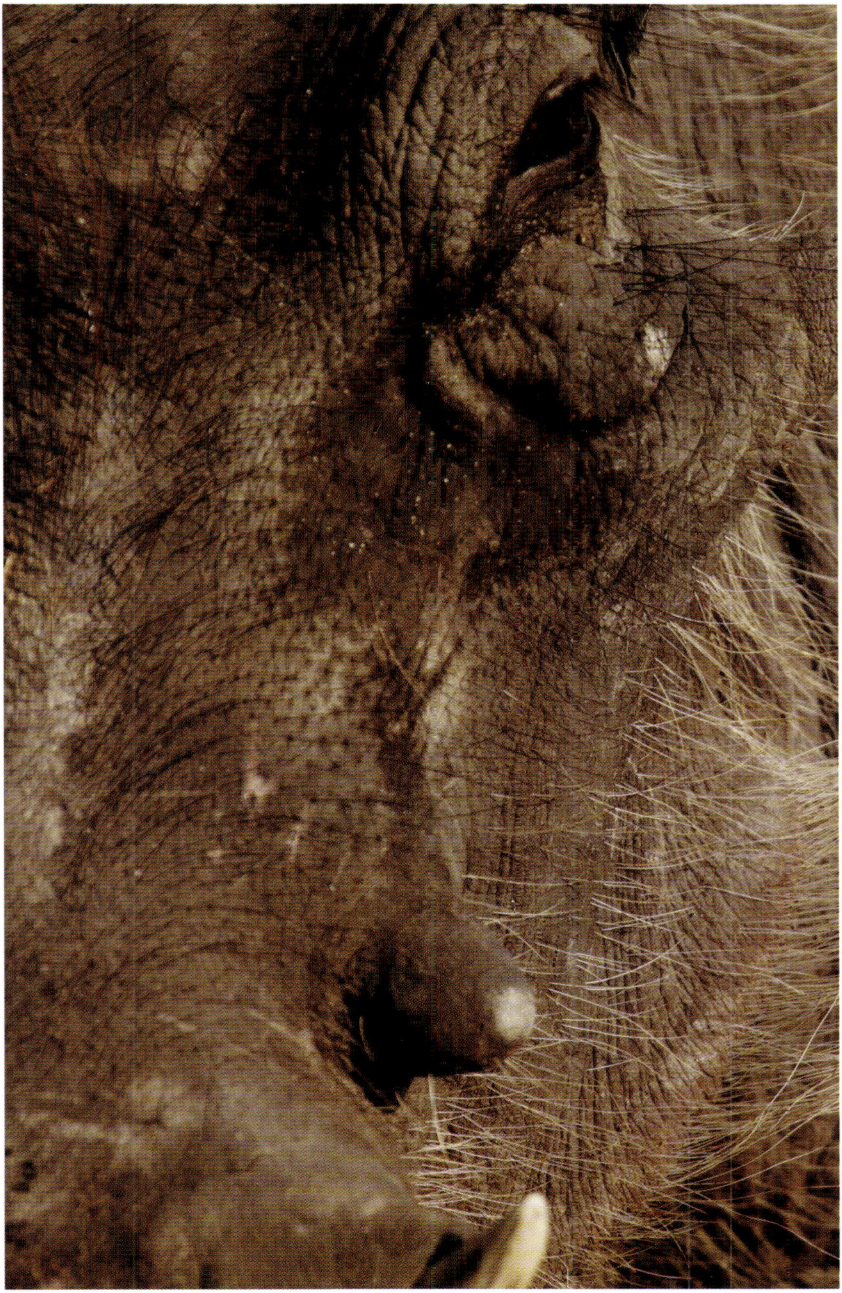

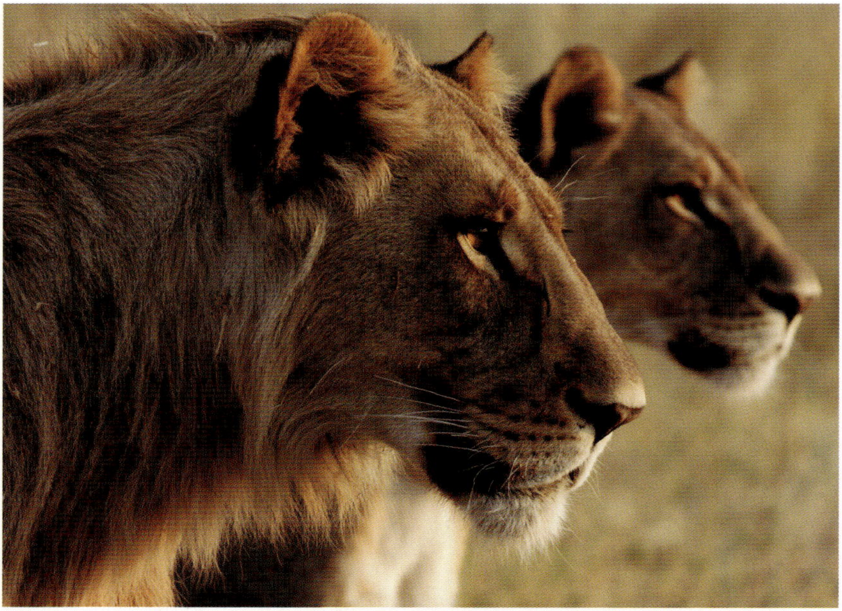

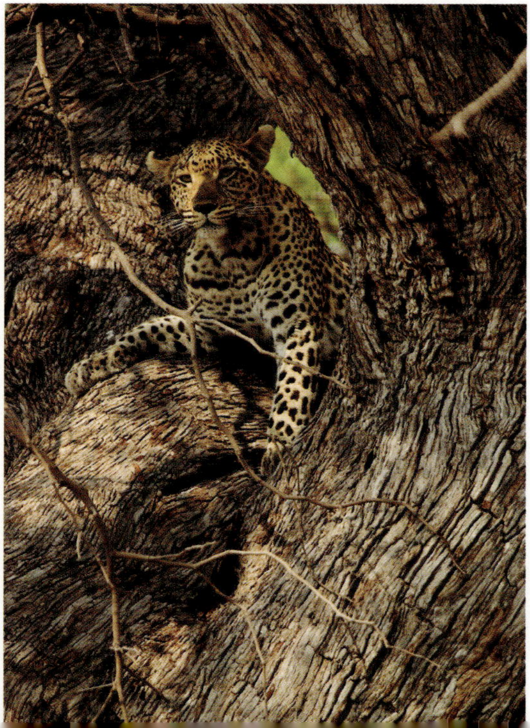

▲ ***Lion, Okavango Delta. DSLR, 100-400mm Lens, f/7.1 @ 1/200, ISO 200***

These two lions are brother and sister of around two years of age. Their mother and aunt were hunting nearby and, as they watched intently, they struck an almost identical pose. The telephoto lens coupled with the distance between the siblings meant that only the male was in focus. **SS**

◀ ***Leopard, Okavango Delta. DSLR, 100-400mm Lens, f/5.6 @ 1/640, ISO 320***

It is always worth looking out for natural elements to frame your portrait. Here, the texture of the bark combined with the shape of the tree trunk was ideal. **JG**

▶ ***African Wild Dog, Savuti, Chobe National Park. DSLR, 100-400mm Lens, f/5.6 @ 1/200, ISO 1600***

These superb looking hunters are endangered with only 3,500 to 5,000 left in the wild, the majority of which are found in Botswana. Although this is a straightforward portrait composition, the animal's lively expression strengthens the image. **SS**

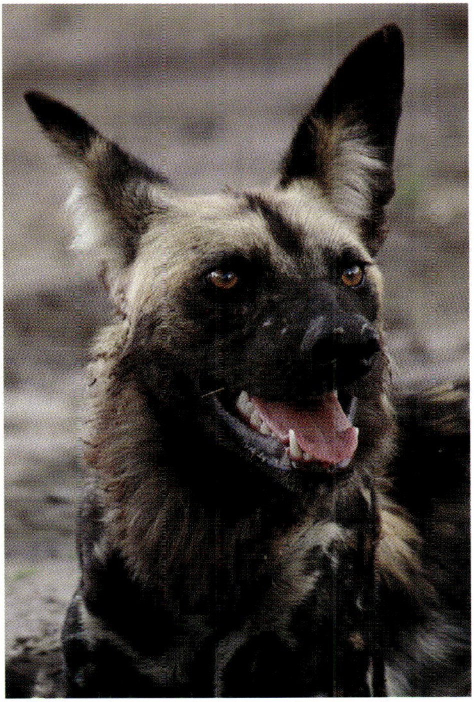

▼ ***Southern Giraffe, Okavango Delta. DSLR, 100-400mm Lens, f/5.6 @ 1/250, ISO 200***

Watching animal behaviour offers one an insight into their daily routines and catching these moments is a rewarding aspect of wildlife photography. Here, a giraffe leans back to groom thus allowing me to capture an unusual angle of this elegant species. **SS**

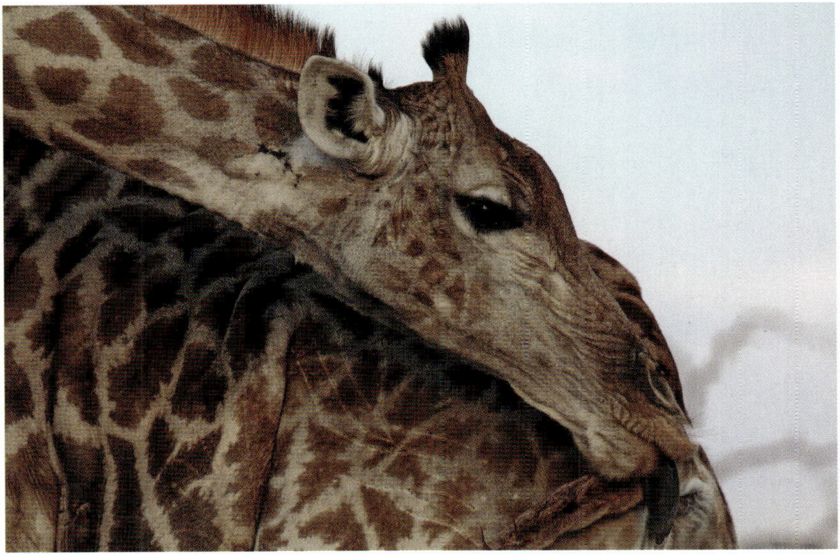

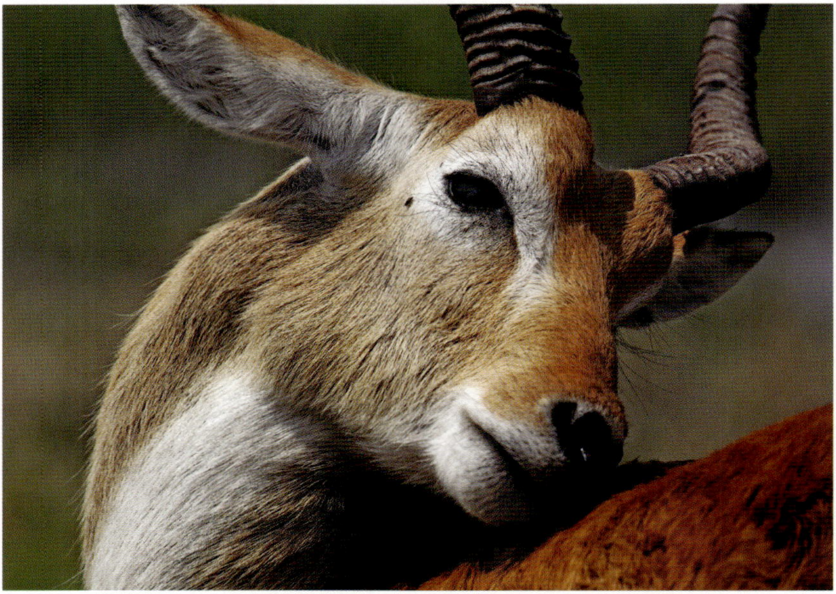

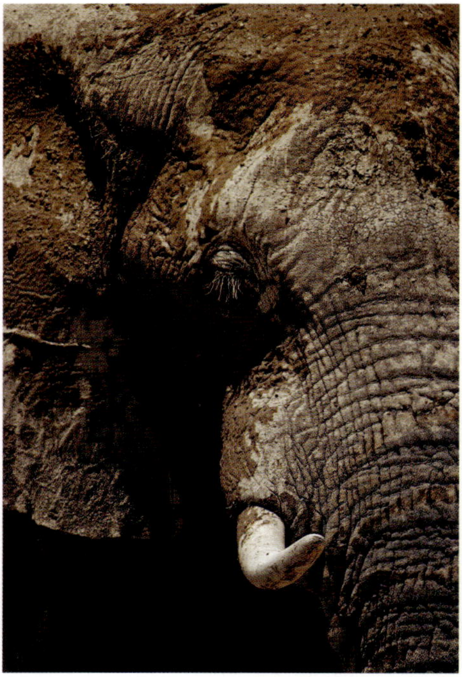

▲ *Red Lechwe, Okavango Delta. DSLR, 100-400mm Lens, f/5.6 @ 1/1000, ISO 100*

Red lechwe are a near-endemic, aquatic antelope that thrive on the shallow flood plains of the Okavango Delta, Chobe River and Namibia's Caprivi Strip. In this image, the rich colours of his coat are accentuated by the Delta's green backdrop. **SS**

◀ *Elephant, Nxai Pan National Park. DSLR, 100-400mm Lens, f/5.6 @ 1/1600, ISO 100*

It is often difficult to create an original perspective from a commonly photographed animal. The contrasting tones (aided by mud patches) help to give this photograph impact, while the fine eyelashes compete with the isolated tusk for the viewer's attention. **JG**

Alternative Portraits

For the vast majority of portraits, the primary focal point should be the eye of the animal so as to maximise the image's impact. However, portraits do not always have to include the animal's head - zooming in on the trunk of an elephant or the flick of a zebra's tail can often portray more character than a traditional face shot. Either way, using a wide aperture to create a shallow depth of field will separate the subject from its surroundings but remember that the background colour is still important.

▶ ***Elephant Tusks, Okavango Delta. DSLR, 100-400mm Lens, f/9 @ 1/1000, ISO 3200***

Photographing elephants has its own set of challenges. Monotone grey skin combined with dark, bulky bodies and tones that throw your light metering off, make it no easy task. However, over the years I have found that with good light and a creative eye, they are extremely rewarding to photograph. Here, two males momentarily line up their tusks whilst feeding. **SS**

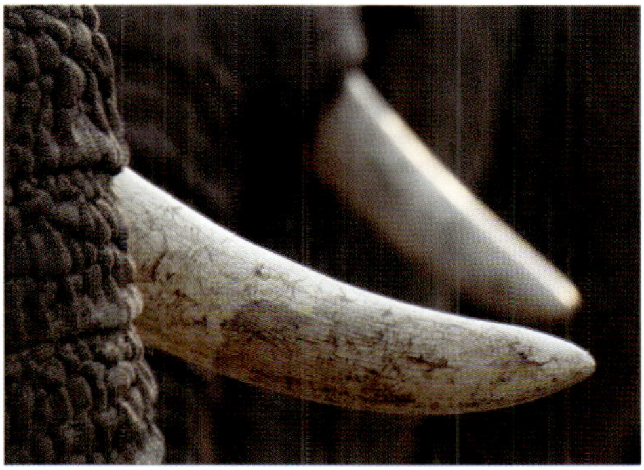

▼ ***Lion Paw Print, Makgadikgadi Pans National Park. DSLR, 100-400mm Lens, f/5 @ 1/640, ISO 100***

Other features or signs of wildlife can constitute an alternative portrait of an animal and tracks are no exception. In the image below, a lion track stands out clearly on the Kalahari sands and with the sun almost directly above the track, it is the combination of shadow and light that make it stand out. **SS**

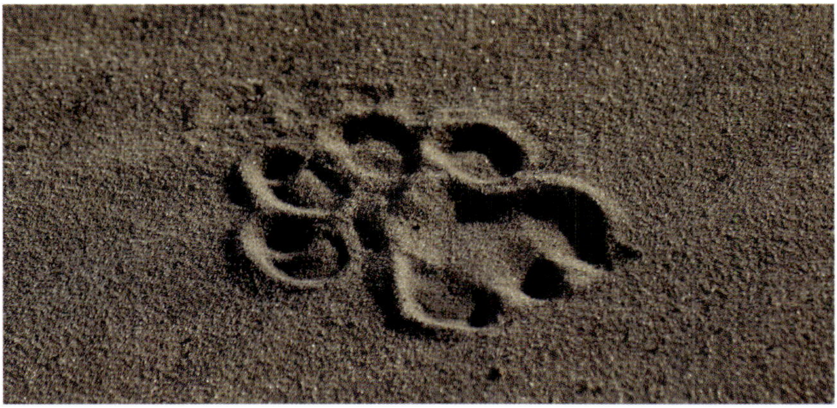

▶ *Warthog & Elephant, Savuti, Chobe National Park. DSLR, 100-400mm Lens, f/5.6 @ 1/640, ISO 250*

Photographing in Savuti during the hottest part of the dry season can be challenging both in terms of subject matter and personal comfort. Yet, watching a family of warthogs scurry around giant elephant legs as they waited to quench their thirst was a memorable sight and this is now one of my favourite photos. **JG**

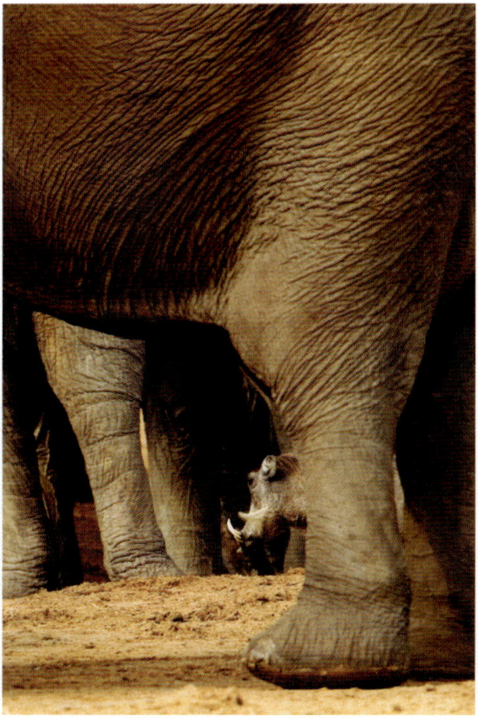

▶▶ *Lioness & Cub, Central Kalahari Game Reserve. 100-400mm Lens, f/5.6 @ 1/1000, ISO 100*

Sometimes animals are like buses - you can wait days to see something special and then one morning everything appears at once. The day I shot this, I had already encountered two separate lion prides before I stumbled upon a third lolling around in the open Kalahari plain. I knew they would soon have to seek shelter from the rising sun so I waited accordingly and this doting mother duly rewarded me for my patience. **JG**

▼ *Meerkats, Makgadikgadi Pans. DSLR, 100-400mm Lens, f/13 @ 1/250, ISO 160*

Occasionally you can portray an animal's character without a face or expression and for me, this photo encompasses the endearing nature of meerkats. **JG**

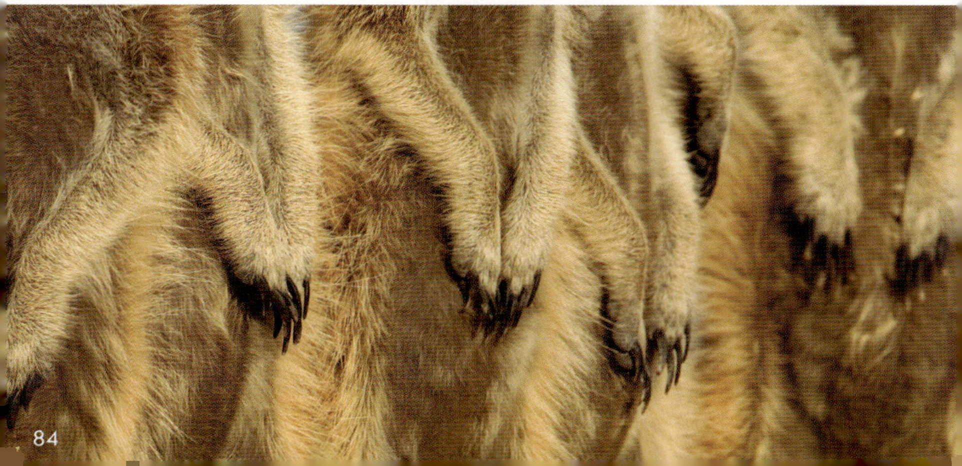

BEHAVIOUR

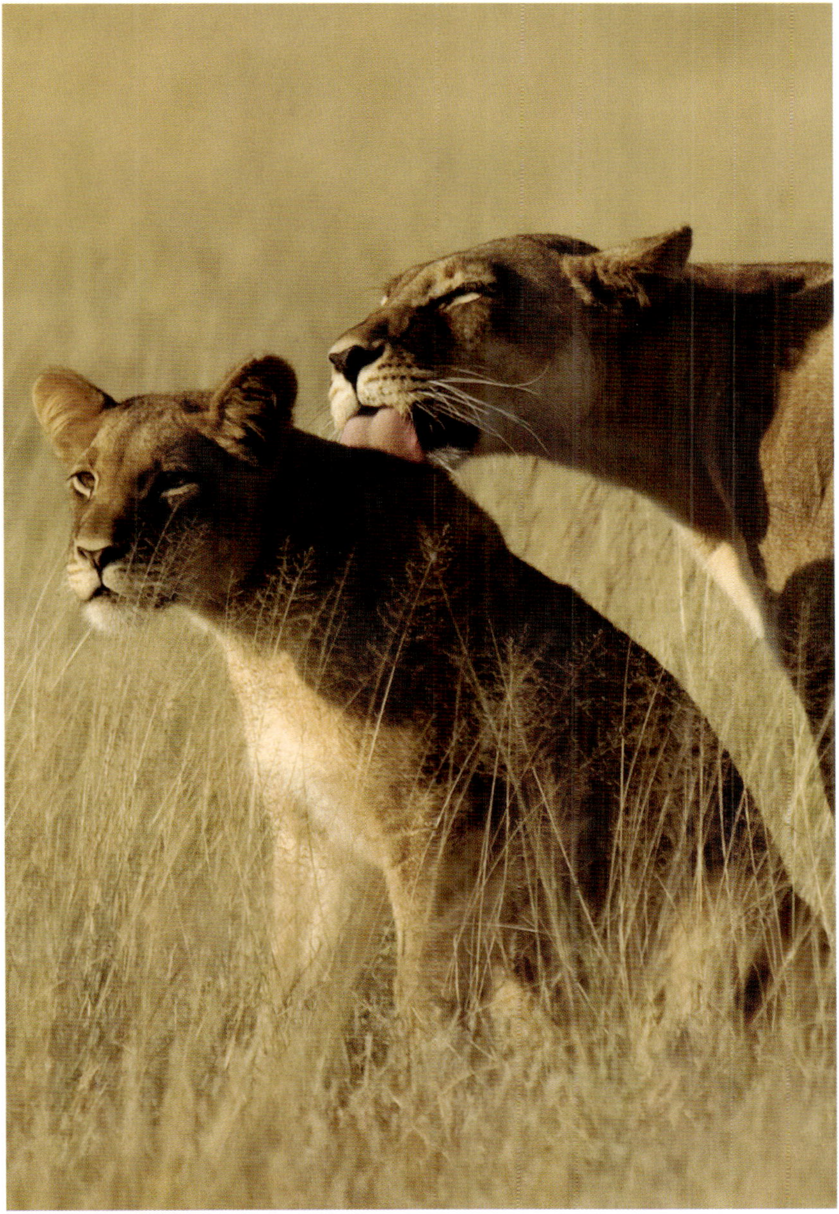

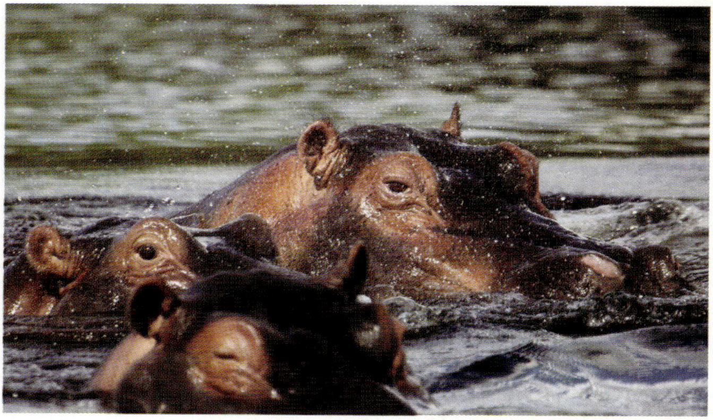

▲ ***Hippopotamus, Chobe River. DSLR, 100-400mm Lens, f/5.6 @ 1/500, ISO 400***

Hippo pods along the Chobe River are wonderful to photograph from a boat. Getting down as low as possible conveys the impression that you are in the water with them. **SS**

▼ ***Spotted Hyena, Savuti, Chobe National Park. DSLR, 100-400mm Lens, f/8 @ 1/500, ISO 100***

The power and strength of the spotted hyena lie in its forequarters. Muscular necks and jaws enable this species to pick up and carry large carcasses. At Maribou Pan we found this hyena trying to walk off with the leg bone of an elephant but due to the lack of meat on the bone, it was not long before he gave up interest. **SS**

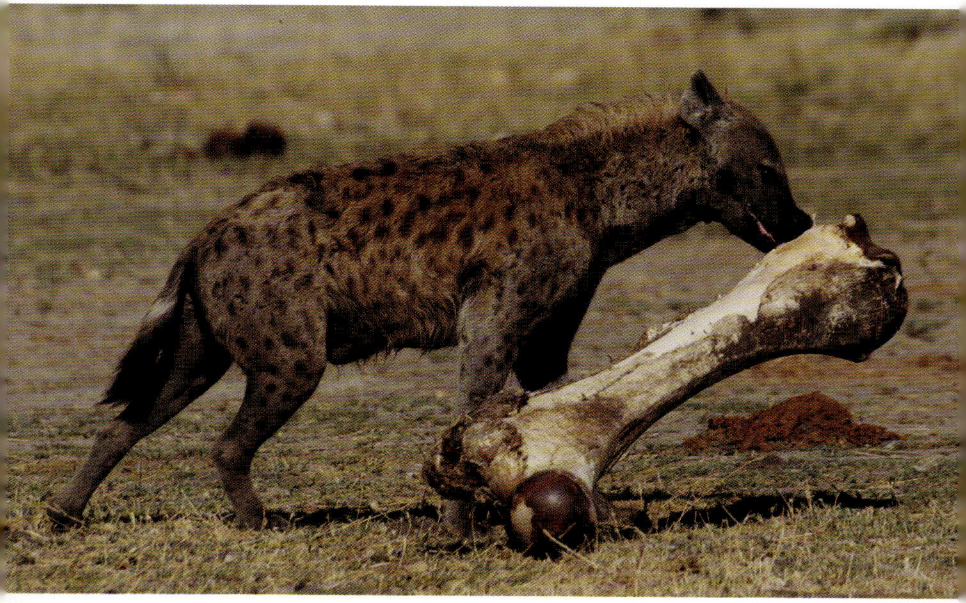

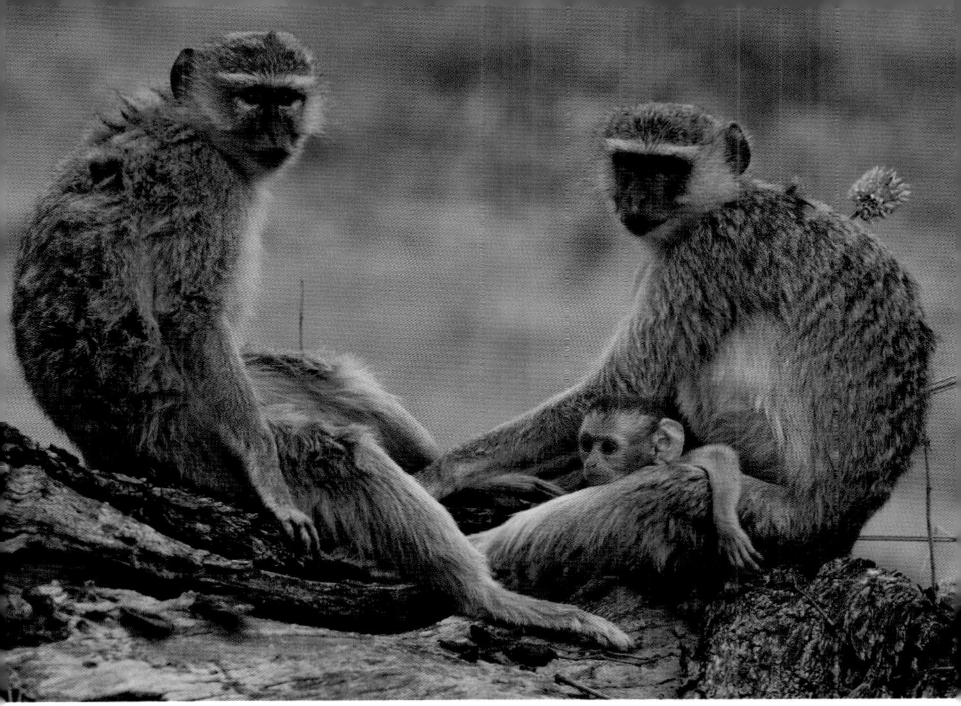

▲ ***Vervet Monkey, Okavango Delta. DSLR, 100-400mm Lens, f/8 @ 1/100, ISO 200***

Young of any kind seem to tug at everyone's heartstrings and photographing social structures can add an extra dimension to your images. I had watched this baby playing around its mother and aunt for some time before it finally settled in its mother's lap. **SS**

Capturing Behaviour

In order to capture animal behaviour, be it a leopard jumping down a tree or a yawning hippo, it is always worth selecting a continuous drive mode in advance. Shooting at a faster burst rate will allow you to capture that unpredictable split second moment and the advent of digital photography has made it easy to delete unwanted images to free up card space.

Try to learn as much as possible about the behavioural traits of each species as this will enable you to alter your camera settings in advance and position yourself accordingly, giving you a better chance of creating the perfect image.

▶ Lion, Nxai Pan National Park. DSLR, 100-400mm Lens, f/5.6 @ 1/1000, ISO 200

Mating lions are a sight to behold. Having witnessed this a few times, it was the different expressions of these two individuals that caught my eye on this occasion. On average they will mate every 20 minutes or so for about four days so, if you do stumble across a mating couple, it is definitely worth hanging around. **SS**

▶ ▶ Chacma Baboon, Chobe National Park. DSLR, 100-400mm Lens, f/5.6 @ 1/500, ISO 200

Try to make the effort to spend some time with a troop of baboons when on safari. Their behaviour is stimulating to watch and their expressive faces are wonderful to photograph. **SS**

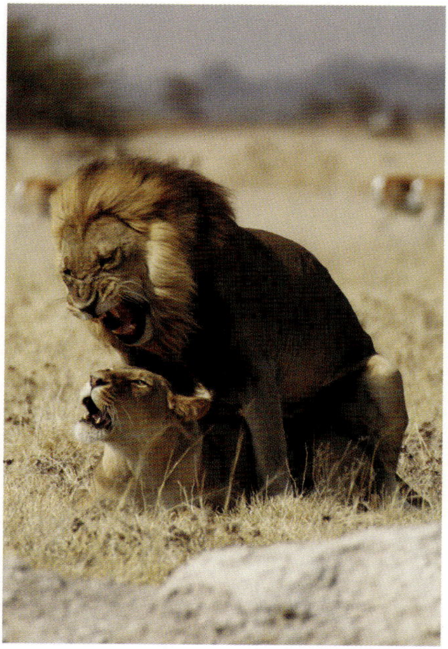

▼ Cheetah, Okavango Delta. DSLR, 100-400mm Lens, f/5.6 @ 1/1000, ISO 100

Intra-species behaviour can be as captivating as the interaction between different species. Grooming can provide life and emotion to what might otherwise be a standard portrait. **JG**

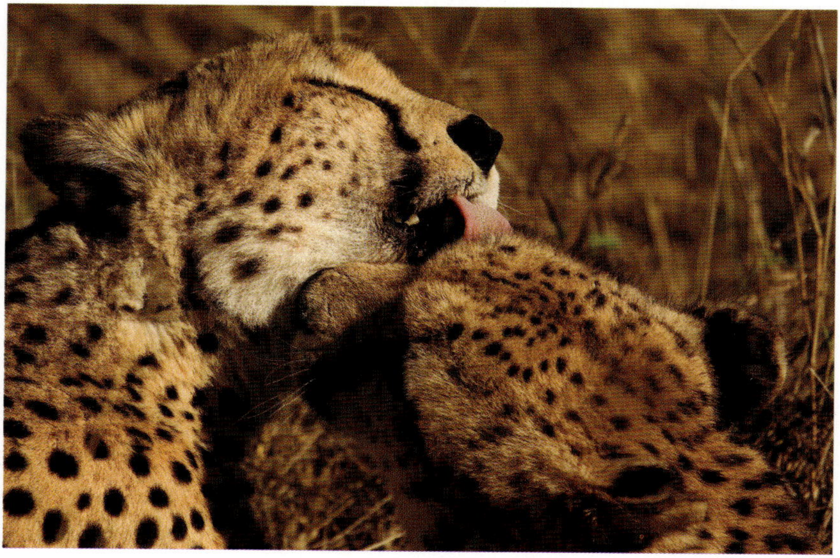

Expressions

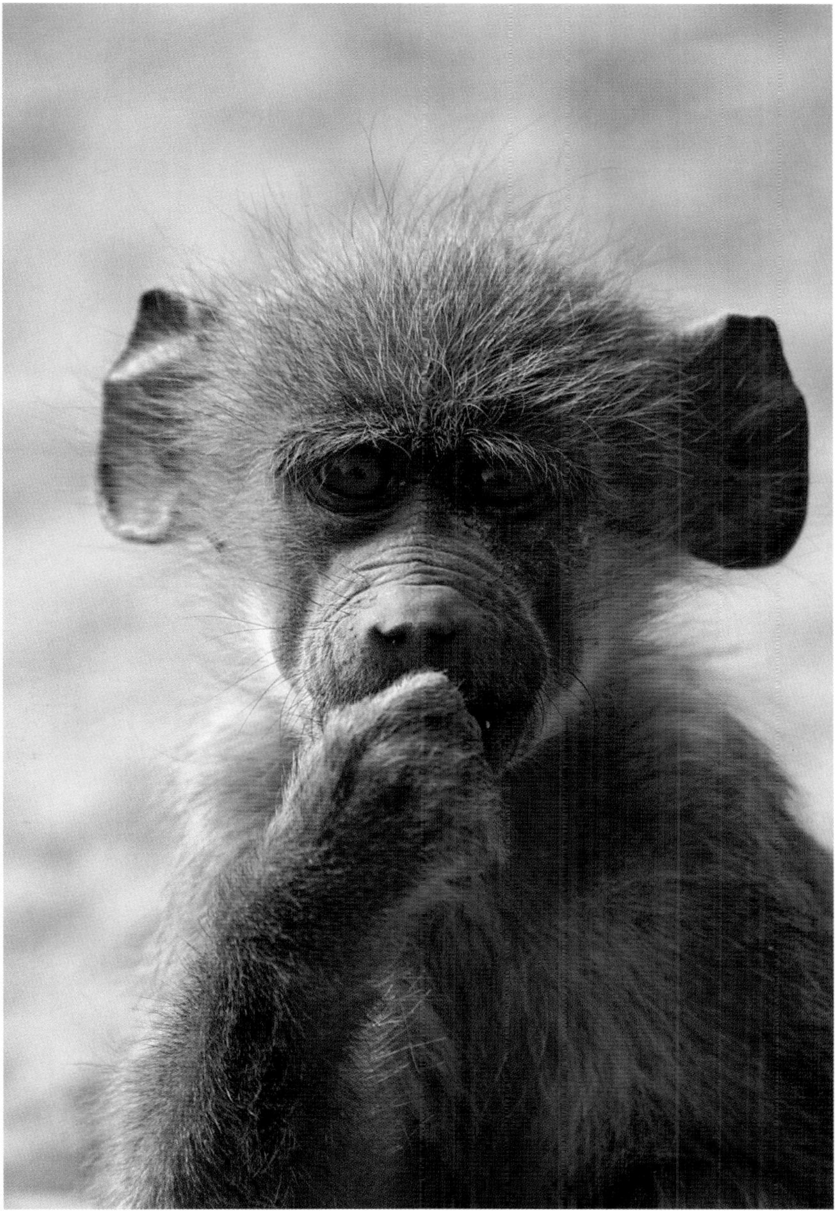

▶ ***Springbok, Central Kalahari Game Reserve. DSLR, 500mm Lens, f/4.5 @ 1/1600, ISO 100***

It is often tempting to drive past frequently seen animals in search of predators but more often than not, the expression of the animal has more impact than the type of species as this toothy springbok demonstrates. **JG**

▼ ***Brown Hyena, Makgadikgadi Pans. DSLR, 100-400mm Lens, f/6.3 @ 1/400, ISO 160***

The golden coat of a brown hyena is at its most beautiful when either backlit by a low sun, or side lit as in this shot. Being careful not to disturb the animal, I had to gradually manoeuvre myself to a standing position to avoid the grass in the foreground. Even then, I still had to wait for several minutes until he sleepily opened his eyes, giving me an almost pensive expression. **JG**

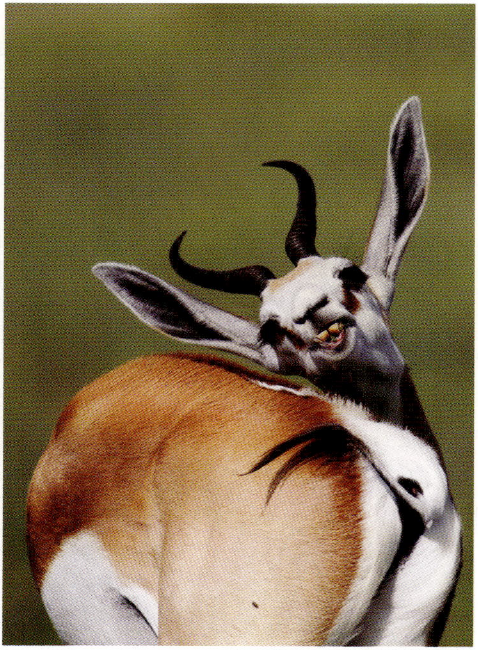

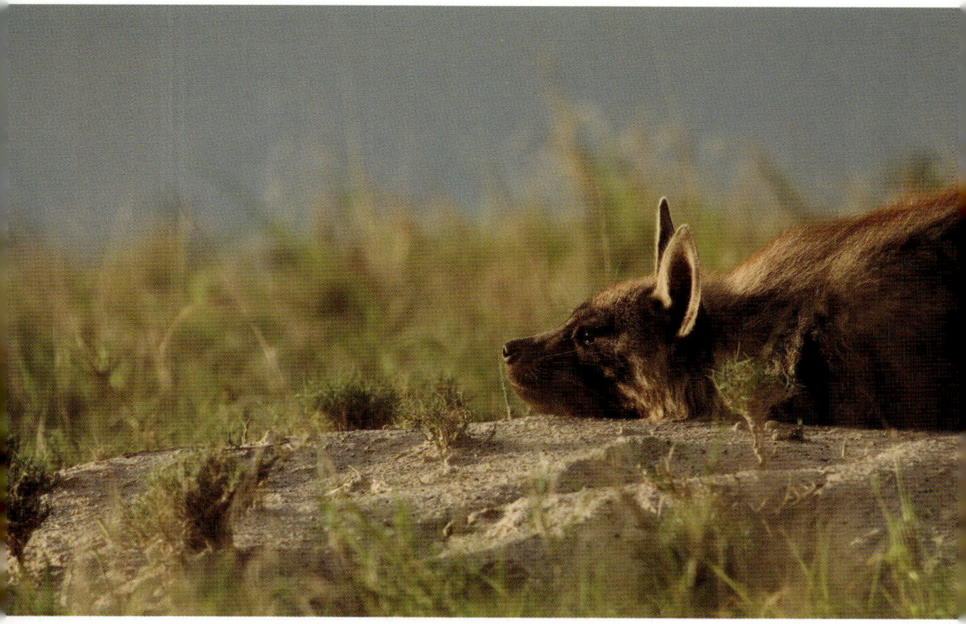

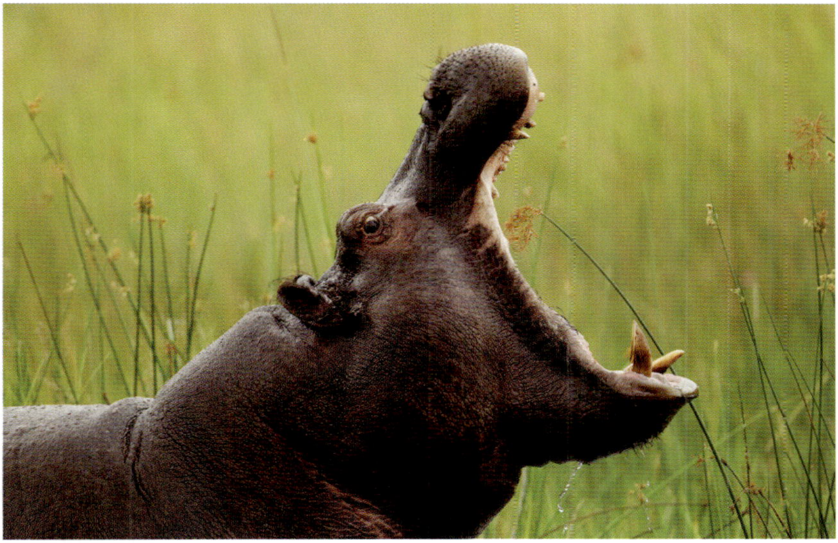

▲ Hippopotamus, Moremi Game Reserve. DSLR, 500mm Lens, f/4 @ 1/640, ISO 4000

It is always nice to capture a hippo out of the water and occasionally a territorial male will oblige with an aggressive, gaping display. Poor light and the need to handhold my heavy telephoto lens forced me to raise the ISO in order to shoot at a fast shutter speed. The composition allowed his cavernous jaws to spill into the empty space. **JG**

▼ Black-backed Jackal, Central Kalahari Game Reserve. DSLR, 100-400mm Lens, f/8 @ 1/160, ISO 400

CKGR is home to an unusually large number of black-backed jackals which give you plenty of opportunity to experiment. Try to take a different type of image at each sighting to practise a variety of techniques. In the image below, the side lighting intensifies the impact of its inquisitive stare. **JG**

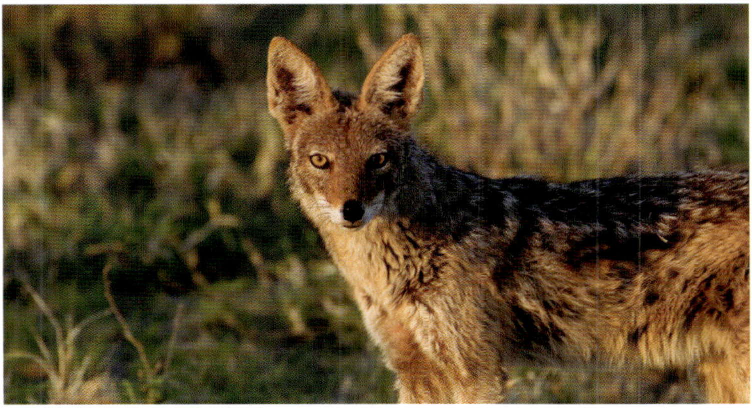

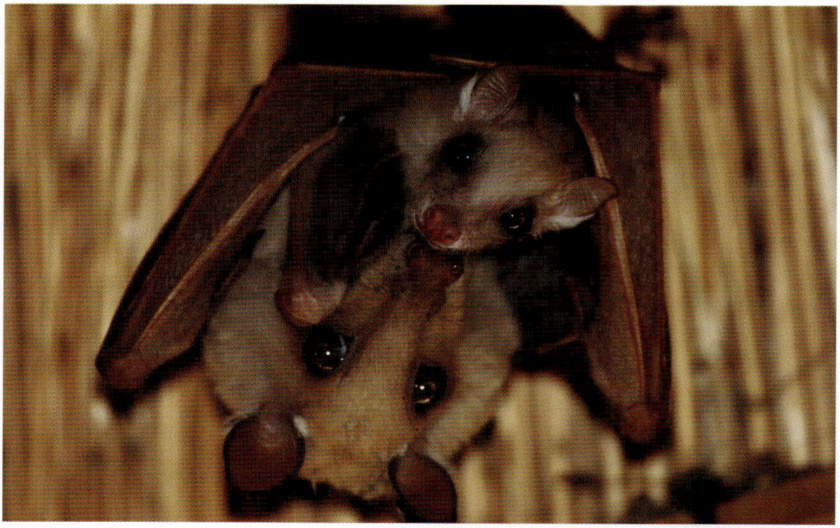

▲ ***Peters's Epauletted Fruit Bats, Okavango Delta. DSLR, 100-400mm Lens, f5.6 @ 1/60, ISO 800***

Lodges in Botswana are a haven for all sorts of animals and we recommend having your camera with you at all times - yes, even at lunch! Here, a Peters's epauletted fruit bat hangs from a thatched roof with her young. Although most of the day is spent resting, there are brief moments when they wake up to groom. I had to lie on my back for some thirty minutes before these two finally stirred. **SS**

▼ ***Cheetah, Okavango Delta. DSLR, 100-400mm Lens, f/5.6 @ 1/500, ISO 200***

Despite being a cliché, everyone loves the yawn of a big cat and capturing it is not hard with sufficient forward planning. First, select high-speed continuous drive mode and then ensure that your shutter speed is going to be fast enough to avoid motion blur. Do this by framing the animal in advance and checking the exposure settings (if not, raise your ISO accordingly). After that, it is a question of patience. Watch the animal through the viewfinder with your finger poised on the shutter button, otherwise by the time you compose the shot, you will have missed the action. **JG**

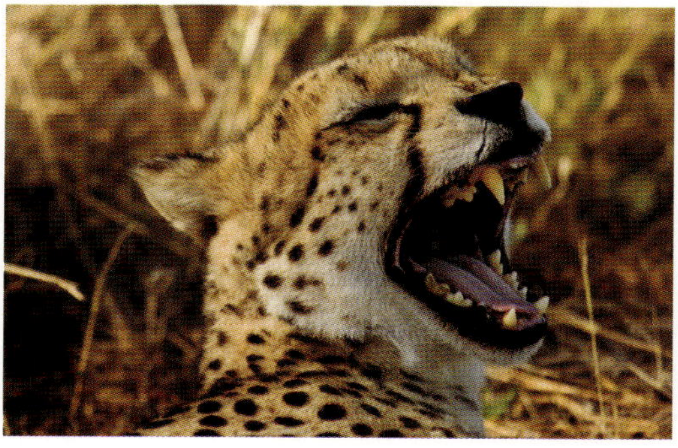

▶ ***Leopard, Okavango Delta. DSLR, 100-400mm Lens, f/5 @ 1/160, ISO 200***

Despite the leopard's shy nature, this female, whose cub was nearby, largely ignored us as she looked towards the rising sun. The golden light of early morning brings out the contrasting colours in her coat and the surrounding trees that make up her world. **SS**

LIGHTING

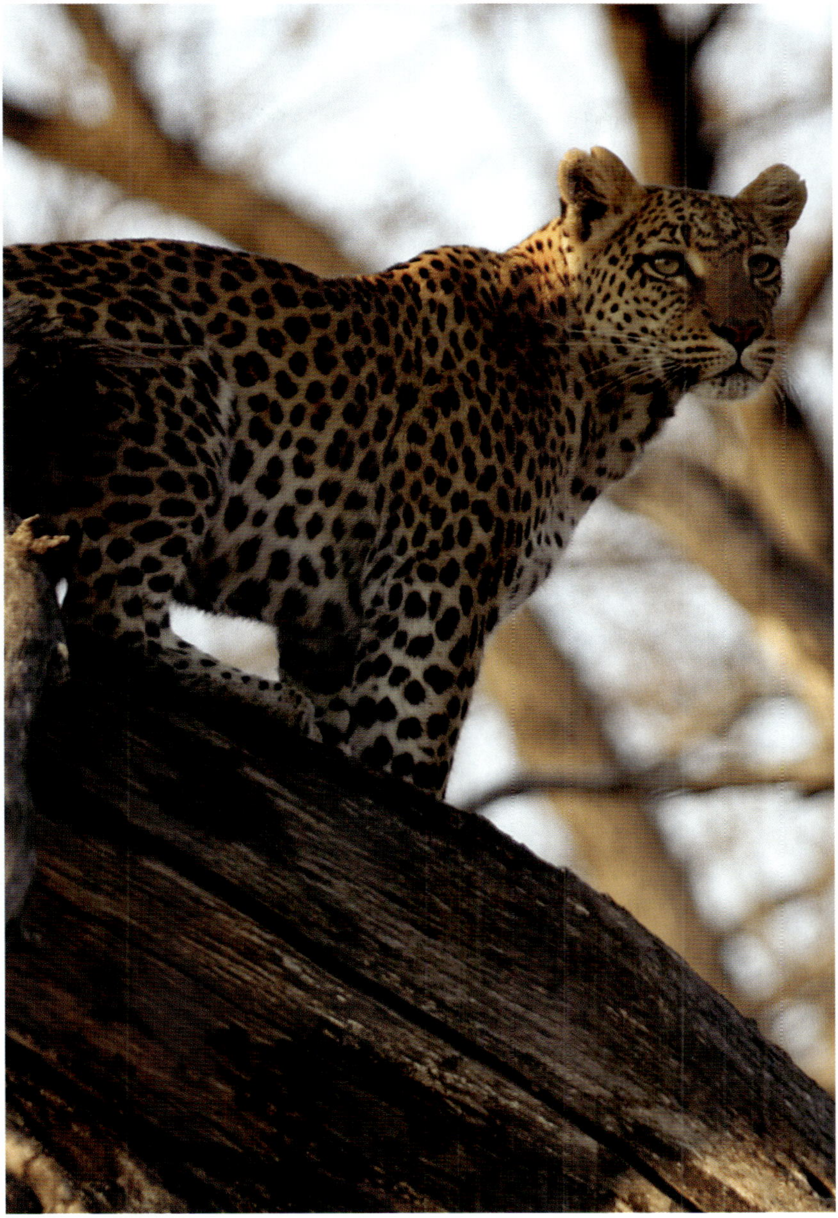

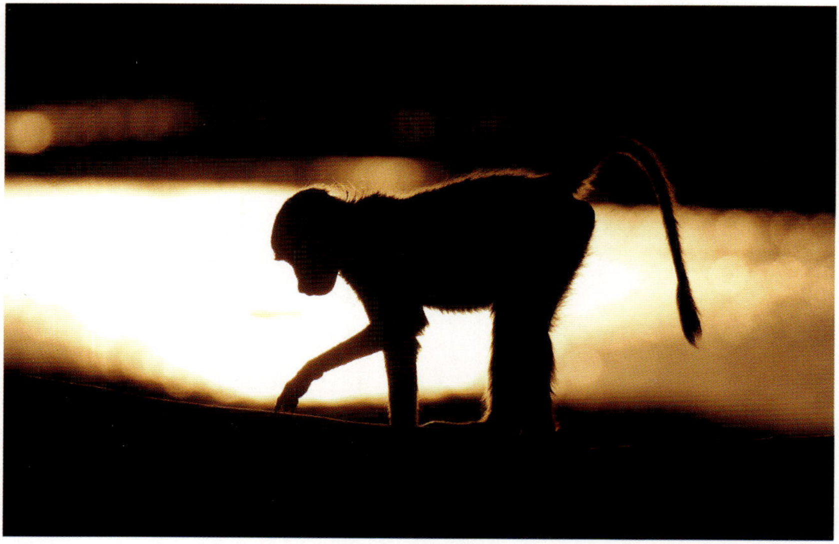

▲ ***Chacma Baboon, Okavango Delta. DSLR, 100-400mm Lens, f/5.6 @ 1/5000, ISO 200***

Late one afternoon, I was lucky to come across a troop of baboons foraging at last light. Instead of using the setting sun to silhouette this individual, I took advantage of the light reflecting on the pool of water behind it. **SS**

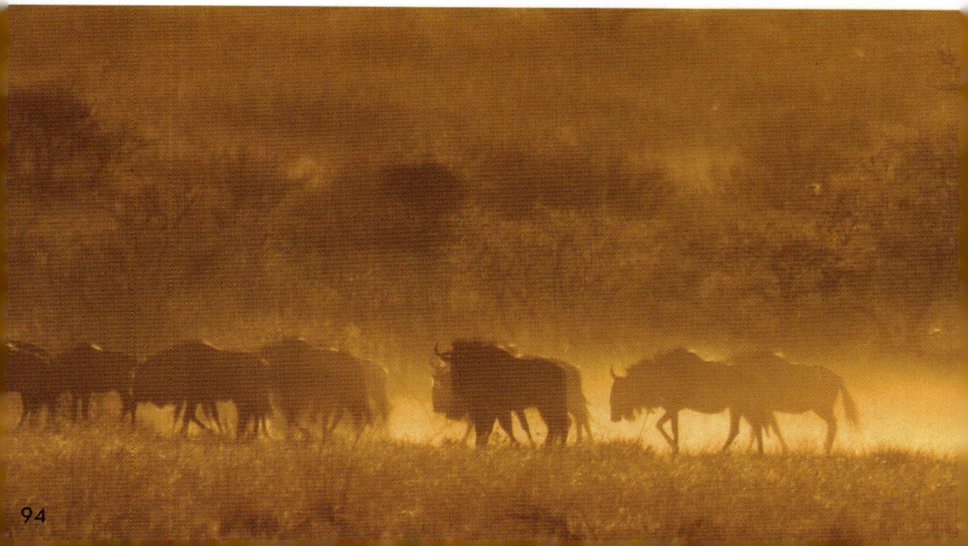

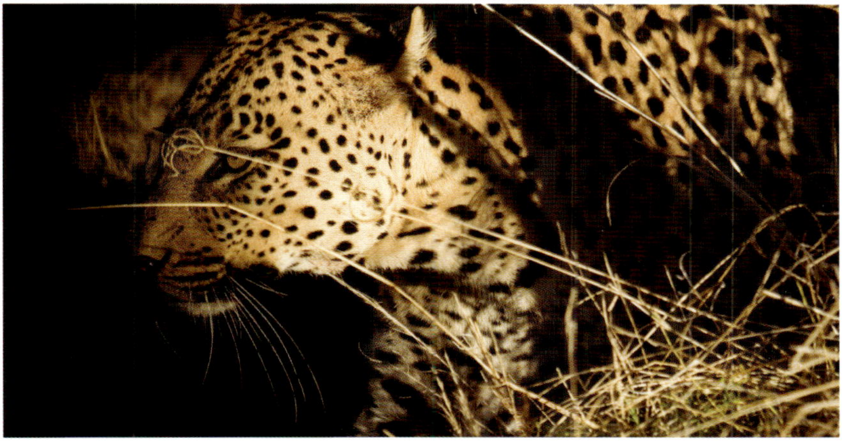

▲ ***Leopard, Okavango Delta. DSLR, 100-400mm Lens, f/5.6 @ 1/1000, ISO 400***

Surprisingly, this shot was actually taken early one morning in natural light as the leopard stalked in the shade of low bushes. Knowing the exposure would be tricky, I switched to spot metering but was not very optimistic as she lurked in the shadows. Fortunately, she finally emerged into the sunlight giving me a dramatic dark background – luck can be a wildlife photographer's best friend! **JG**

▼ ***Blue Wildebeest, Central Kalahari Game Reserve. DSLR, 100-400mm Lens, f/5.6 @ 1/1250, ISO 160***

Often the dust stirred up from a moving herd will create beautiful shafts of gold when reflected in the early morning sunlight. With its expansive plains, the Central Kalahari is one of the best places to witness this. **JG**

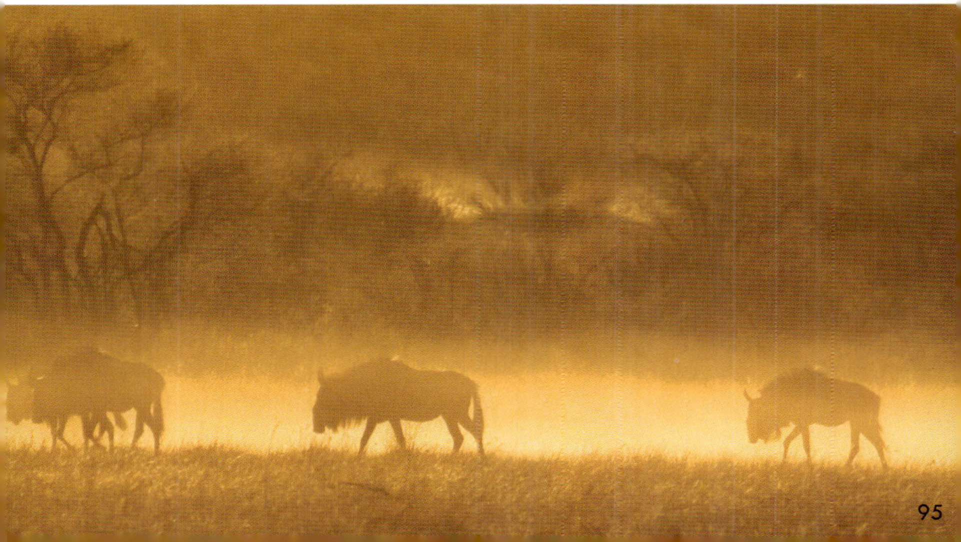

▶ *Greater Kudu, Makgadikgadi Pans National Park. DSLR, 100-400mm Lens, f/5.6 @1/800, ISO 400*

Side lighting can often create a more interesting portrait than a front lit subject. The key is to try to capture the sunlight in one of the eyes so that it is the first thing the viewer is drawn to in the photograph. Early morning or late afternoon, the low sun will create an even greater contrast between the two sides of the animal and therefore a more striking effect. **JG**

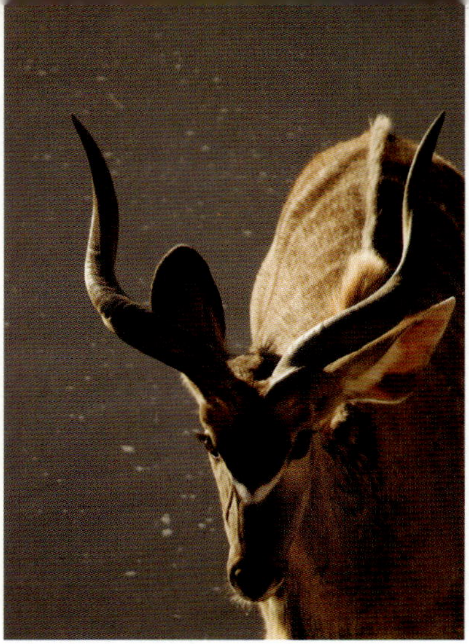

▼ *Burchell's Zebra, Makgadikgadi Pans. DSLR, 100-400mm Lens, f/10 @ 1/800, ISO 800*

Shooting directly into the sun can be challenging in terms of auto-focus and exposure but it is worth persisting and experimenting. Switch to manual focus if necessary. You only need one of the images to succeed to make the effort worthwhile. **JG**

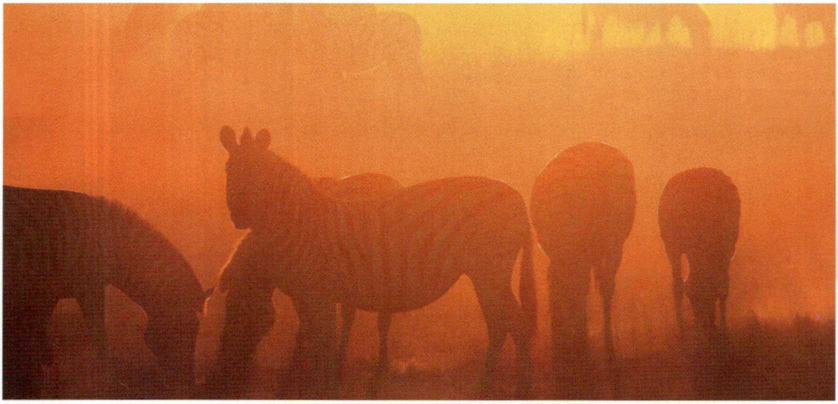

NON-GOLDEN OPPORTUNITIES

The soft light in the early morning and late afternoon is often quoted as the best time to photograph wildlife, but you can still capture good images in the middle of the day. A polariser will saturate the sky and create a vivid blue backdrop, while the contrast in harsh lighting situations is often ideal for dramatic black and white images, so don't pack the camera away just because your watch says so. Challenging lighting conditions also force you to think more creatively which will improve your photographic skills.

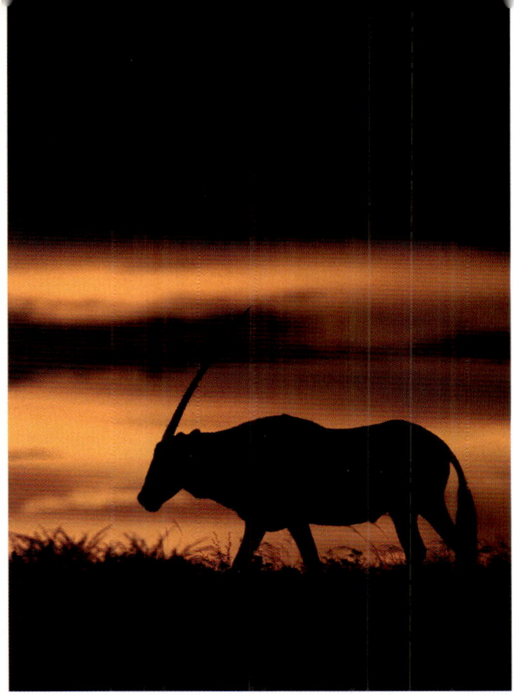

▶ ***Gemsbok, Central Kalahari Game Reserve. DSLR, 500mm Lens, f/6.3 @ 1/1250, ISO 100***

This is a great example of the importance of checking the exposure of your images while shooting. I initially spot metered on the sunset but having quickly viewed the brightness histogram, I decided to underexpose by 2/3 of a stop in order to redden the sunset further and to darken the overhanging clouds. This created a much more dramatic effect. **JG**

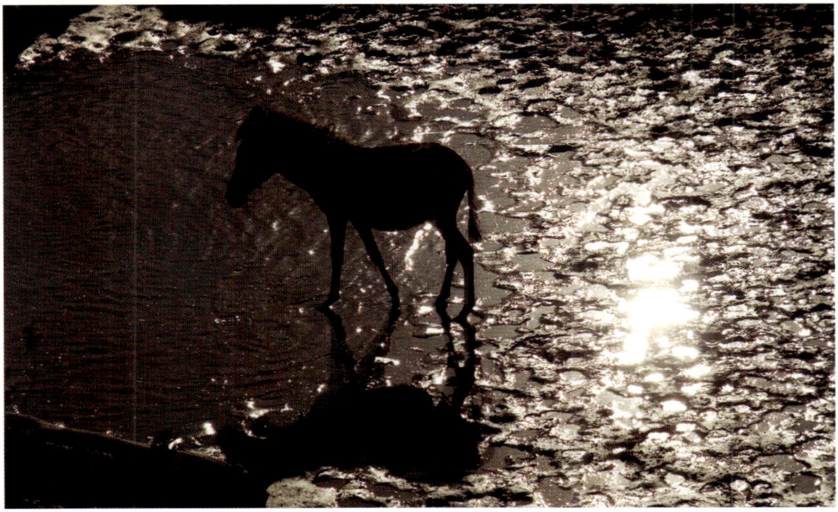

▲ ***Zebra Foal, Makgadikgadi Pans National Park. DSLR, 17-85mm Lens, f/10 @ 1/2500, ISO 400***

Even with harsh lighting (this was taken mid-afternoon), it is possible to create an interesting image if you think in tones rather than colours. I initially intended to convert this image to black and white but when editing, found that the lack of saturation made this unnecessary. **JG**

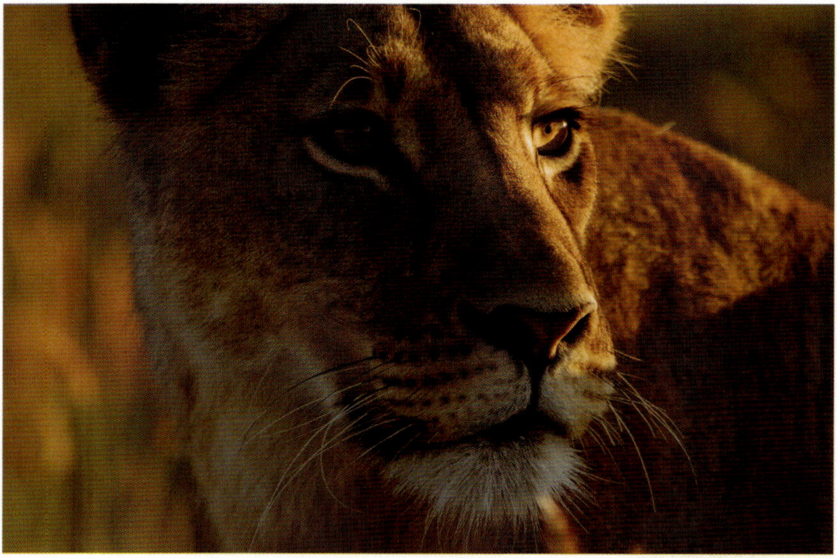

▲ ***Lioness, Central Kalahari Game Reserve. DSLR, 100-400mm Lens, f/5.6 @ 1/320, ISO 200***

Another example of the effect of side lighting creating a striking image. With the majority of the lioness in the shade, the sunlight in her left eye provides the perfect focal point for the viewer. **JG**

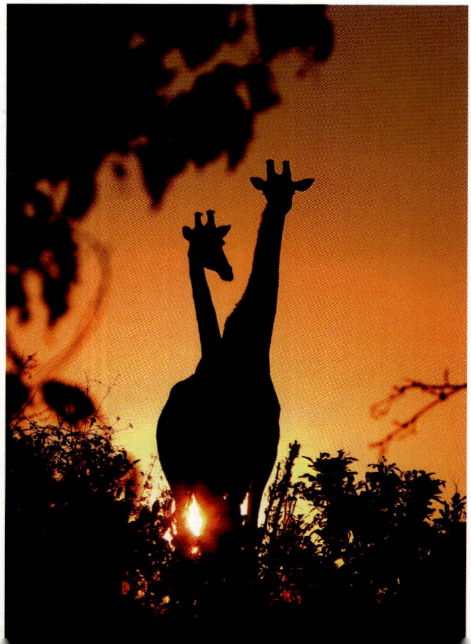

◀ ***Southern Giraffe, Savuti, Chobe National Park. DSLR, 100-400mm Lens, f/9 @ 1/640, ISO 200***

Sunset in Savuti and two giraffe cross each other's path. Silhouettes are a much sought after image for a wildlife photographer and to achieve the best exposure, it is necessary to meter on a light part of the image, usually a patch of sky near the sun. **SS**

▶ ***Gemsbok, Central Kalahari Game Reserve. DSLR, 100-400mm Lens, f/5.6 @ 1/1250, ISO 100***

From December to April, the summer rains transform the Kalahari into a lush green landscape peppered with flowers. If you are fortunate enough to visit as the rains are finishing, you will encounter scenes like this which lend themselves perfectly to the rule of thirds (see p.64). **JG**

Groups

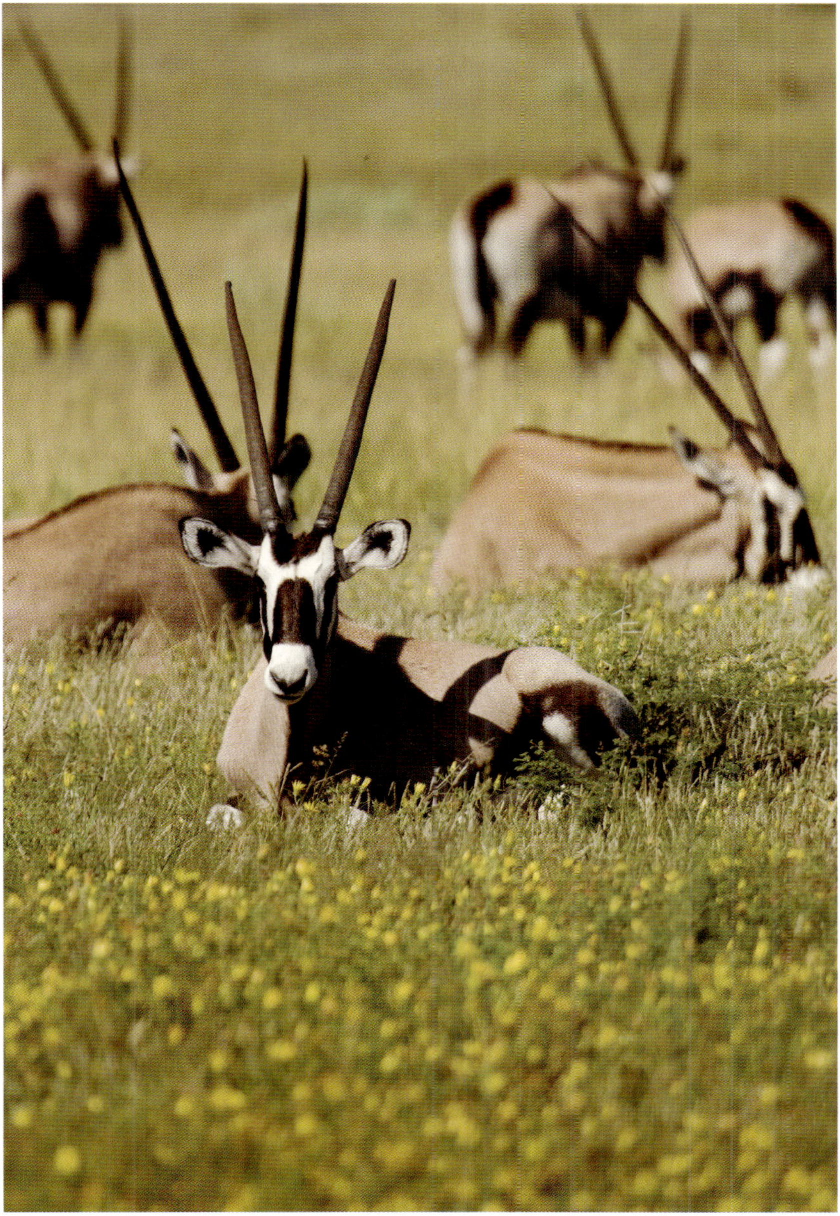

▶ *Elephant, Savuti, Chobe National Park. DSLR, 100-400mm Lens, f/10 @ 1/400, ISO 250*

The density of elephants in the Savuti will give you plenty of opportunity to experiment with different compositions. Try to use natural shapes whenever possible so as to add originality to your images. Including additional animals in the background will help maintain a sense of their environment. **JG**

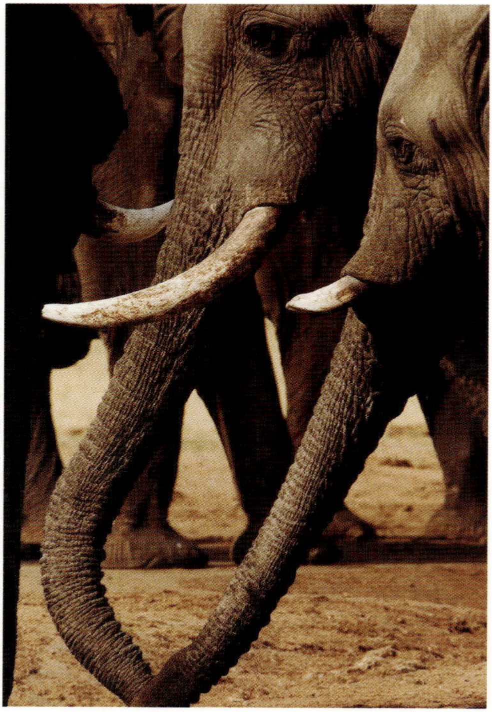

▼ *Tsessebe, Okavango Delta. DSLR, 100-400mm Lens, f/5.6 @ 1/400, ISO 100*

This fleet-footed antelope, said to be the fastest antelope in Africa, is seen mostly in the Okavango Delta. This herd is grouped nicely with their foreheads characteristically caked in mud. **SS**

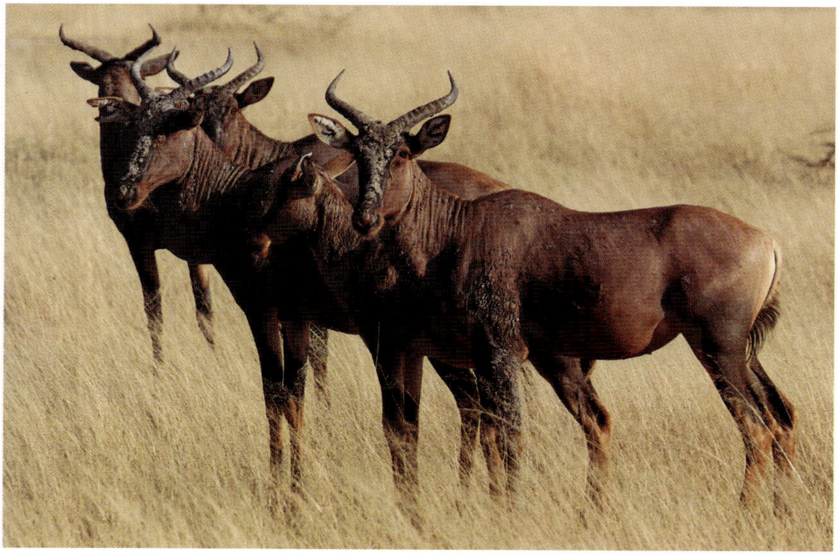

▶ Common Waterbuck, Okavango Delta. DSLR, 100-400mm Lens, f/5.6 @ 1/250, ISO 100

Wildlife is never quite where you would like it to be and often herds disperse whilst feeding. However, something caught the attention of these waterbuck and they immediately grouped together to stand and listen for any danger. More eyes and ears on the job will help in detecting a threat. **SS**

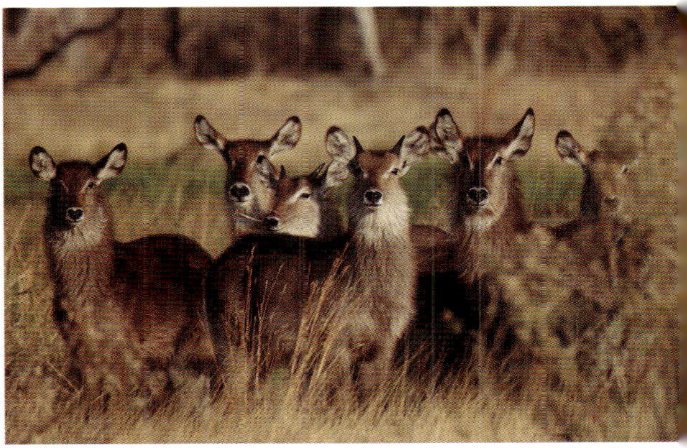

▼ Burchell's Zebra, Makgadikgadi Pans National Park. DSLR, 100-400mm Lens, f/6.3 @ 1/800, ISO 250

You do not always need to capture a whole herd of animals to convey an idea of their numbers. Zebras' vulnerability whilst drinking means they will often get spooked, creating splashing water and unusual poses. A high shutter speed is necessary to freeze motion, but by not going above 1/800, I was still able to express some movement of the water. **JG**

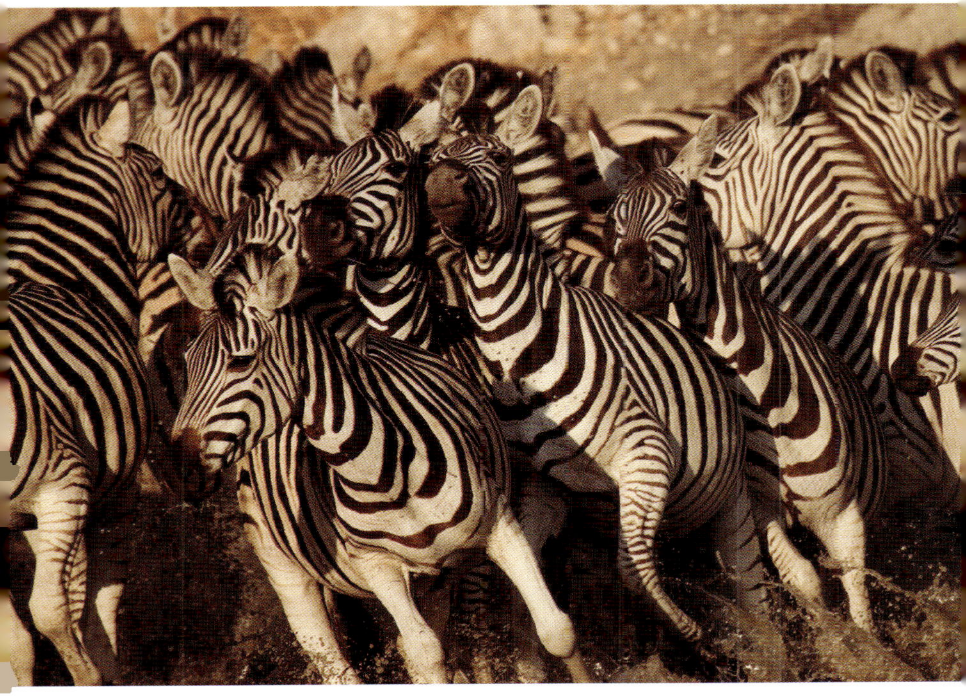

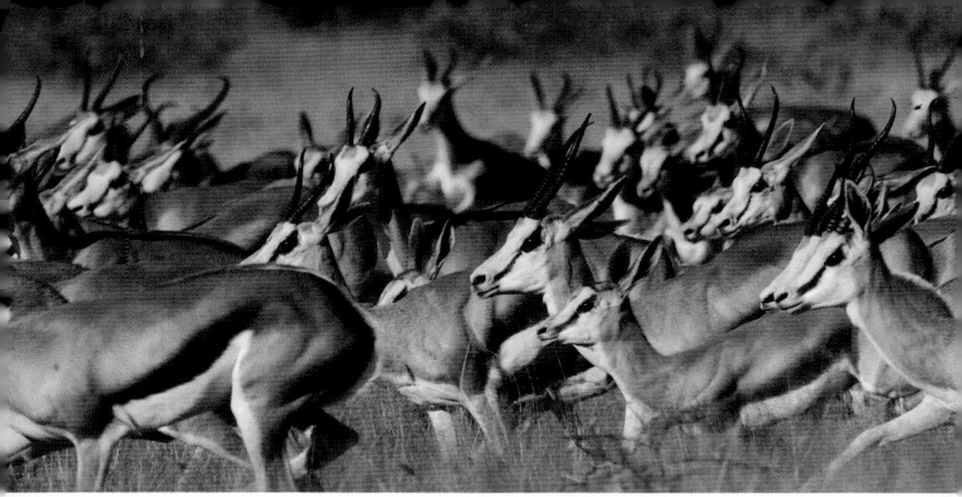

▲ ***Springbok, Central Kalahari Game Reserve. DSLR, 100-400mm Lens, f/5.6 @ 1/1250, ISO 100***

This springbok herd were evading a pair of inexperienced lioness hunters with relative ease. I zoomed in closely on them as they ran past to convey a feeling of being amongst the herd. **JG**

▼ ***Lion, Savuti, Chobe National Park. DSLR, 100-400mm Lens, f/5.6 @ 1/400, ISO 200***

While sitting at a pan in Savuti, this pride of lion emerged from a nearby mopane forest to drink. The golden light allowed for a high shutter speed and a wide aperture thereby softening the pair in the background to give the image depth. SS

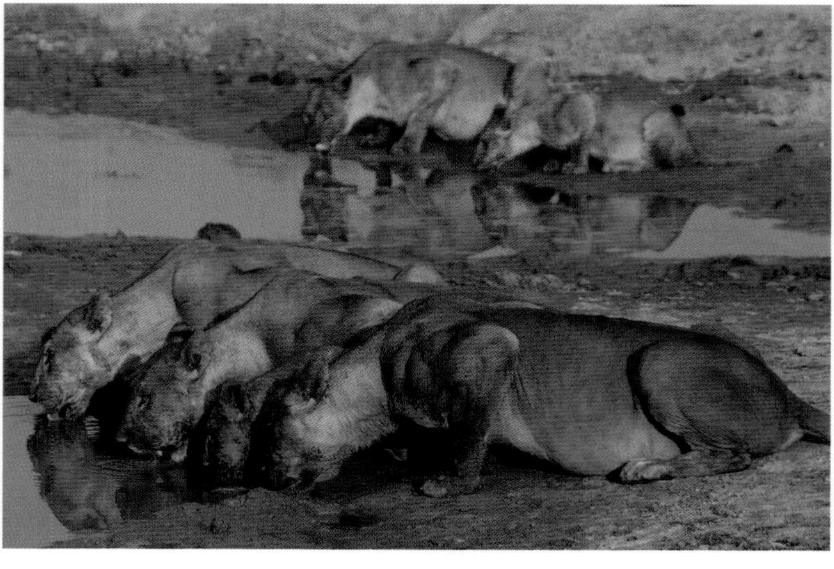

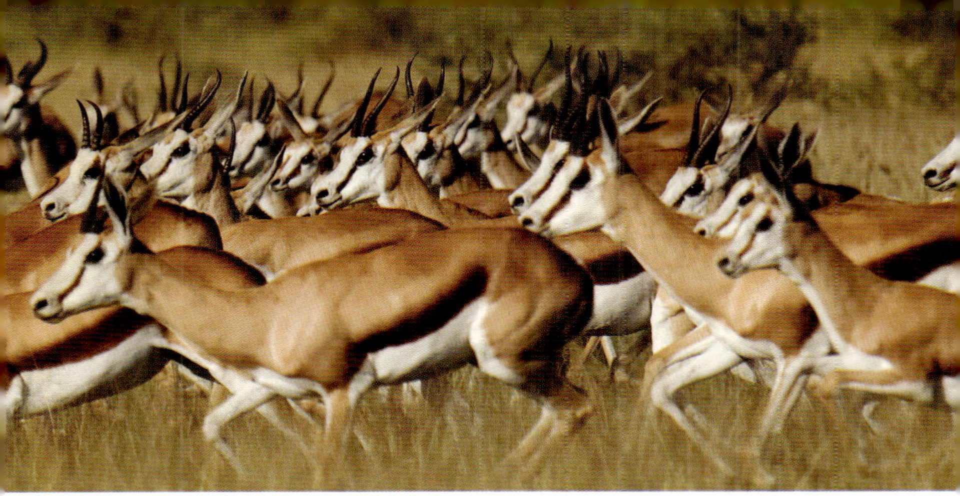

Playing with Numbers

Rather than adjusting your focal length to fit all the animals into the image, cropping in tight to capture the character of a few individuals can create a sense of being part of the herd. Alternatively, having individuals entering and exiting the sides of your image can help portray movement. To emphasise large numbers, frame your image so that both foreground and background contain members of the herd and experiment with different apertures to throw some individuals out of focus.

▼ ***Greater Kudu, Okavango Delta. DSLR, 100-400mm Lens, f/5.6 @ 1/320, ISO 100***

Once in a while, wildlife creates obvious compositions making the photographer's task a lot easier. When this trio of kudu aligned themselves perfectly, then waited for me to take the shot, I couldn't believe my luck. **JG**

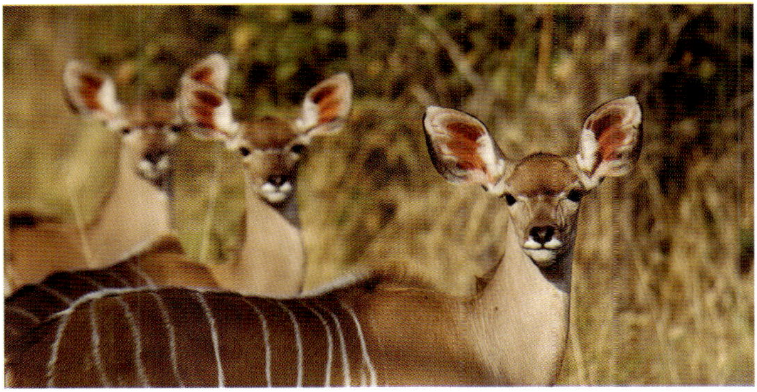

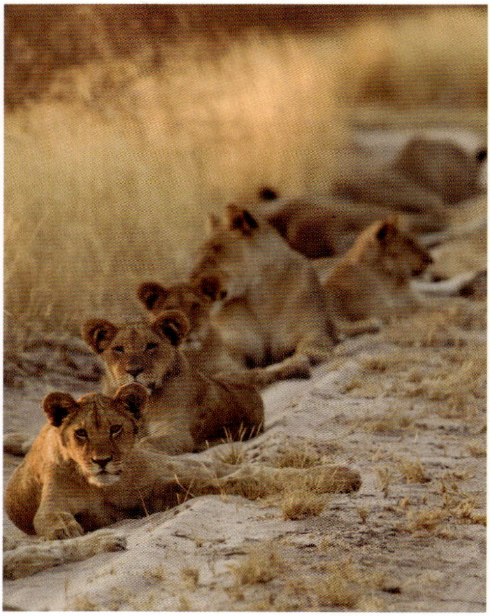

◀ Lion, Central Kalahari Game Reserve. DSLR, 100-400mm Lens, f/6.3 @ 1/200, ISO 400

One by one, this pride of nine females and cubs emerged from the bushes and conveniently lay in a line in the road. In the dwindling light, my beanbag enabled me to shoot at a slower shutter speed, avoiding the need to raise the ISO any higher. **JG**

▶ Leopard, Savuti, Chobe National Park. DSLR, 18-55mm Lens, f/10 @ 1/250, ISO 200

Spotting an impala carcass in the top right hand branch of a tree, I anticipated that the owner would eventually return to feed. Having visualised this type of image for many years, it was only recently that the opportunity for this classic silhouette finally presented itself. **SS**

▶ Elephant, Okavango Delta. DSLR, 100-400mm Lens, f/5.6 @ 1/500, ISO 100

When elephants come to water, it is usually in close-knit herds. The water's edge can be a dangerous place with predators lying in wait so they often bunch together whilst drinking as a security measure. Here, a family group enjoy the cool waters of the Khwai River. **SS**

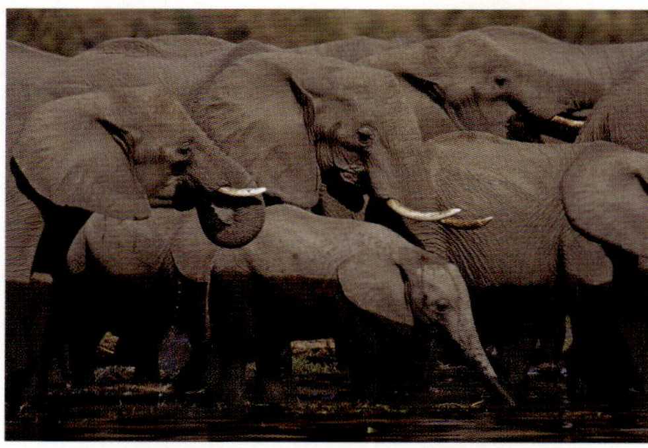

▶ Bat-eared Fox, Central Kalahari Game Reserve. DSLR, 100-400mm Lens, f/5.6 @ 1/1250, ISO 320

Even with two animals you can create a more interesting effect than a simple portrait by using a shallow depth of field. **JG**

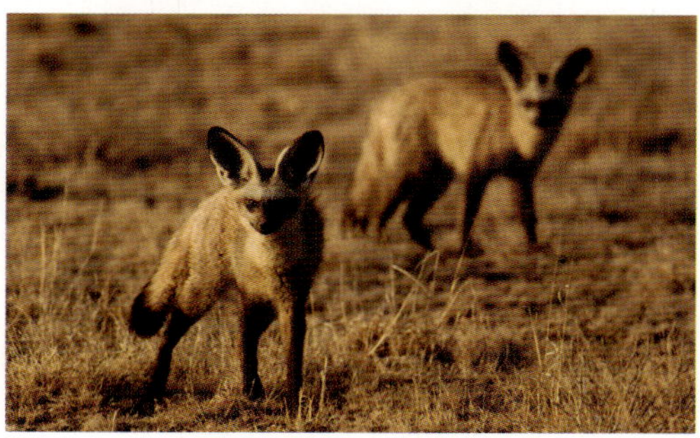

Environment

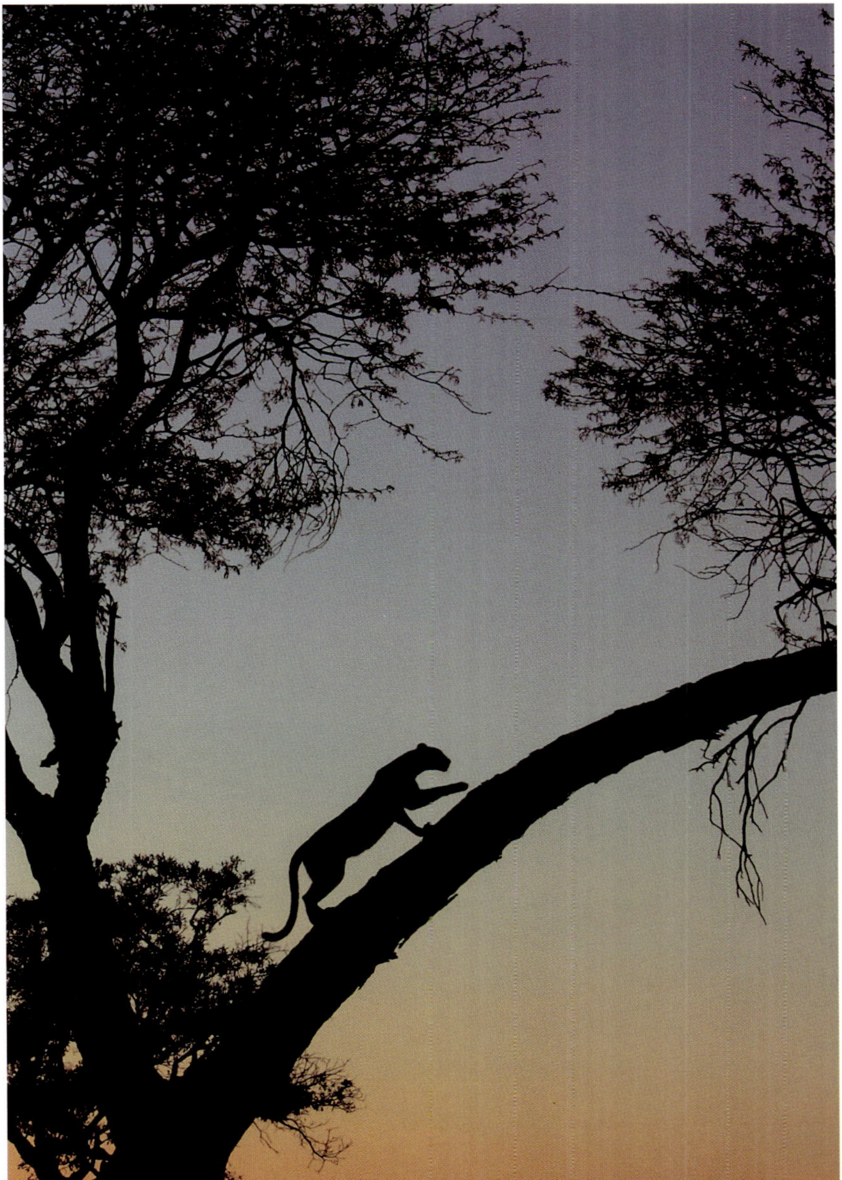

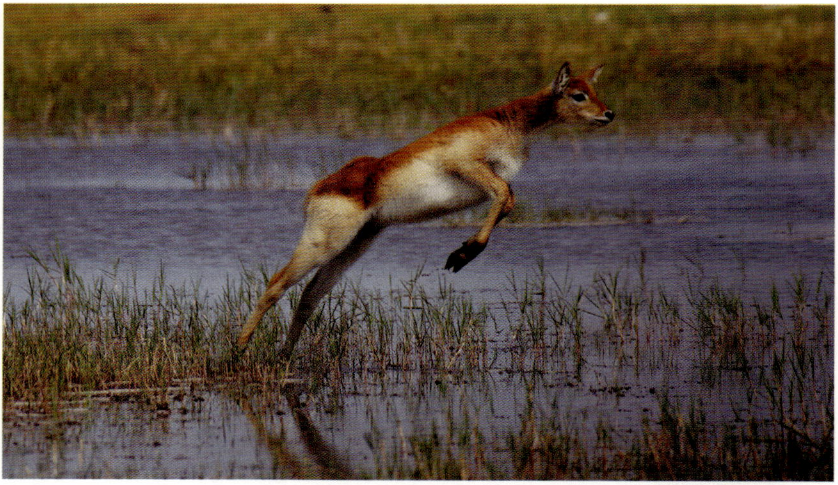

▲ ***Red Lechwe, Okavango Delta. DSLR, 100-400mm Lens, f/5.6 @ 1/1000, ISO 100***

Powered by their muscular hindquarters and aided by their splayed and elongated hooves, this aquatic antelope will escape predation by leaping into deeper water. Using continuous drive mode meant I could capture the precise moment she leapt. **SS**

▼ ***Cheetah, Moremi Game Reserve. DSLR, 100-400m Lens, f/7.1 @ 1/800, ISO 100***

One morning we found two cheetahs sleeping on a termite mound. Despite their apparent lethargy, we waited several hours and eventually they moved on around the edge of a floodplain. This tree caught their attention and one of them used a branch to work his claws and stretch his back, striking an unusual pose. Stay with your subject for as long as is possible - you never know when something interesting will happen. **SS**

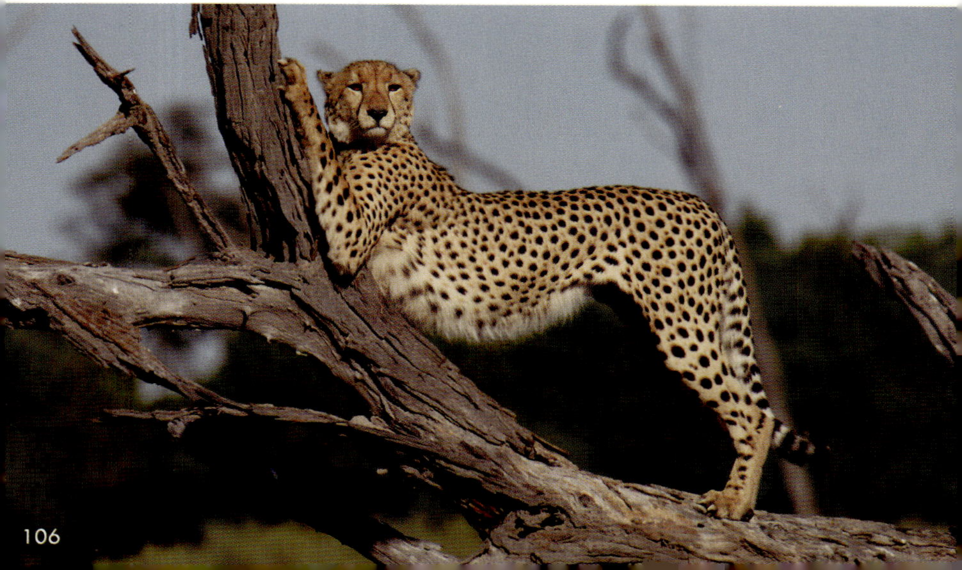

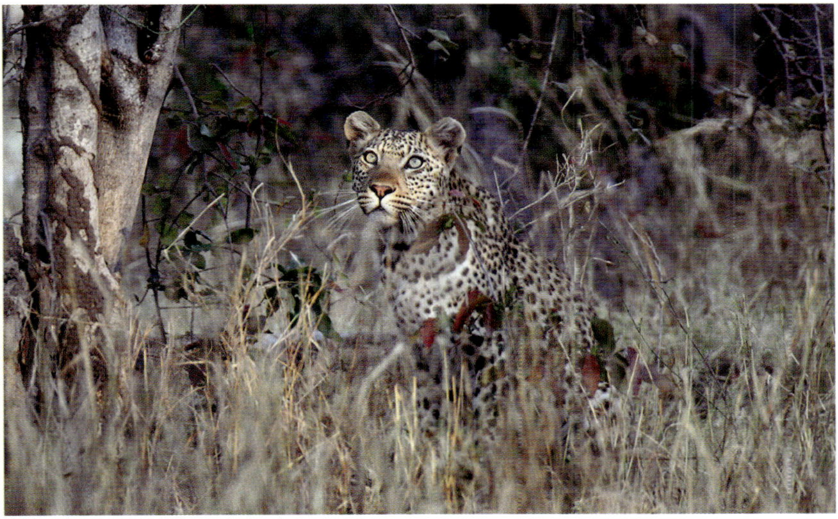

▲ *Leopard, Moremi Game Reserve. DSLR, 100-400mm Lens, f/5.6 @ 1/100, ISO 1600*

This image, shot in the soft rays of the setting sun, is all about light. The vivid colours of her coat visibly stood out against the shadowy backdrop as she started her evening hunt. Unusually, the light also made her eyes appear to be of different colours. **SS**

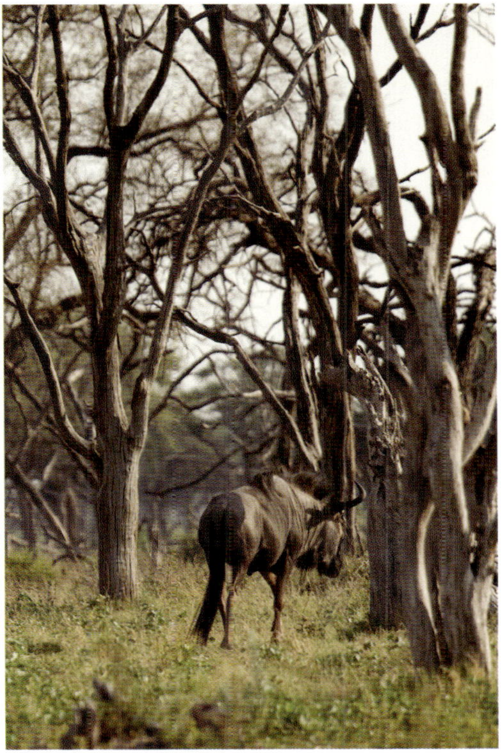

▶ *Blue Wildebeest, Okavango Delta, DSLR, 100-400mm Lens, f/5.6 @ 1/800, ISO 250*

Try to make a conscious decision whether to shoot in landscape or portrait orientation every time you take a picture. By turning the camera on its side to photograph this wildebeest, I was able to emphasise the height of the trees so that the habitat became as important an element to the image as the animal itself. **JG**

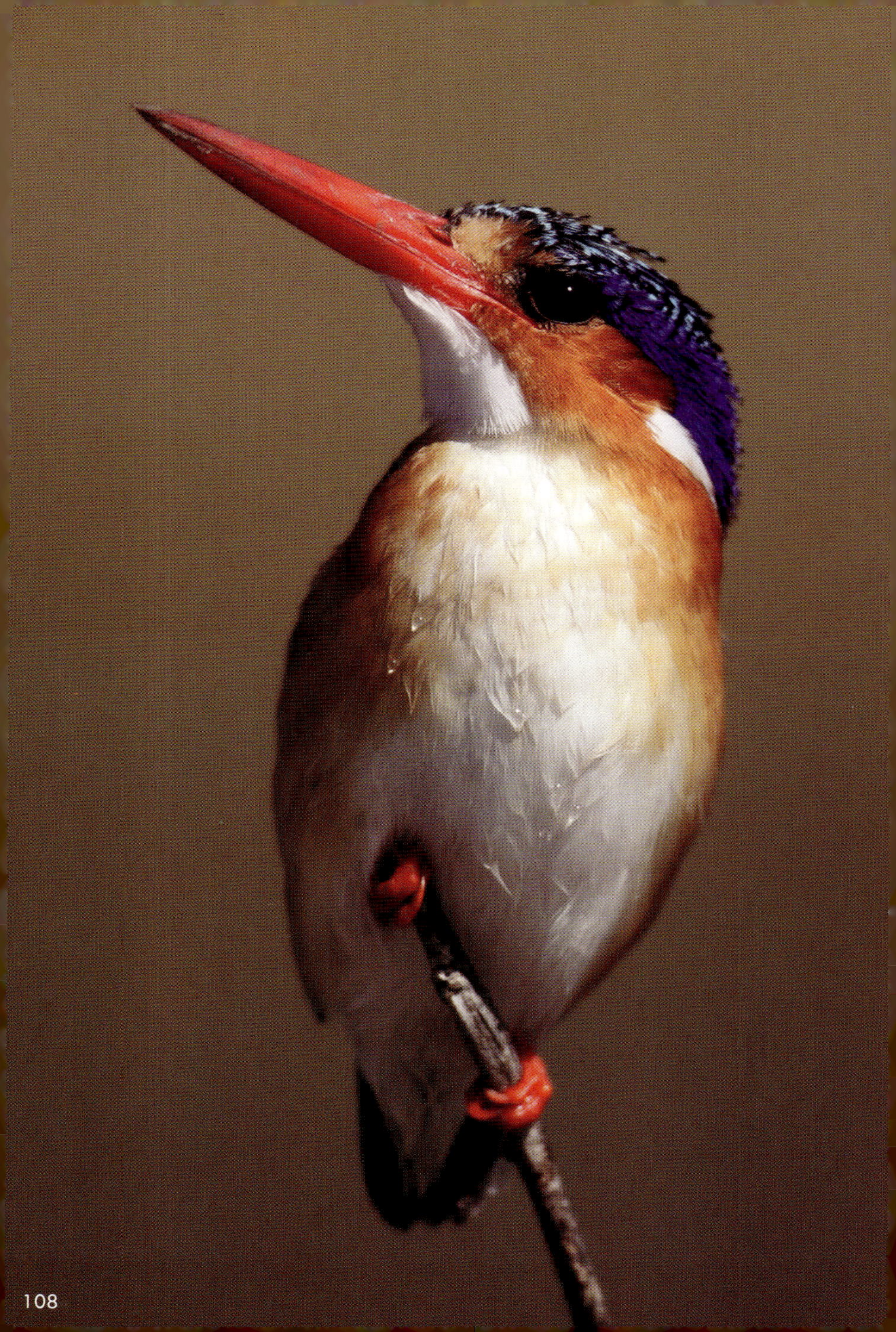

BIRDS
LIFE ON THE WING

"It is not only fine feathers that make fine birds." *Aesop*

Birds

Bird photography encompasses a diverse range of colour, shape, form and habitat. With over 500 species inhabiting desert and wetland ecosystems, Botswana offers immense avian potential. Capturing the moment presents all sorts of challenges but this aspect of wildlife photography is hugely rewarding.

Portraits

▶ ***Pearl-spotted Owlet, Makgadikgadi Pans. DSLR, 17-85mm Lens, f/6.3 @ 1/250, ISO 250***

Of all the birdcalls you are likely to encounter whilst on safari, the rising scale of a pearl-spotted owlet is one of the easiest to identify and if you approach carefully, you may get the chance to photograph one up close. In contrast to its diminutive stature, its large eyes provide instant appeal. This head-on stare was therefore ideal to maximise impact. **JG**

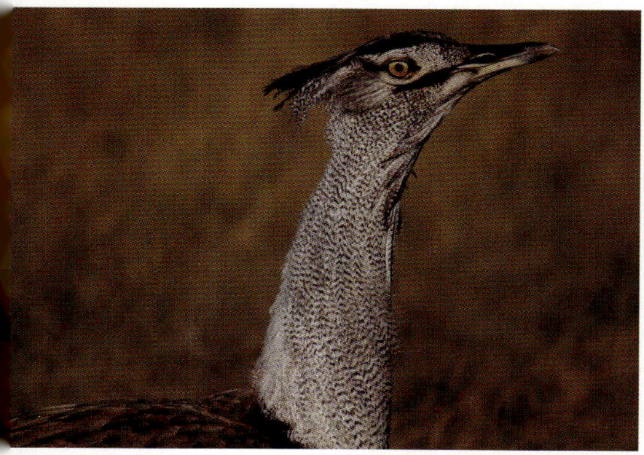

◀ ***Kori Bustard, Okavango Delta. DSLR, 100-400mm Lens, f/5.6 @ 1/2500, ISO 200***

The Kori Bustard's claim to fame is that it is the heaviest flying bird in Africa. Although you will mainly see them walking through open grasslands, their huge wingspans and heavy wing beats slowly get them airborne. Here, a wide aperture blurs the background pushing the subject to the fore. **SS**

◀ ***Malachite Kingfisher, Okavango Delta. DSLR, 500mm Lens, f/4 @ 1/2500, ISO 200***

This tiny kingfisher is often seen whizzing along the waterways of the Delta. We found this one perched along the Khwai River and the clean, neutral background really accentuates its beautiful colours. **SS**

Bird Portraits

Make sure that your focus is on the eye of the bird and that it is well lit - a glinting eye will breathe life into your image. The surrounds of lodges and campsites are a surprisingly good place to photograph birds as they are slightly more used to a human presence.

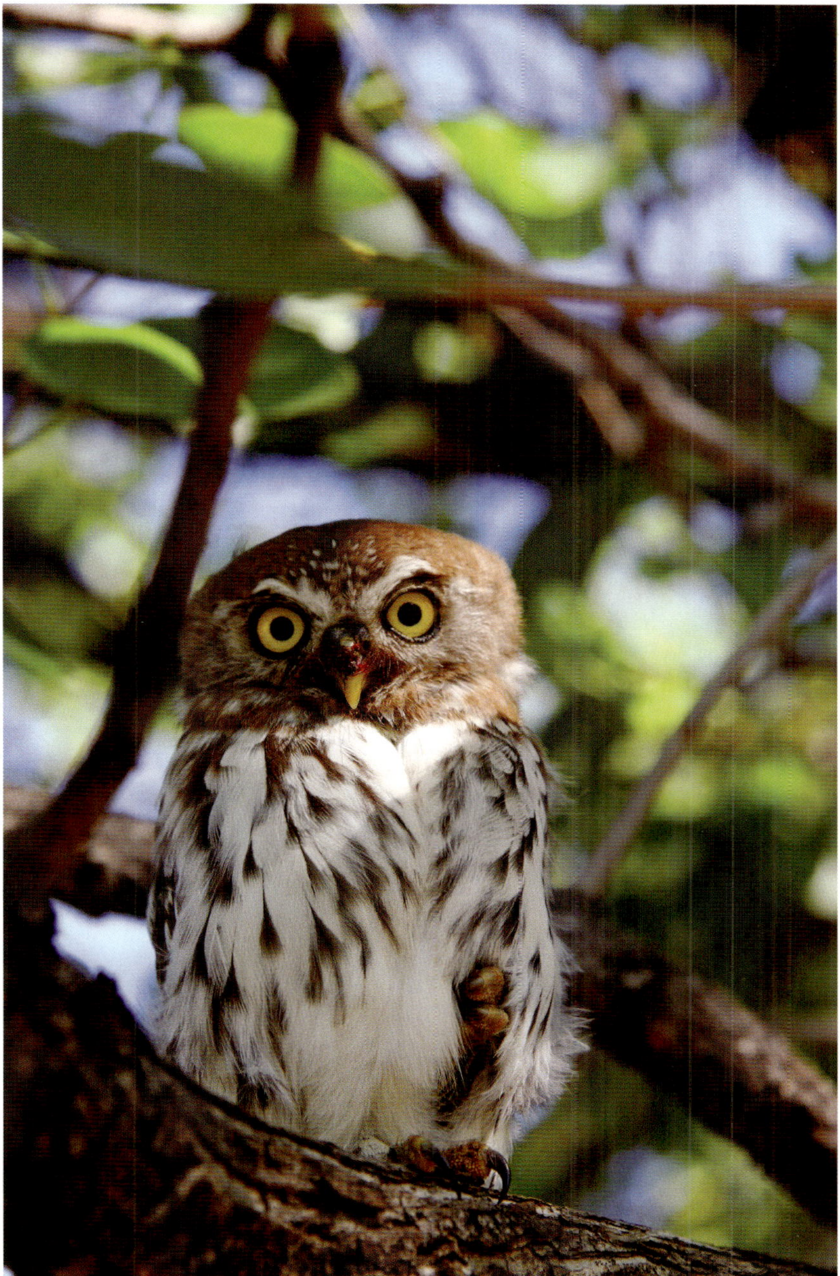

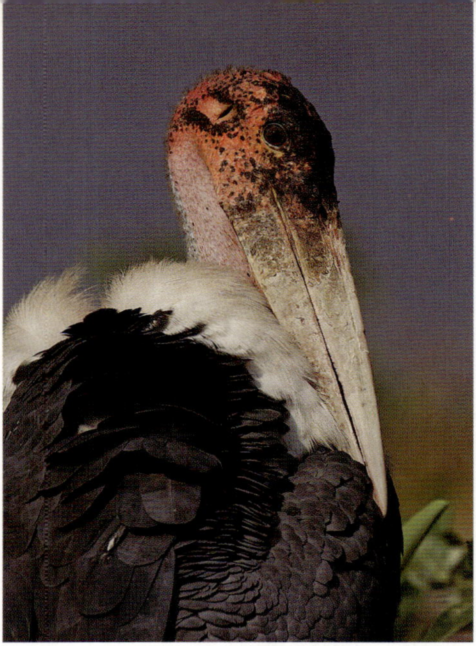

◀ ***Maribou Stork, Okavango Delta. DSLR, 100-400mm Lens, f/8 @ 1/500, ISO 100***

There are several heronries or rookeries in the Okavango Delta that are worth visiting, especially for close-up images. Each year hundreds of storks, herons, egrets and ibises nest on islands out in the open waters. The sheer numbers, coupled with the ability to get up close, means that many hours (and memory cards) can be spent here. Try to visit the heronry in the early morning or late afternoon so that the sun lights up your subjects well. **SS**

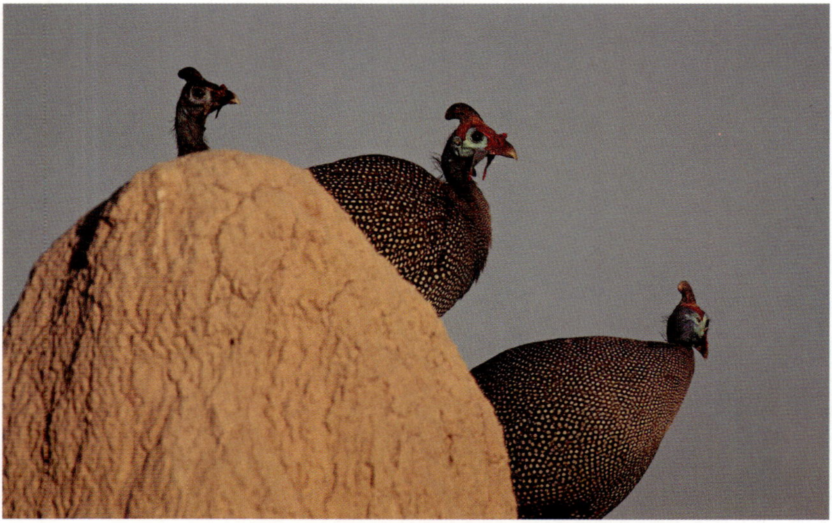

▲ ***Helmeted Guineafowl, Okavango Delta. DSLR, 100-400mm Lens, f/5.6 @ 1/1250, ISO 200***

The helmeted guineafowl is a wonderful character of the African bush. Spending their days on the ground feeding, they fly to roost in the safety of trees with the onset of dusk. The raised termite mound led to the rare opportunity to frame these individuals against the sky, forming an interesting compositional portrait. **SS**

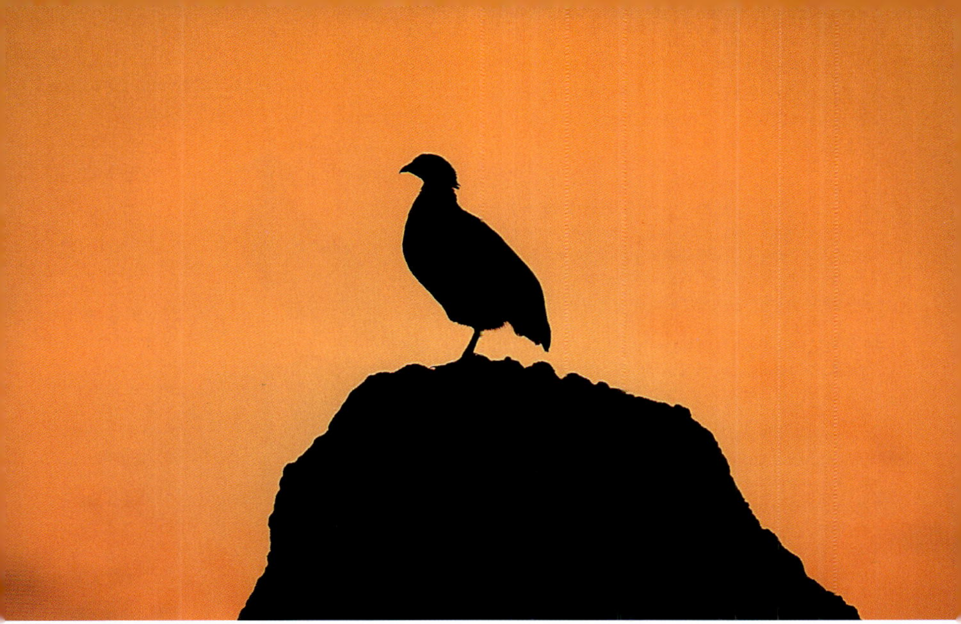

▲ ***Red-billed Francolin, Okavango Delta. DSLR, 100-400mm Lens, f/8 @ 1/640, ISO 200***

As the dying embers of the sun turned the sky orange, we passed this francolin offering its evening call atop a termite mound. This is a classic example of how a simple composition of a common subject can still create a powerful image. **SS**

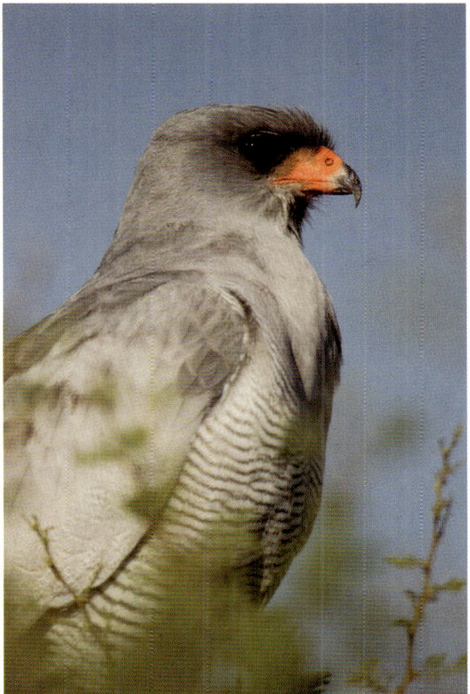

▶ ***Pale Chanting Goshawk, Central Kalahari Game Reserve. DSLR, 100-400mm Lens, f/5.6 @ 1/1000, ISO 100***

Despite being one of the more widespread raptors in the Kalahari, pale chanting goshawks can be frustrating to shoot as they tend to take flight as soon as you approach. Fortunately, this one was relaxed enough for me to drive past its chosen perch, thereby positioning the sun behind me to capture its head against the blue sky. **JG**

▶ *Secretary Bird, Central Kalahari Game Reserve. DSLR, 500mm Lens, f/5.6 @ 1/500, ISO 250*

If you are patient, secretary birds can provide some great photographic opportunities. As specialist snake hunters, they are mostly seen stomping through the grass but occasionally raise their wings creating a more dramatic portrait. **JG**

▶▶ *Cattle Egrets, Okavango Delta. DSLR, 100-400mm Lens, f/5.6 @ 1/2500, ISO 200*

A rainstorm tends to reduce the dust in the atmosphere generating crystal clear skies. As we were watching a herd of buffalo, squadrons of cattle egrets arrived to feed on the insects disturbed by their hooves. The strong light meant that high shutter speeds could freeze the action. **SS**

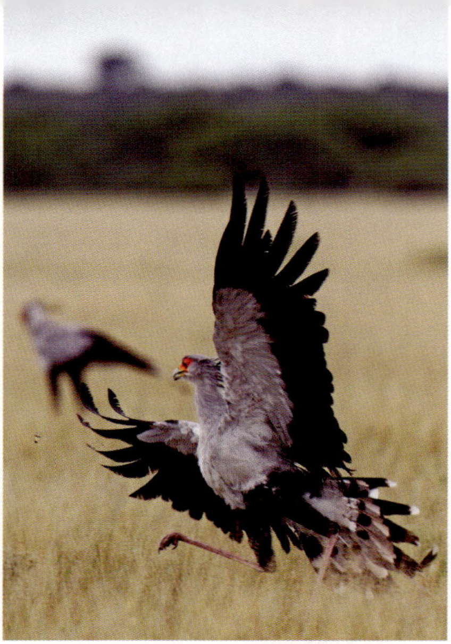

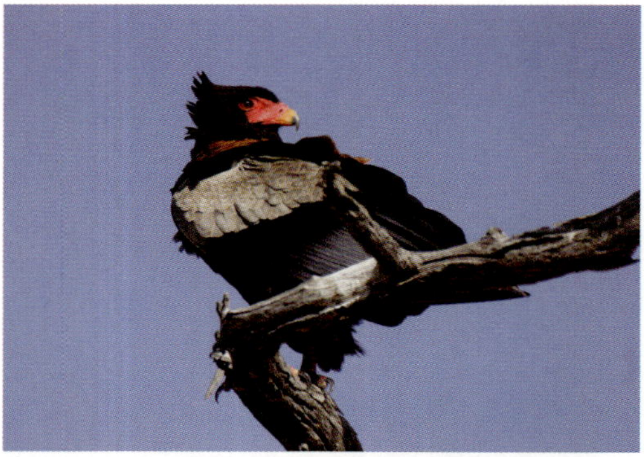

◀ *Bateleur Eagle, Okavango Delta. DSLR, 100-400mm Lens, f/7.1 @ 1/400, ISO 100*

The beautifully marked bateleur eagle is more commonly seen flying overhead in its characteristic glide. They can spend hours on the wing but when perched, they can often be found in dead trees. A slight breeze ruffled this individual's head and neck feathers giving the image extra character. **SS**

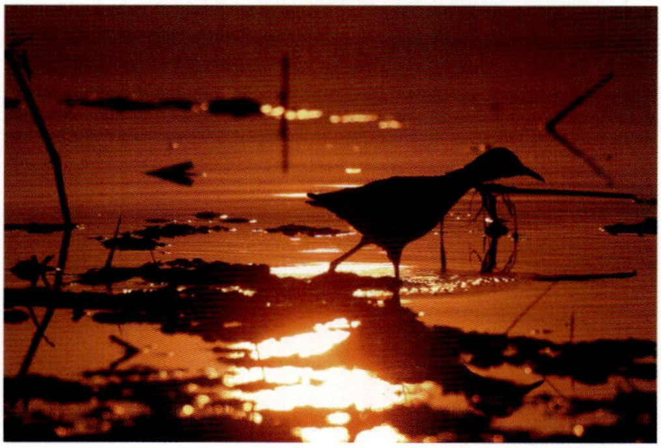

◀ *African Jacana, Okavango Delta. DSLR, 100-400mm Lens, f/5.6 @ 1/500, ISO 100*

Another frequently seen bird, the African jacana, has long legs and toes which allow it to walk across the tops of aquatic plants. As it continued its search for food, the setting sun transformed the water into a perfect golden backdrop. **SS**

In Flight

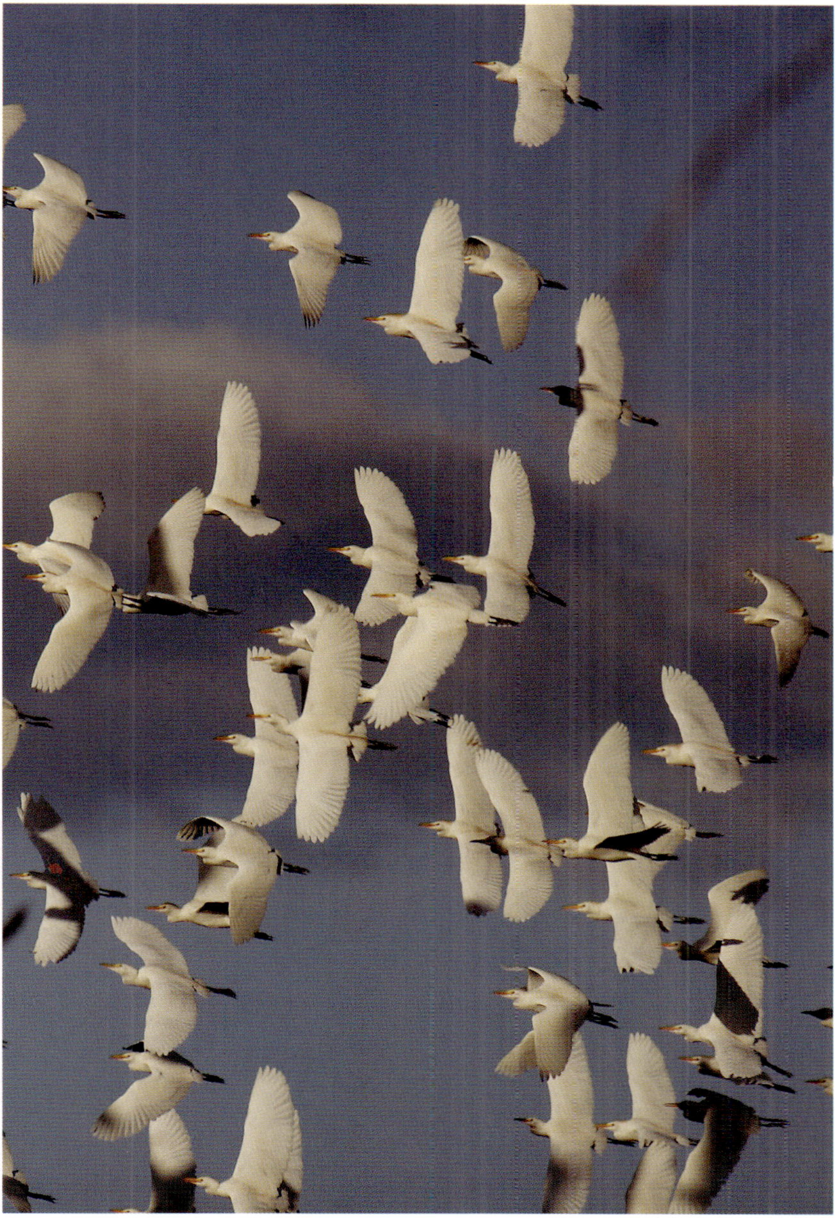

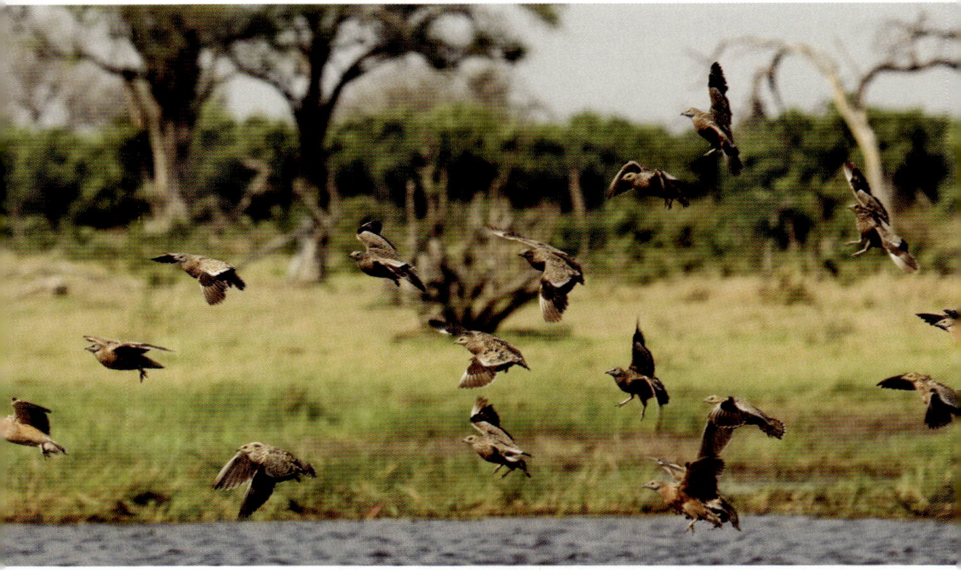

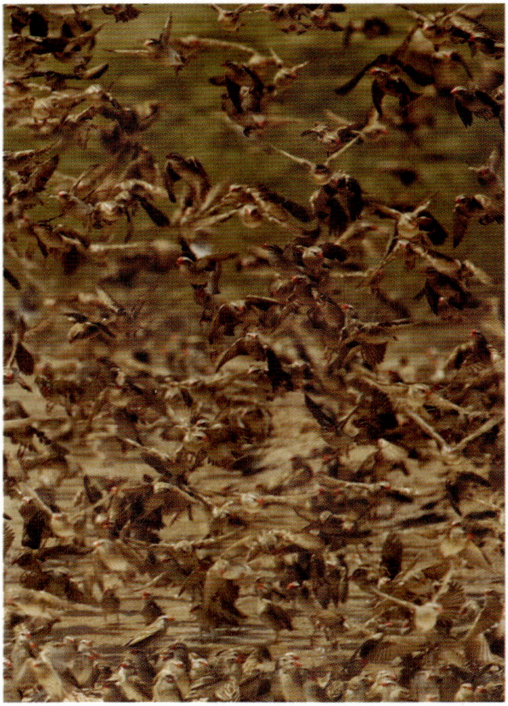

▲ Burchell's Sandgrouse, Okavango Delta. DSLR, 100-400mm Lens, f/5.6 @ 1/1250, ISO 200

Catching images of birds as they are close to landing (or taking-off) with legs splayed often makes for a more appealing photograph. Interestingly, sandgrouse are normally found in pairs and will only group together when they come to drink. **JG**

◀ Red-billed Quelea, Makgadikgadi Pans National Park. DSLR, 100-400mm Lens, f/6.3 @ 1/1600, ISO 400

It took several attempts to capture this image of a flock of red-billed quelea drinking as the contrasting tones of the birds, together with the split backdrop, made obtaining correct exposure more difficult than normal. The combination of different poses and shallow depth of field help to convey the confusion of flying in a large flock. **JG**

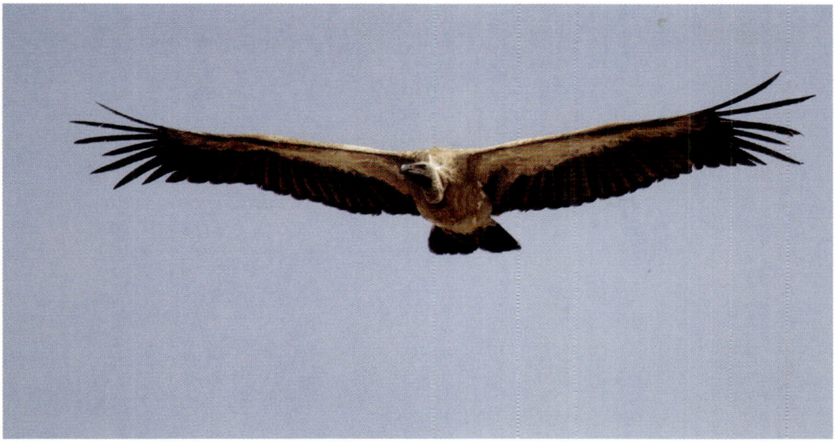

▲ ***White-backed Vulture, Makgadikgadi Pans National Park. DSLR, 100-400mm Lens, f/5.6 @ 1/1250, ISO 100***

Any photograph of a flying bird will have more impact the closer you are to its eye-level. Although I was several metres below this vulture, the relatively shallow shooting angle ensured its head was below the wingspan thus creating a more interesting composition than if shooting from directly below. Having the late sun behind me was vital to be able to record the detail. **JG**

▼ ***Rufous-naped Lark, Savuti, Chobe National Park. DSLR, 100-400mm Lens, f/6.3 @ 1/4000, ISO 400***

Early one morning in Savuti, we were greeted by the melodic sounds of a rufous-naped lark displaying at dawn. The golden back lighting highlights the finer details of its feathers. **SS**

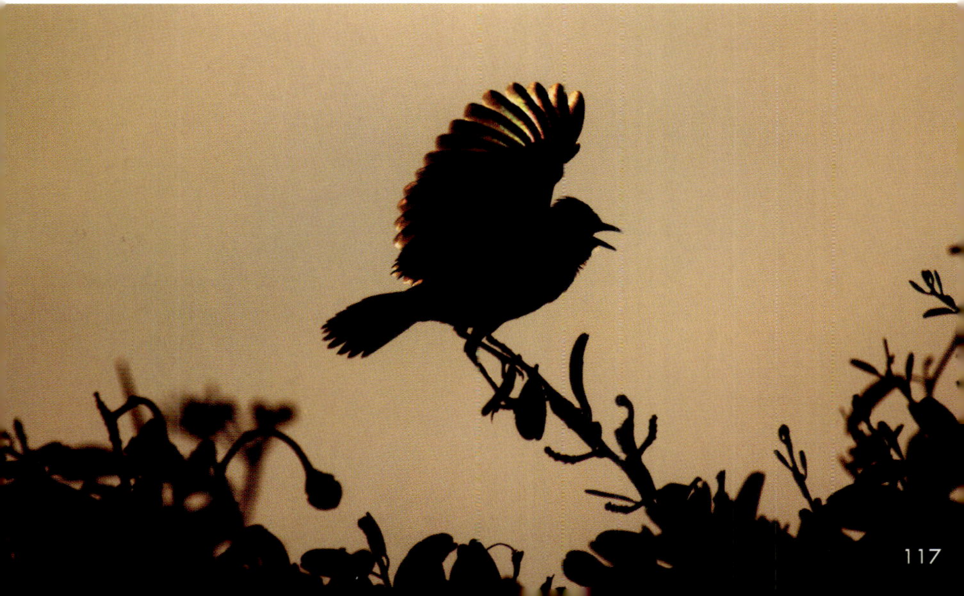

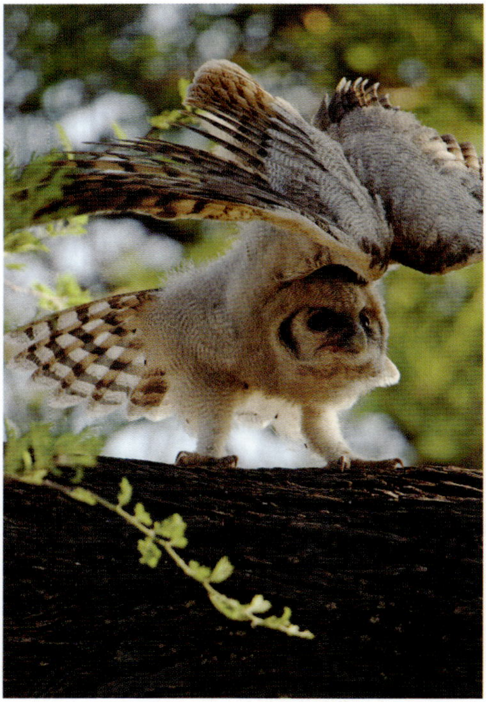

◀ ***Giant Eagle Owl Chick, Makgadikgadi Pans National Park. DSLR, 100-400mm Lens, f/5.6 @ 1/500, ISO 400***

We spotted this juvenile giant eagle owl just before locating its parents in nearby trees. Although the youngster was restless, jumping from branch to branch, its parents seemed oblivious to its constant calling. The combination of sunlight behind and foreground shade meant spot metering was necessary to avoid underexposing. **JG**

▶ ***Chin-spot Batis, Okavango Delta. SLR, 100-400mm Lens, Fuji Provia 100F***

A small cup of twigs wrapped in a spider's web and covered in lichen protect the newly-hatched chick concealed below this adult. Once the parents had become accustomed to my presence, they carried on as normal flitting back and forth to feed. **SS**

Learning to Fly

Photographing birds in flight is a challenging proposition requiring you to adjust your camera settings in advance. The constantly changing distance between yourself and the bird means continuous focus (AI-Servo) is vital to ensure a sharp image. Switching to automatic focal point selection will let the camera track the bird even if it moves into a different part of the viewfinder (this will be more successful against an evenly coloured sky than against a backdrop of vegetation).

If the sky is bright and you are able to keep the subject in the centre of the viewfinder, spot metering on it will reduce the risk of underexposed silhouettes. Most importantly, you will need high shutter speeds (at least 1/800) so raise your ISO accordingly, in case the bird flies into a darker environment before you get a chance to change your settings

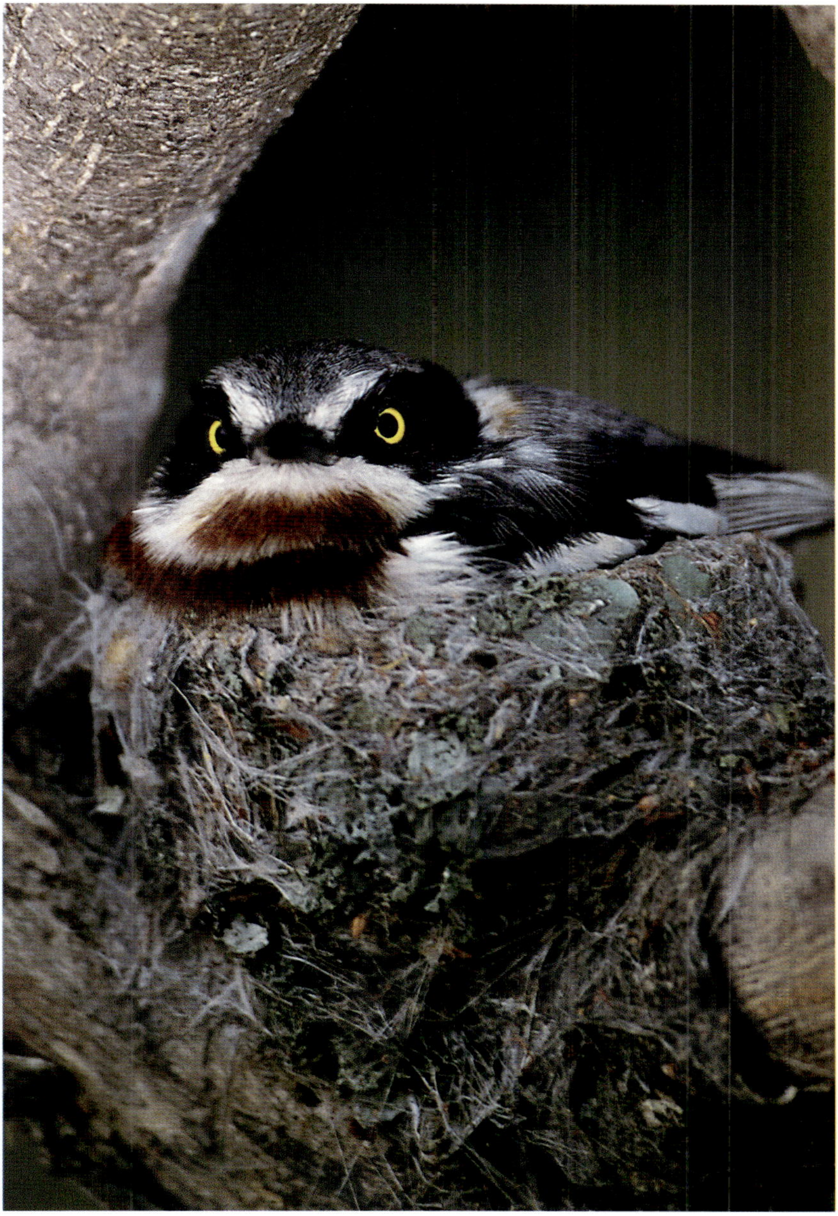

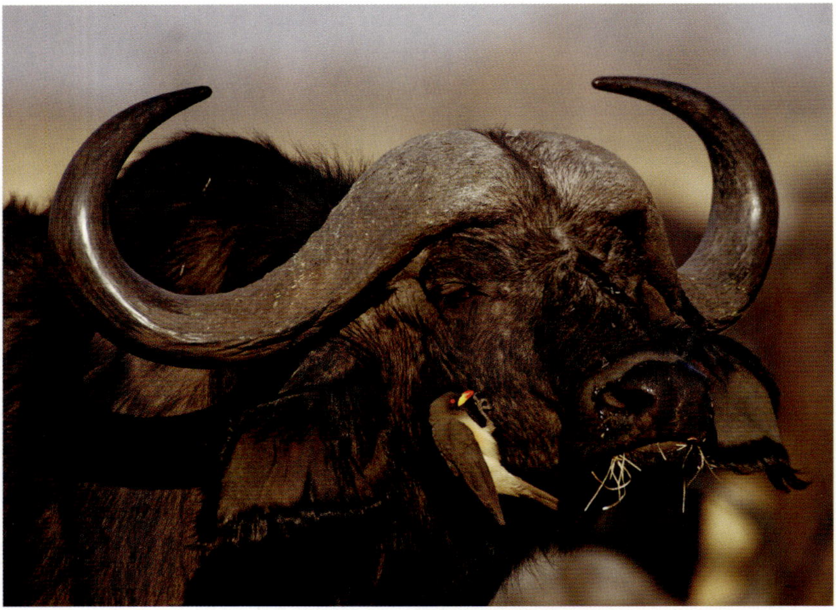

▲ ***Yellow-billed Oxpecker & Cape Buffalo, Okavango Delta. DSLR, 100-400mm Lens, f/5.6 @ 1/320, ISO 100***

Oxpeckers are masterful climbers and use their tails for support. They not only seek out parasites on the fur of mammals but, as recent research suggests, they also feed on blood in and around cuts on the host animal. **SS**

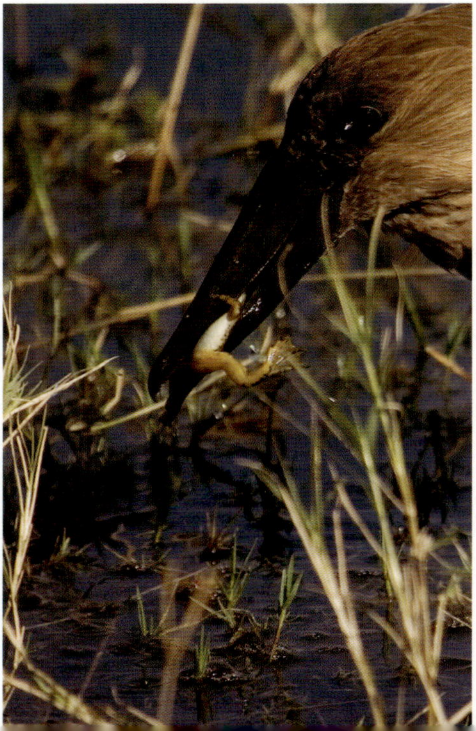

▶ ***Hamerkop, Okavango Delta. DSLR, 100-400mm Lens, f/5.6 @ 1/500, ISO 100***

The Okavango is a great place to photograph birds hunting, either for fish or small frogs. From storks and herons to this hamerkop, the time spent watching and waiting can be much more photographically satisfying than a traditional big game shot. Furthermore, you will often get more than one chance to create the best composition and use of light. **JG**

▶ ***Paradise-flycatcher, Okavango Delta. DSLR, 100-400mm Lens, f/5.6 @ 1/400, ISO 200***

Paradise-flycatchers arrive in Botswana each summer to build their intricate nests of twigs and spider webs. Here, the chicks cry out for sustenance brought to them by the female. Obtaining correct exposure in dappled light can be tricky. You can either try spot or evaluative metering modes. If you have the time experiment with both, but either way be ready as the parents visit the nest rather quickly. **SS**

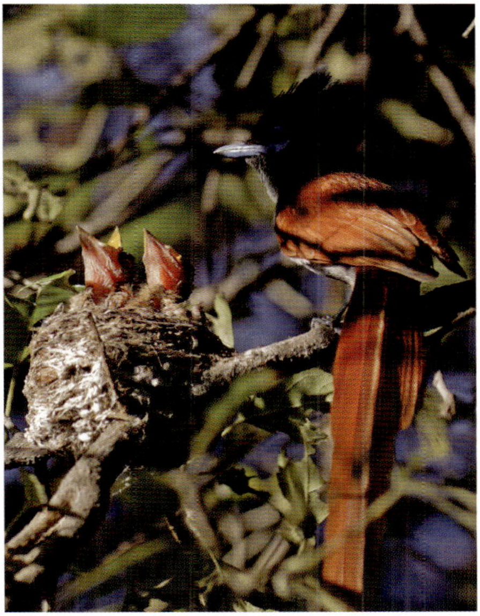

▼ ***Tawny Eagle & Lilac-breasted Roller, Moremi Game Reserve. DSLR, 500mm Lens, f/4 @ 1/2000, ISO 100***

Smaller birds will often mob potential predators as a primary mode of defence and the counter-intuitive image of a smaller bird chasing a larger one adds an extra dimension to the photograph. **JG**

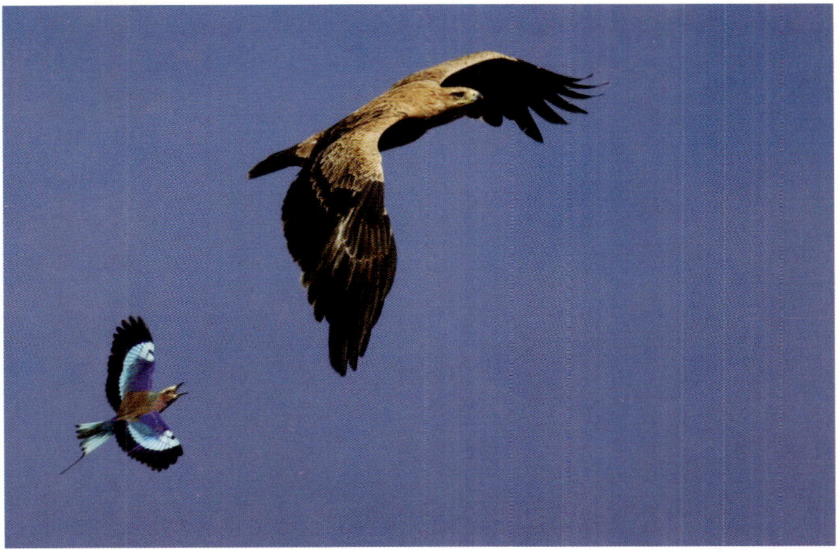

▶ ***Yellow-billed Stork & Egyptian Geese, Okavango Delta. DSLR, 100-400mm Lens, f/5.6 @ 1/4000, ISO 200***

Competition at feeding spots can be fierce. Although these two species tolerated each other at first, suddenly it became too much and the male goose launched a brief attack to scare the stork away. I had only a few seconds to catch this unpredictable moment. **SS**

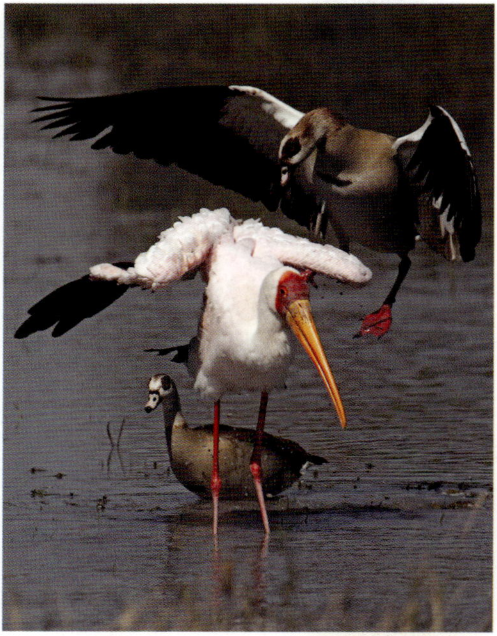

▼ ***Pied Kingfishers, Okavango Delta. DSLR, 100-400mm Lens, f/8 @ 1/500, ISO 2000***

Parenting sounds pretty difficult at the best of times. Here, a pied kingfisher has her work cut out with four or five offspring needing to be taught how to hunt and survive. She is using the fish to encourage the young to take flight and follow her lead. **SS**

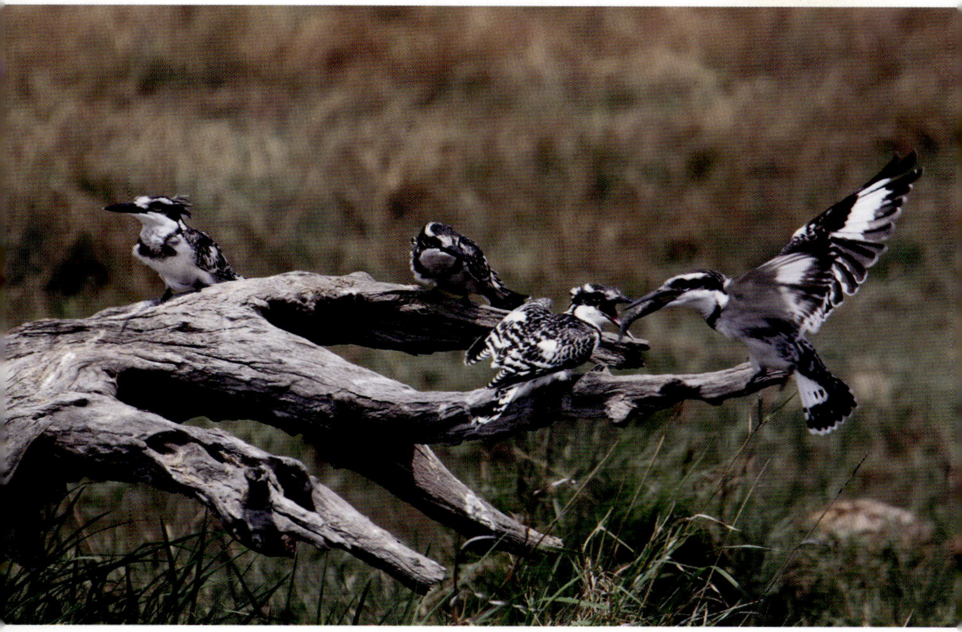

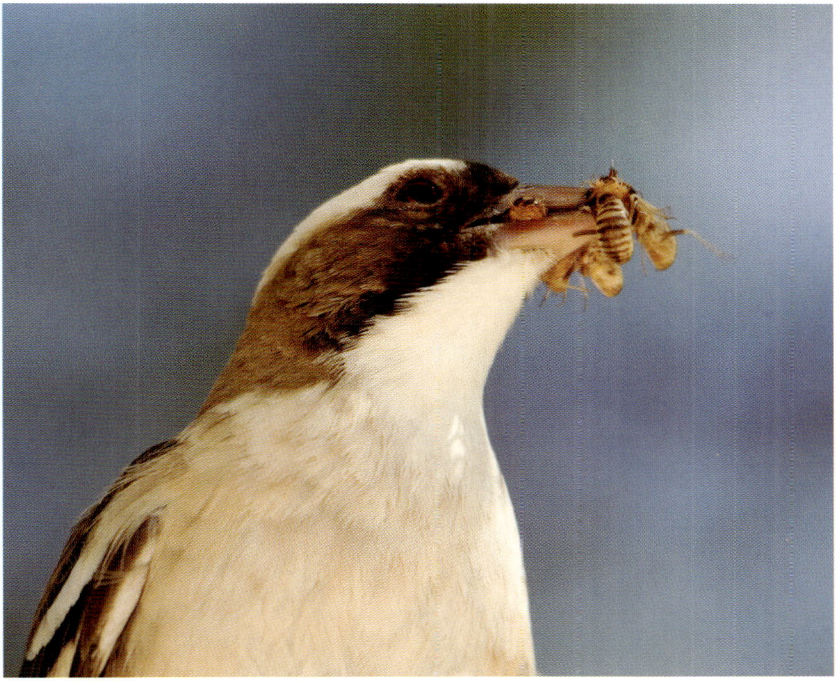

▲ ***White-browed Sparrow Weaver, Central Kalahari Game Reserve. DSLR, 100-400mm Lens, f/5.6 @ 1/250, ISO 100***

I shot this at half past one in a campsite - proof that photographic opportunities occur throughout the day. With six weaver nests in a tree, several parents were simultaneously fetching food and carrying it to their chicks. After twenty minutes, one finally perched for a fleeting moment and posed for the camera before darting inside its nest. **JG**

Bird Behaviour

Events happen quickly in the bush. Anticipation, patience and strong knowledge of your equipment are therefore vital. Birds in particular, are fast moving and capturing a nuance of their behaviour requires the fastest shutter speed available to you. If you are experiencing low shutter speeds, open your aperture or increase your ISO.

Birds also occupy a myriad of habitats and can be photographed at any time of day. Keep your camera handy at all times, even during meals and tea breaks, as you never know when something could happen close to you.

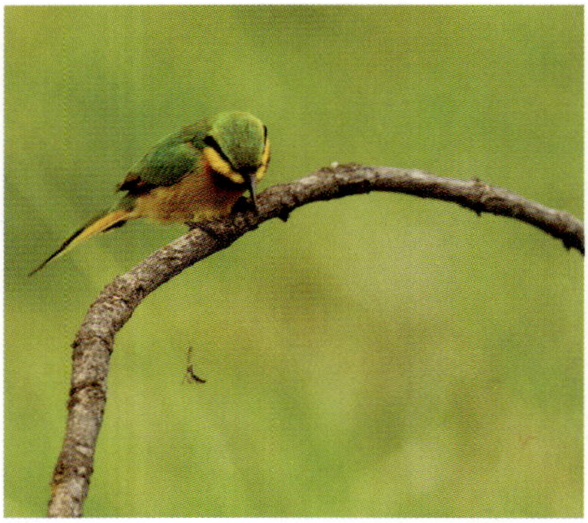

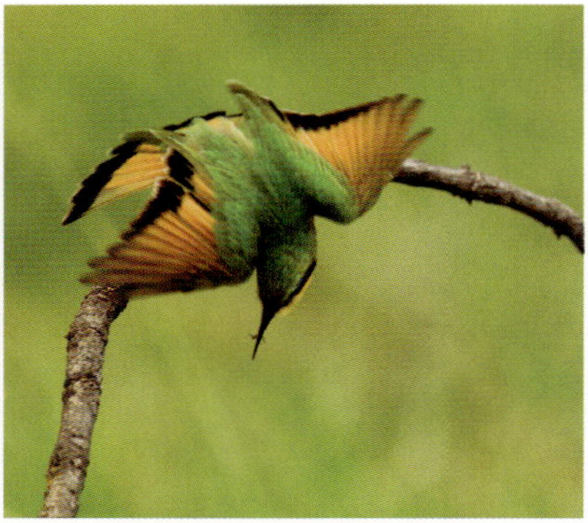

▲ *Little Bee-eater, Moremi Game Reserve. DSLR, 500mm Lens, f/5.6 @ 1/1250, ISO 800*

Bee-eaters often fly from their perch only to return a few seconds later. Rather than tracking them, keep your camera focused on the branch and your finger poised until they return. In this case, the bird caught an insect, returned to the tree, dropped it, then caught it again milliseconds later - testament to their incredible reaction times. **JG**

▶ *Coppery-tailed Coucal, Okavango Delta. DSLR, 100-400mm Lens, f/5.6 @ 1/500, ISO 200*

I still find it amazing that a bird can perch comfortably on flimsy reeds, but this coucal seemed perfectly relaxed. The angled lines of the reeds complement the coucal's gaze to draw you into the shot. **JG**

▼ *African Fish Eagle, Chobe River. DSLR, 100-400mm Lens, f/5.6 @ 1/2500, ISO 400*

The call of the fish eagle is synonymous with Africa and the Chobe River offers fantastic opportunities to photograph them from both boat and car. We got underneath this one by boat giving us a good angle and we were lucky enough to capture him drying his wings thereby giving this portrait a different flavour. **SS**

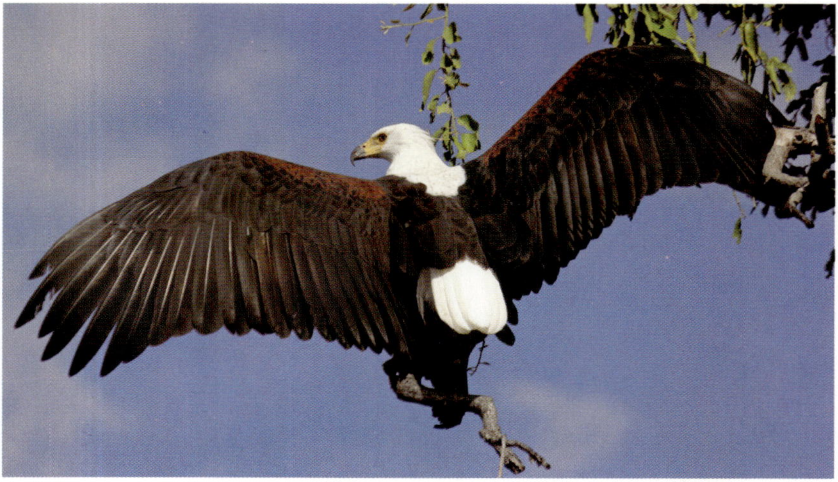

Environment

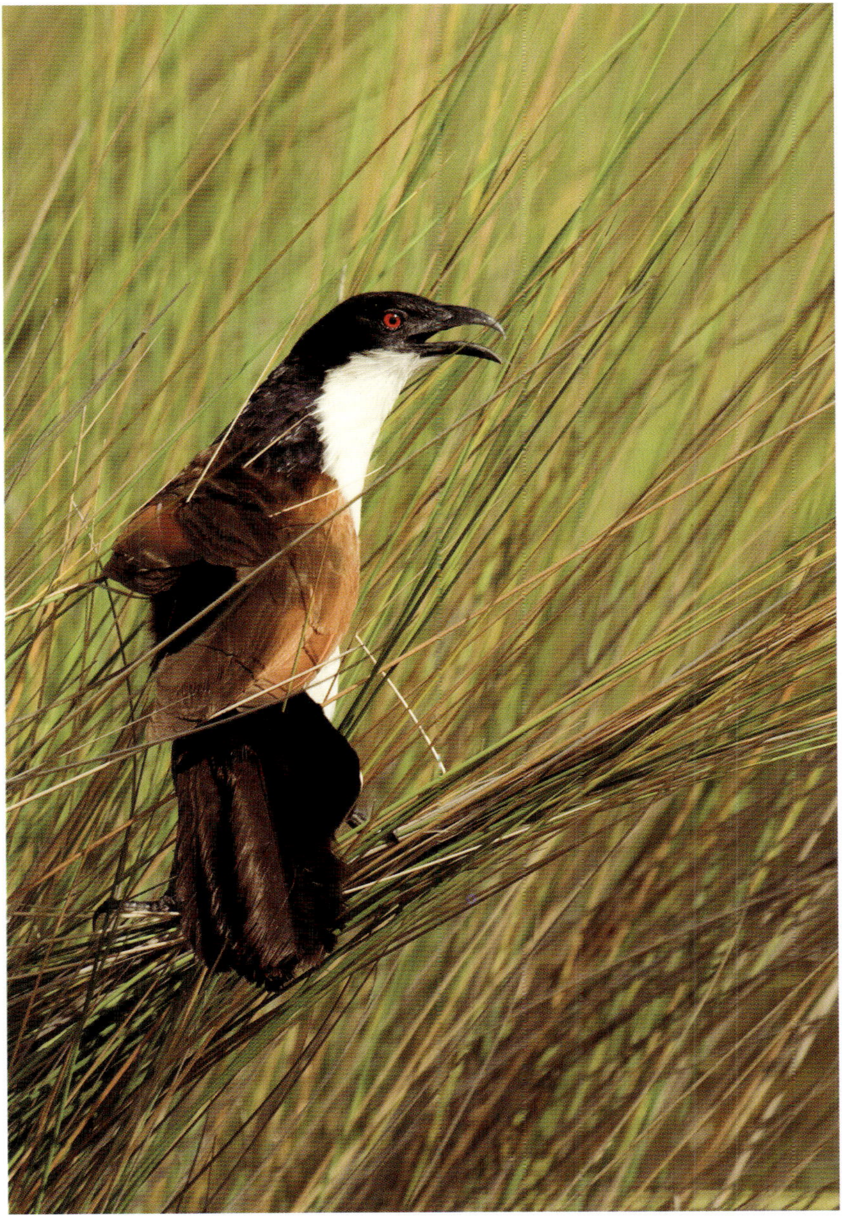

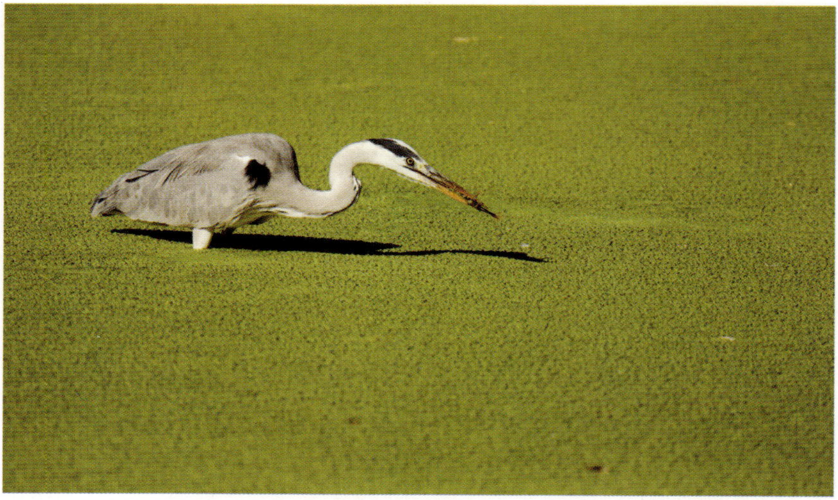

▲ ***Grey Heron, Okavango Delta. DSLR, 100-400mm Lens, f/5.6 @ 1/1000, ISO 100***

Using the environment to add to an image does not necessarily mean you have to zoom out from your subject. Here, the green algae demonstrates the importance of the colour of the backdrop which can transform an ordinary image into a good one. **JG**

▼ ***Squacco Heron, Okavango Delta. DSLR, 100-400mm Lens, f/5.6 @ 1/1000, ISO 200***

Marshy wetlands are home to this common resident. The aquatic vegetation makes the subject stand out as well as highlighting its preferred habitat. **SS**

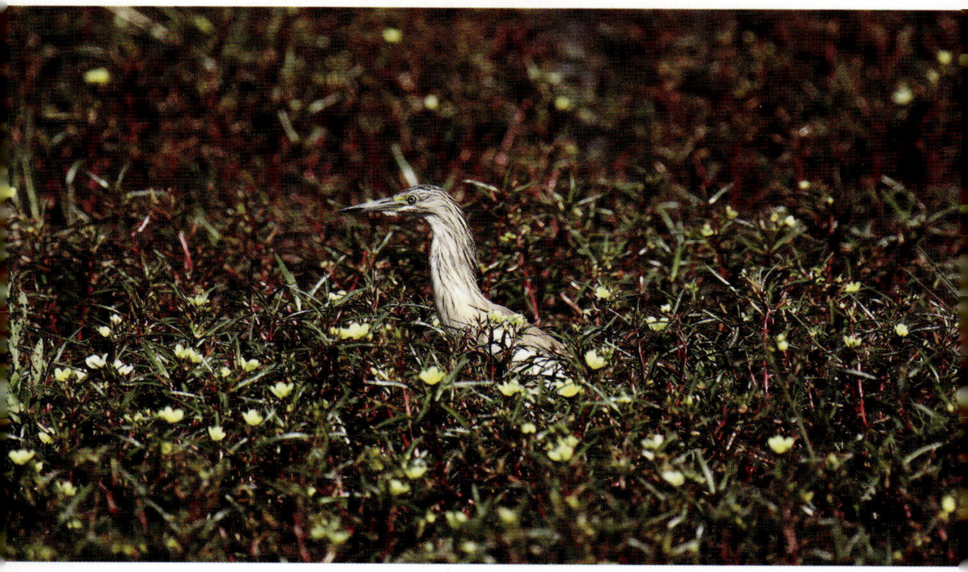

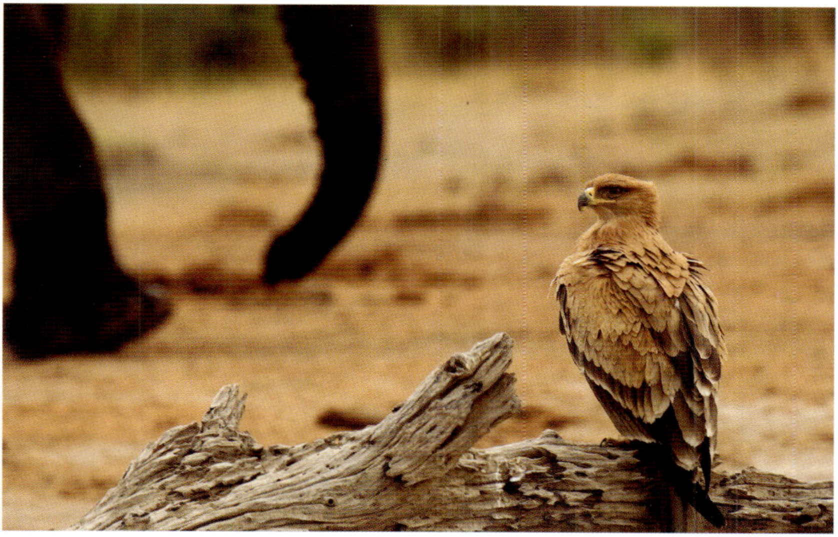

▲ ***Tawny Eagle, Savuti, Chobe National Park. DSLR, 100-400mm Lens, f/5.6 @ 1/1250, ISO 250***

Unfortunately I arrived at this waterhole too late as a number of tawny eagles had been hunting red-billed quelea moments earlier, using their wings to knock the quelea off balance. Waiting in vain for the quelea to return, a passing elephant enabled me to catch a more engaging portrait of this eagle. **JG**

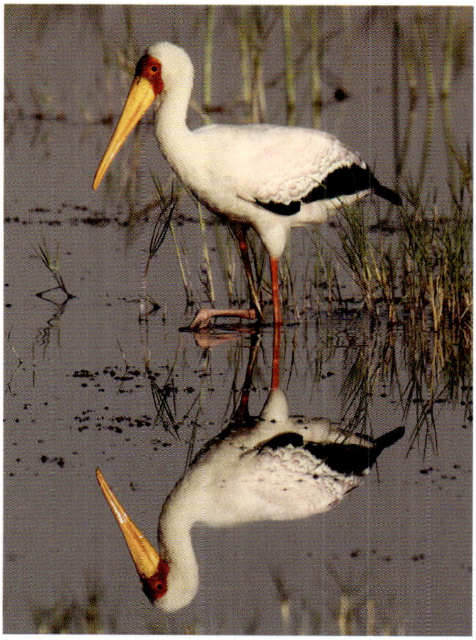

▶ ***Yellow-billed Stork, Okavango Delta. DSLR, 100-400mm Lens, f/8 @ 1/640, ISO 200***

The striking colours of the yellow-billed stork are brought out by the strong water reflection. This image was taken at first light and the low angle of the sun in the early morning really accentuates its colours. **SS**

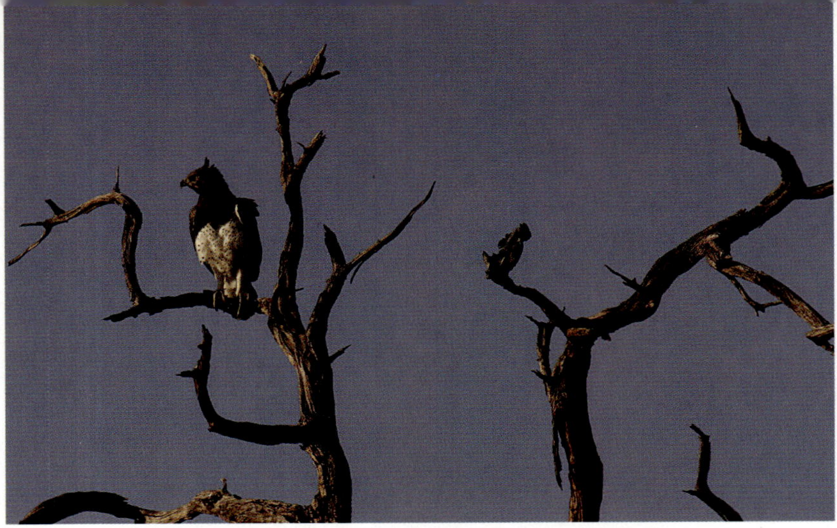

▲ ***Martial Eagle, Okavango Delta. DSLR, 100-400mm Lens, f/9 @ 1/640, ISO 200***

Perched on a dead tree, a martial eagle watches dutifully for an opportunity to hunt. For this image, I deliberately placed the subject in the left hand side of the frame to illustrate more of its environment. This large eagle can sometimes capture small antelope such as steenbok and young impala. **SS**

▼ ***Ostrich with Chicks, Nxai Pan National Park, DSLR, 100-400mm Lens, f/6.3 @ 1/640, ISO 160***

Parents will often look after ostrich chicks in large crèches which can create some endearing photographs. This is particularly so given the size difference between the parents and their young. **JG**

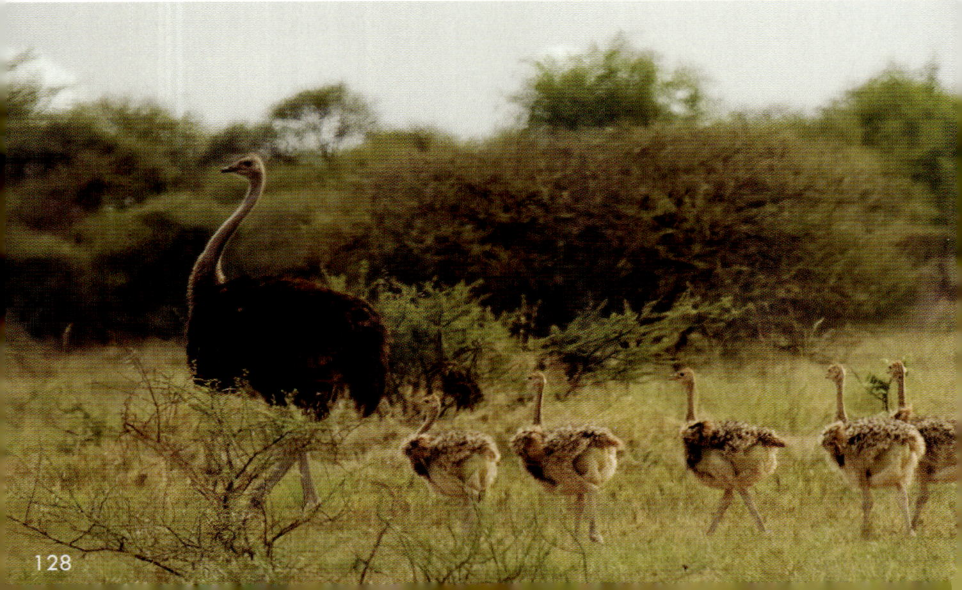

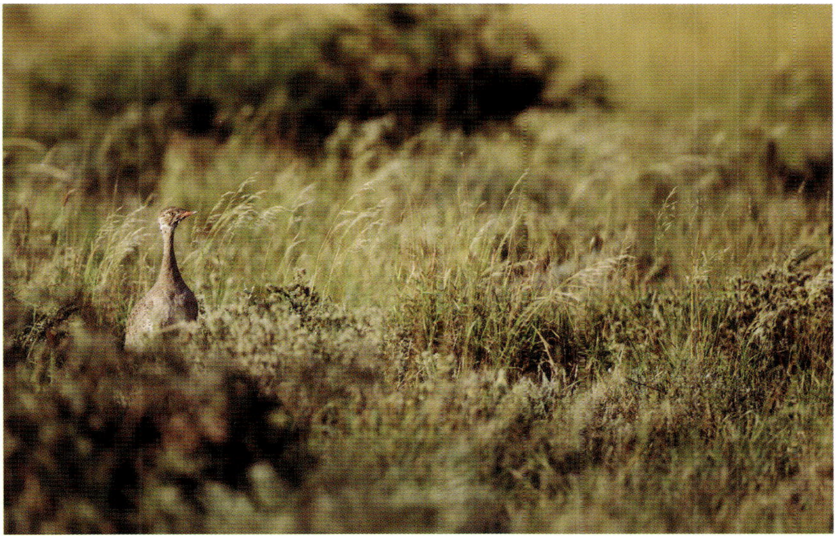

▲ ***Northern Black Korhaan, Central Kalahari Game Reserve. DSLR, 500mm Lens, f/4 @ 1/800, ISO 100***

The idea behind this image was to encourage the viewer to identify with the Korhaan's environment and view of the world. Using a wide aperture of f/4 but ensuring the waving grasses were in the same focal plane (and therefore relatively sharp), achieved the right balance between highlighting the subject and its habitat. **JG**

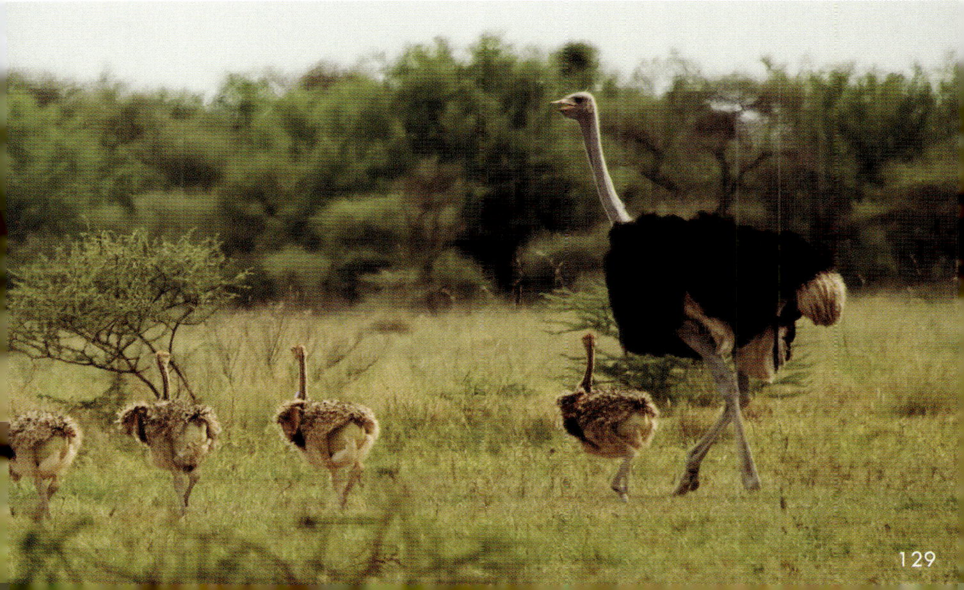

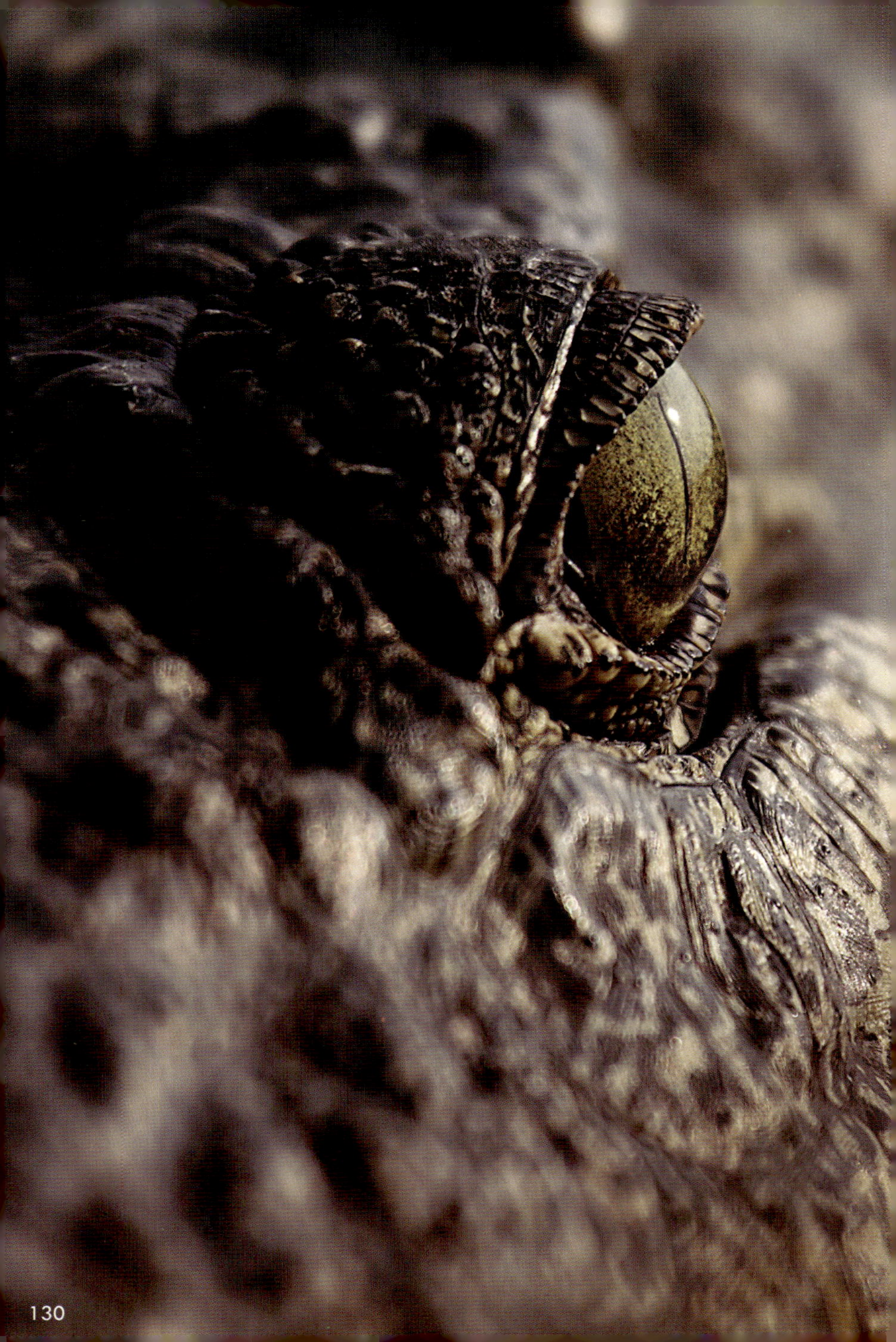

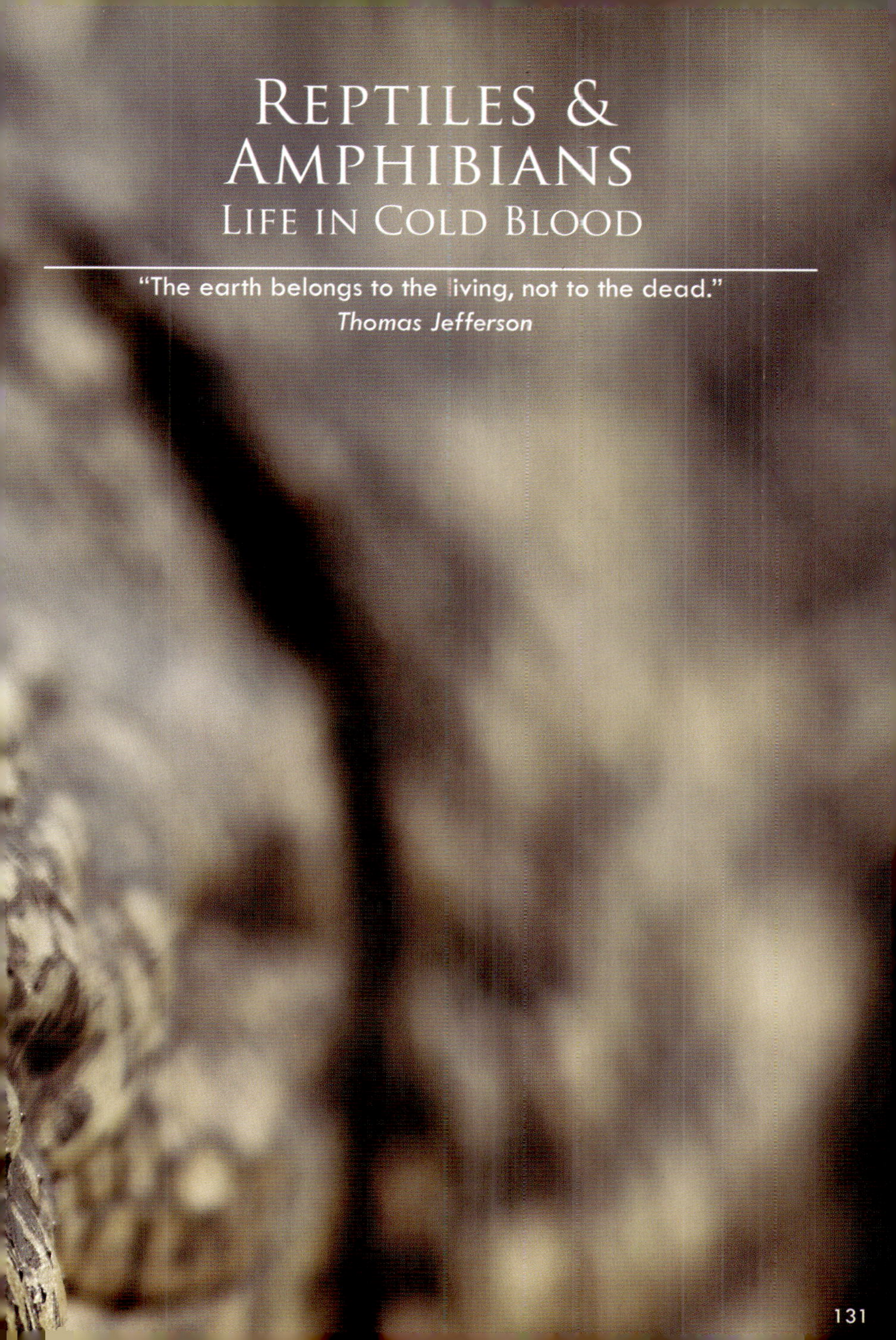

Reptiles & Amphibians
Life in Cold Blood

"The earth belongs to the living, not to the dead."
Thomas Jefferson

Reptiles & Amphibians

At some point on your travels in Botswana you will probably come across some interesting reptiles and amphibians. Crocodiles are certainly going to feature but there is also a large variety of frogs, snakes and lizards. This fascinating world offers the photographer a wide subject range found in a multitude of different habitats.

▶ ***Marsh Terrapin, Makgadikgadi Pans. DSLR, 17-85mm Lens, f/5.6 @ 1/500, ISO 100***

Always drive carefully during the wet season in the Makgadikgadi as large puddles may be home to terrapins. This adult was crossing the road (albeit slowly) and did not mind me joining him at his level for a better perspective. By getting so close to the subject the depth of field becomes even shallower so that by focusing on the eye, I could blur the nose slightly. **JG**

▼ ***Guttural Toads, Okavango Delta. DSLR, 100-400mm Lens, f/5.6 @ 1/500, ISO 200***

Guttural Toads pair up during the rainy season. Here, the different expressions of the mating couple and the light reflecting off the water are key to the image's appeal. **SS**

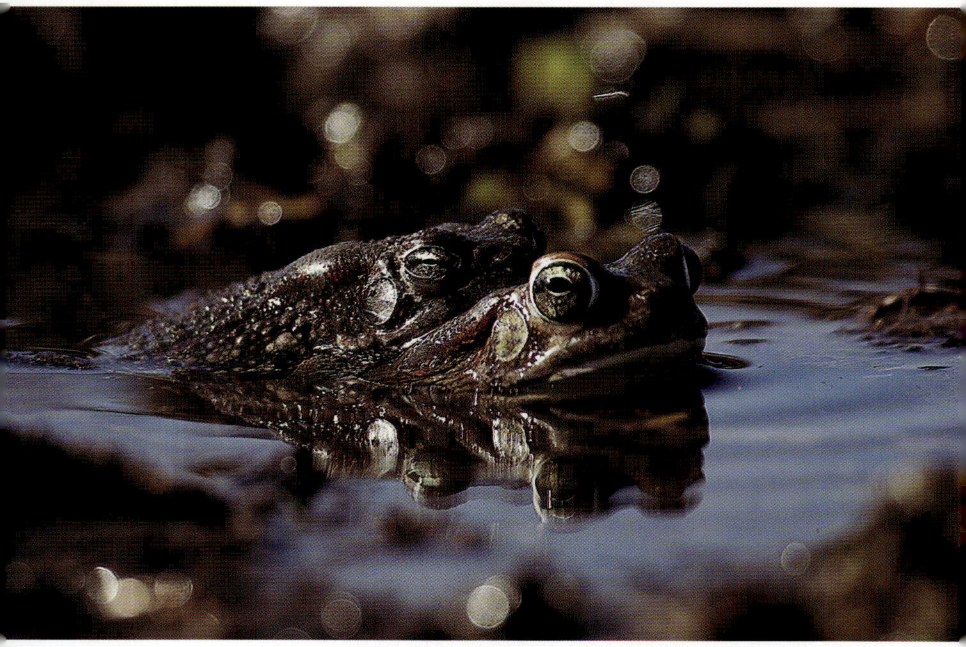

◀ ***Nile Crocodile, Chobe River. DSLR, 100-400mm Lens, f/5.6 @ 1/800, ISO 200***

Nictating membranes and lachrymal glands protect and clean the eyes of the Nile crocodile. Drifting in slowly by boat is a good way of getting close to this well-known reptile which can be found along the banks of the Chobe River and the Okavango Delta. **SS**

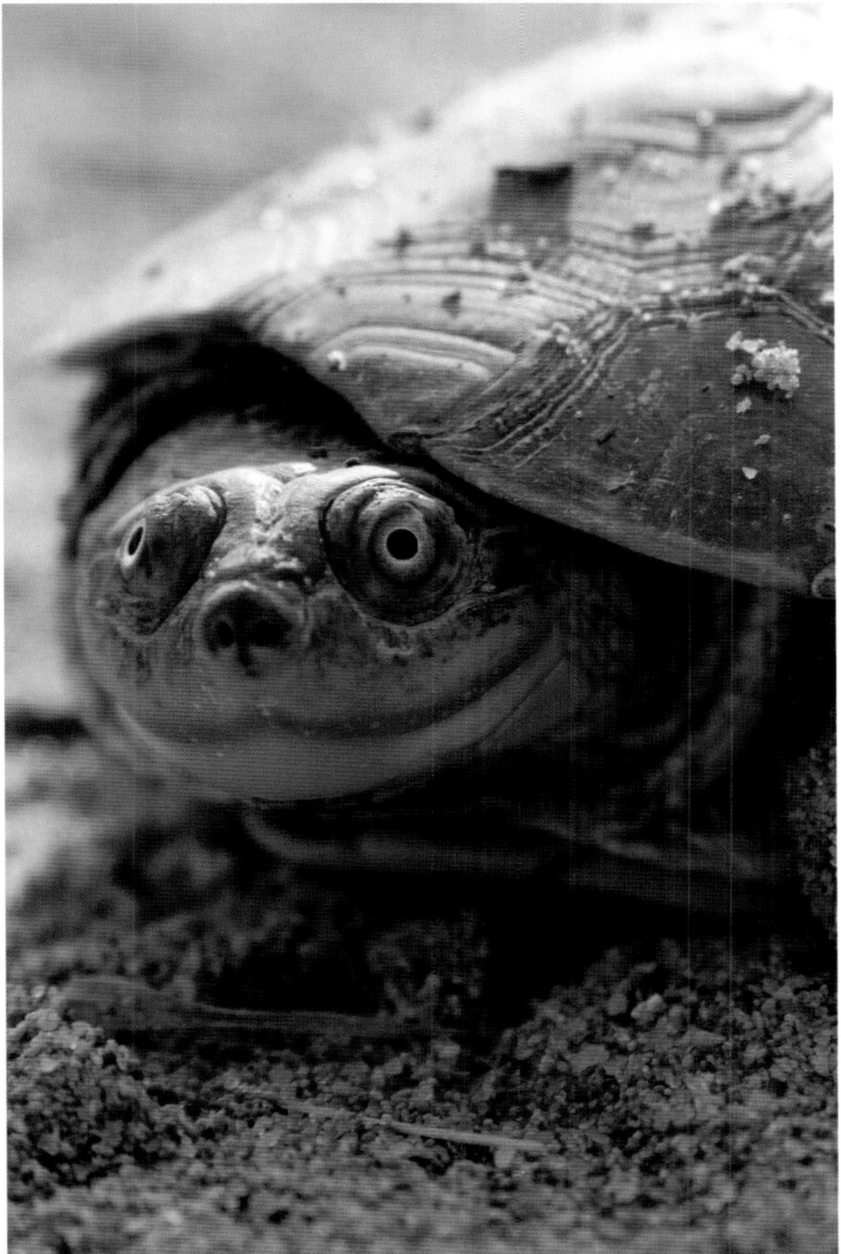

DON'T GET EATEN...

Be careful of getting too close and agitating the animal, especially crocodiles and venomous snakes - long lenses will do the job nicely. Ask your guide to give you advice on safe shooting distances. If you are not with a guide, err on the side of caution.

▶ ***Flap-necked Chameleon, Okavango Delta. SLR, 18-55mm Lens, Fuji Provia 100F***

Flap-necked chameleons, with their independently moving eyes and ability to change colour according to mood, are fascinating to photograph. We came across this individual on a bushwalk in the Delta. **SS**

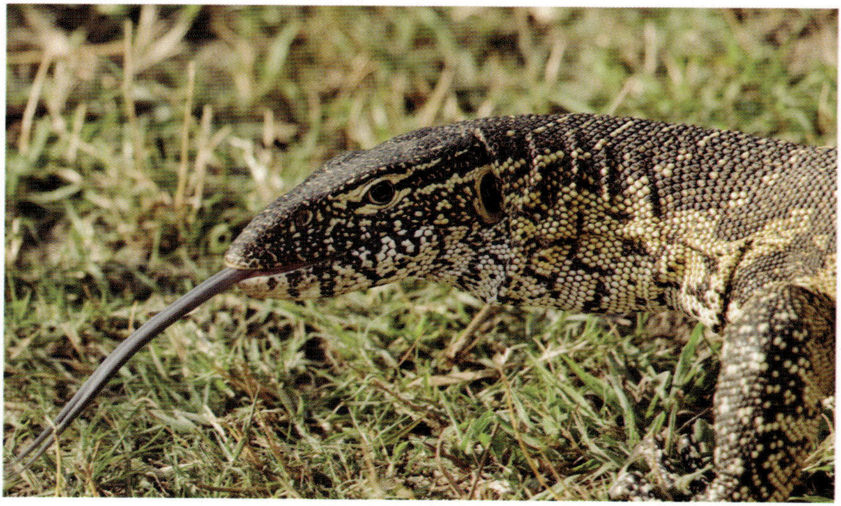

▲ ***Water Monitor, Okavango Delta. DSLR, 100-400mm Lens, f/5.6 @ 1/160, ISO 100***

The patterns and colours of a water monitor are sufficient to create an aesthetically attractive image. However, it is the forked tongue (used for smell) that really epitomises this animal's dragon-like character. **JG**

▶ ***African Giant Bullfrog, Okavango Delta. DSLR, 100-400mm Lens, f/5.6 @ 1/60, ISO 200, Flash***

When the rains come to Botswana in the summer months - November to April - bullfrogs emerge at night from below ground to feast upon the thousands of insects that propagate during this time of plenty. I used my built-in flash to add a slight glint to his eye. **SS**

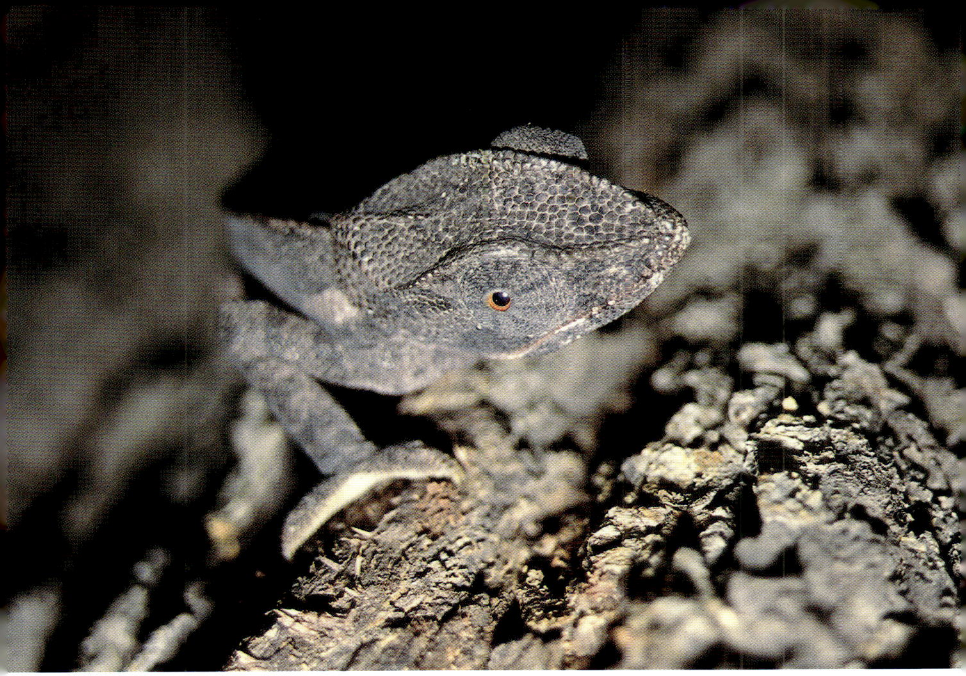

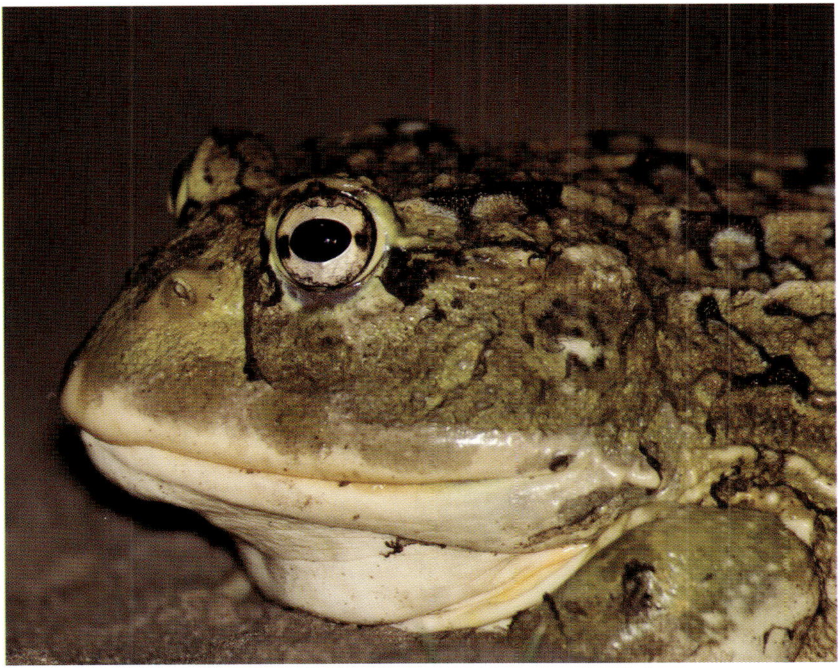

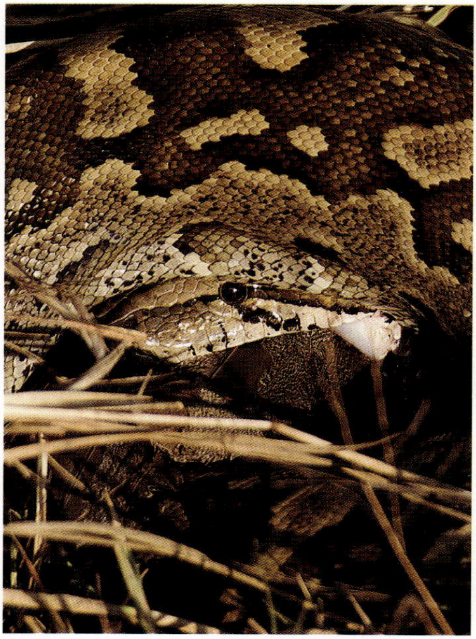

◀ ***African Rock Python, Okavango Delta. DSLR, 100-400mm Lens, f/5.6 @ 1/500, ISO 200***

Success for an African rock python as it begins to devour a francolin. A split second window when the eye of the snake was visible through the grasses enabled me to capture this striking image. Pythons can grow to between 4 and 5 metres and are the only protected reptile species in Botswana. **SS**

▶ ***Mozambique Spitting Cobras, Okavango Delta. SLR, 100-400mm Lens, Fuji Provia 100F***

One of the increasing challenges facing a wildlife photographer is the desire to record rare behaviour. Although spitting cobras are known to cannibalise, images documenting this are hard to come by, so I was grateful to be in the right place at the right time. **SS**

▼ ***Leopard Tortoise, Okavango Delta. DSLR, 100-400mm Lens, f/5.6 @ 1/500, ISO 100***

The widely distributed leopard tortoise is more commonly observed in the summer months. These animals have wonderful textures on their shells and skins and the grass stalk in this image adds a splash of colour. **SS**

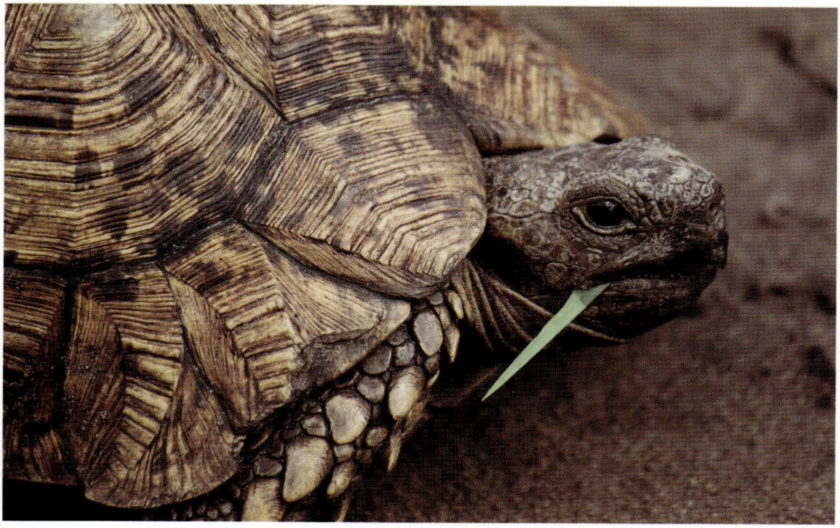

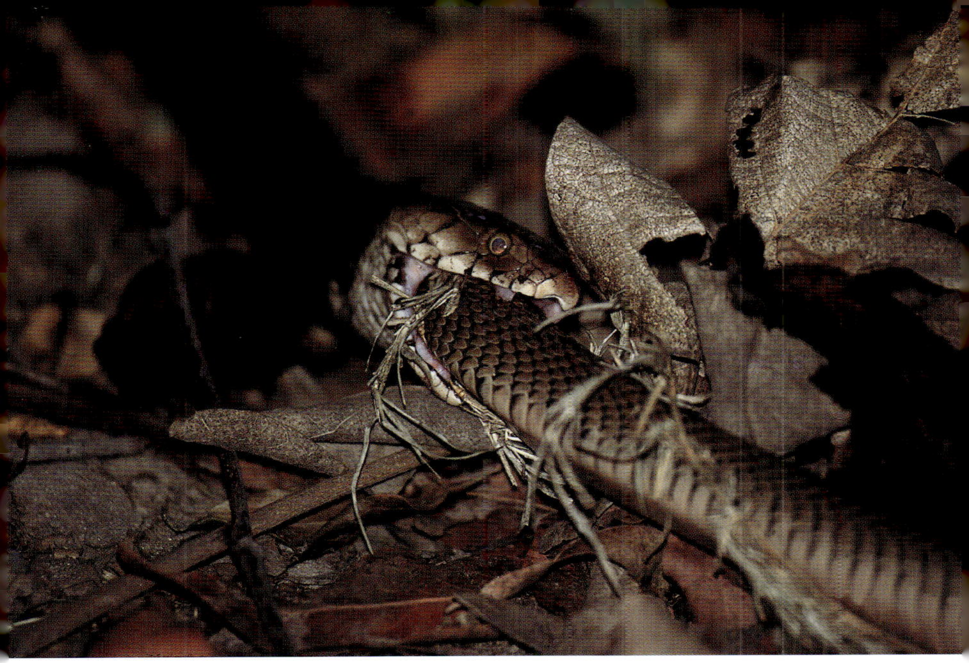

▼ *Rock Monitor, Chobe National Park. DSLR, 100-400mm Lens, f/7.1 @ 1/500, ISO 200*

A rock monitor basks on a termite mound. Reptiles are less active in the cooler mornings as they need to warm up, making it a good time to get a bit closer to your scaly subject. **SS**

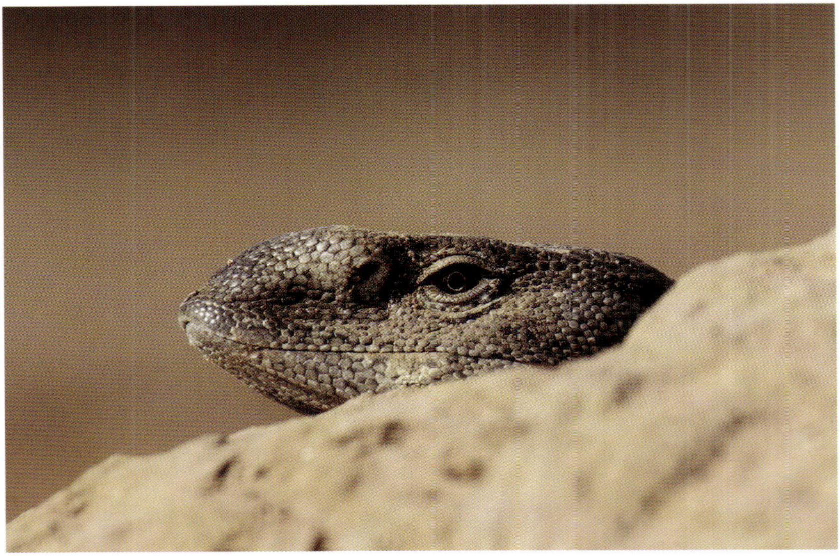

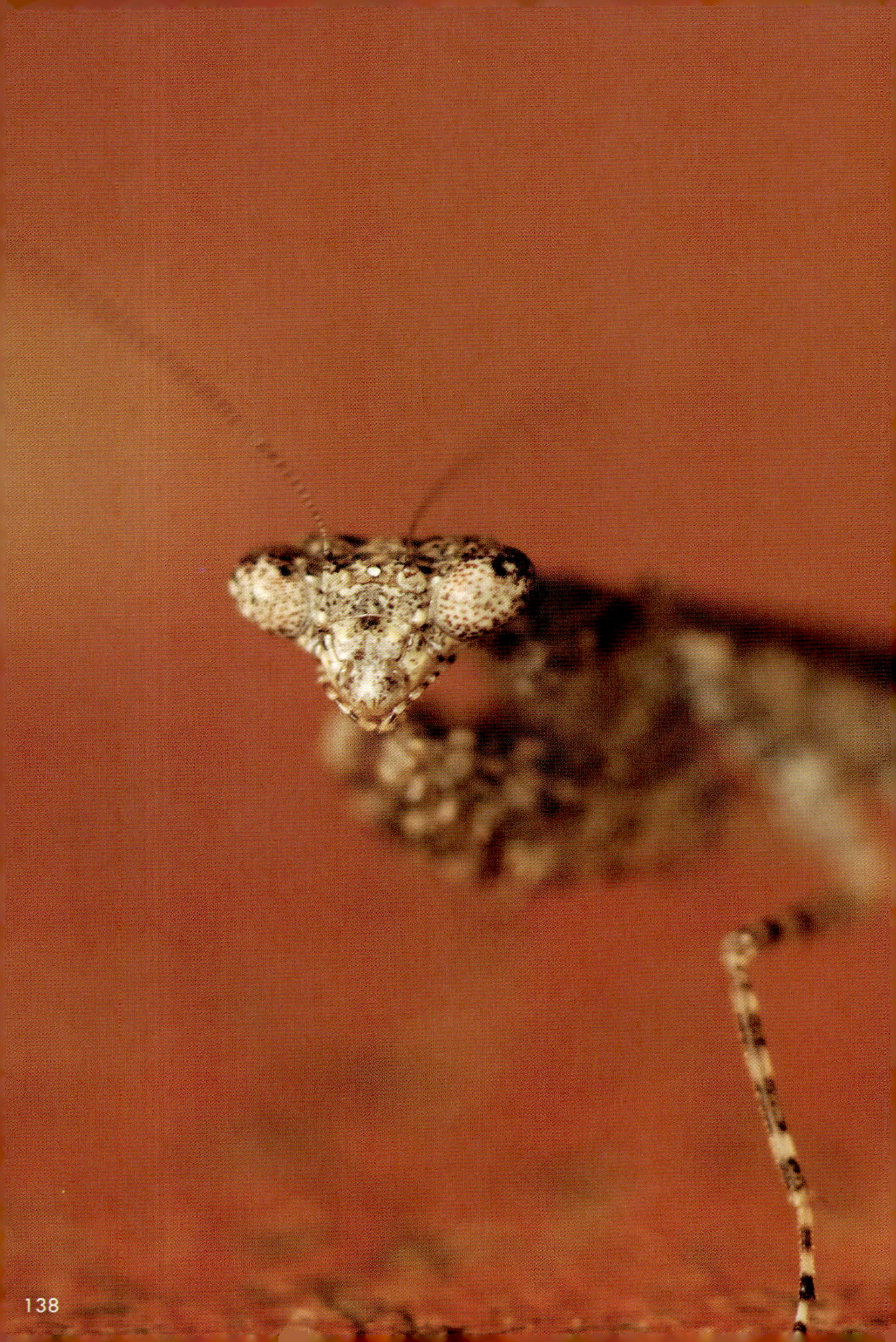

MACRO
THE LITTLE BIG PICTURE

"Sometimes you can tell a large story with a tiny subject."
Eliot Porter

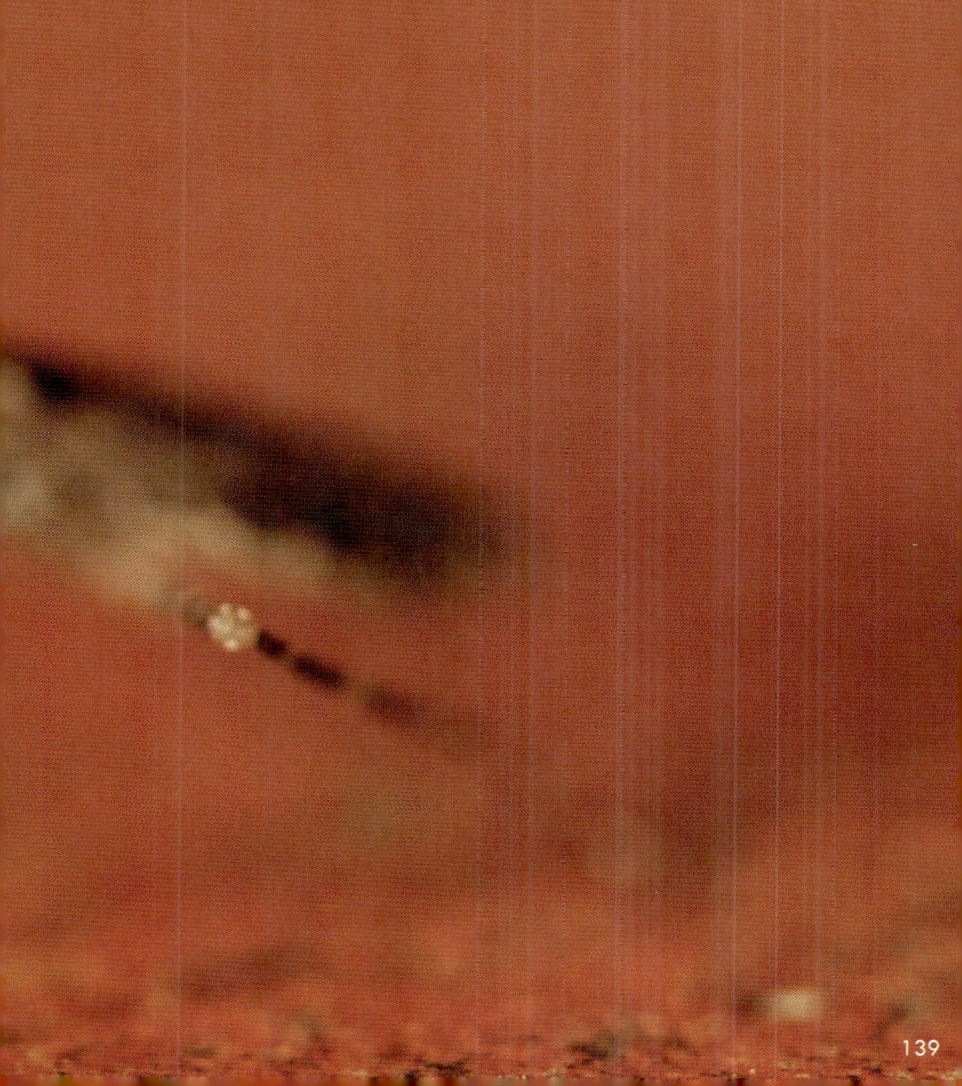

Macro

Given the vast choice of big game subject matter, it is easy to forget that there is a fascinating miniature world that exists right under our noses, yielding stunning photographic opportunities. Although many kit lenses can also be used for close-up photography, investing in a dedicated macro lens will raise the quality of your images to a different level. Macro is all about vivid colours and depth of field. Your background colour is very important as, even with relatively narrow apertures, the incredibly short focal distances will blur a leafy bush into a blanket of green.

▶ ***Foam Nest Frog, Okavango Delta. SLR, 50mm Macro Lens, Fuji Provia 100F***

This is a good example of the impact of depth of field in macro photography and the importance of focusing on the correct part of your subject. In this instance, I hand-held the camera and using manual focus adjusted my position until the frog's eye was sharp. **SS**

◀ ***Preying Mantis, Maun. DSLR, 100mm Macro Lens, f/3.5 @ 0.4, ISO 400, Tripod***

Shot inside on a tiled floor, this image took several attempts before I was finally successful. Not wanting to raise the ISO above 400, the poor internal lighting forced a slow shutter speed of almost half a second. I lay on the floor and used a mini tripod for stabilisation which allowed me to photograph at eye-level. It was then a question of continuing to shoot until the mantis stayed still long enough to capture a sharp image. **JG**

▼ ***Wild Flower, Maun. DSLR, 100mm Macro Lens, f/4.5 @ 3.2, ISO 400, Tripod***

Water droplets on any object constitute great macro subjects, particularly if you can catch glimpses of sunlight in them. This image also aptly illustrates the impact of different combinations of colour. **JG**

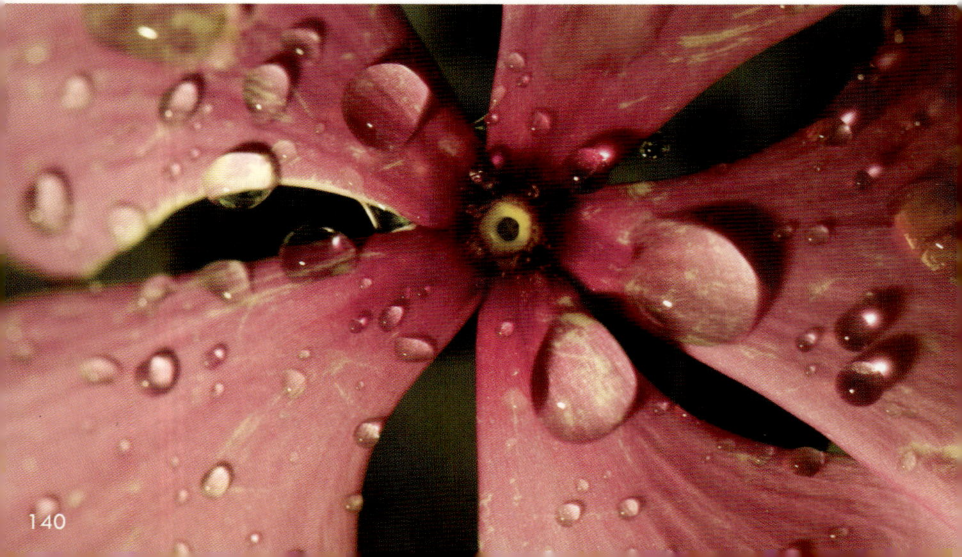

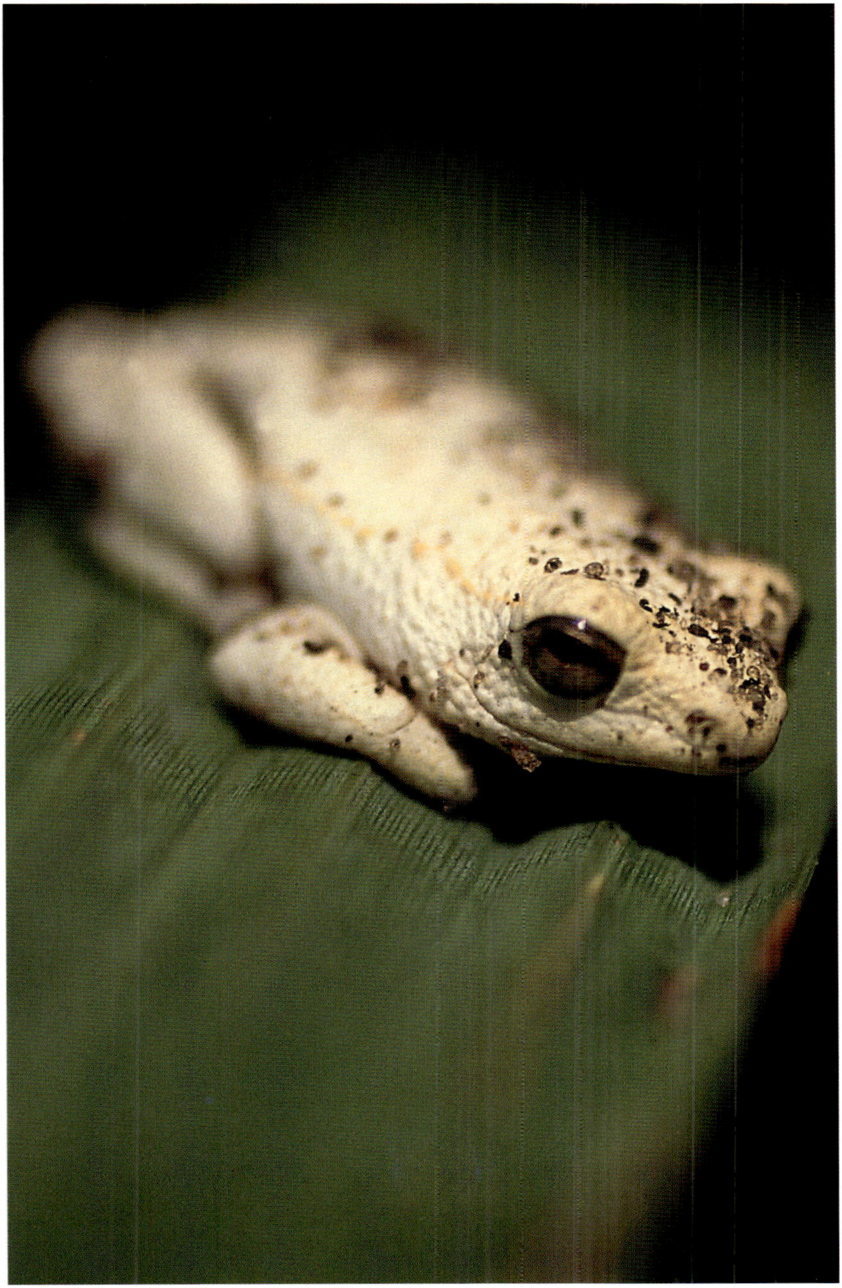

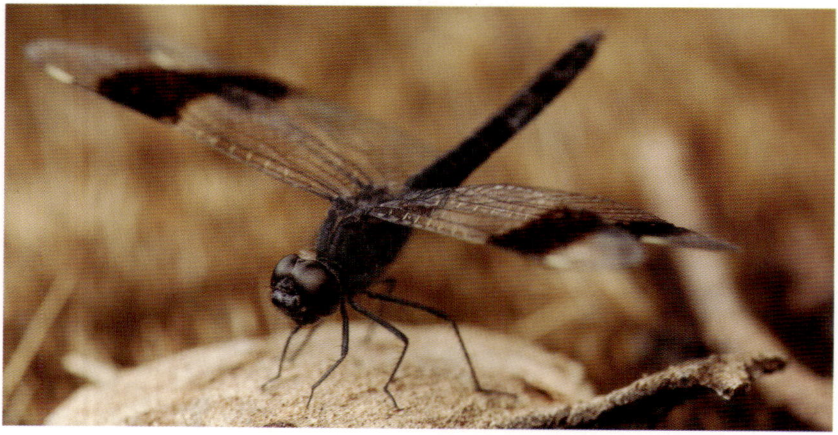

▲ ***Banded Groundling Dragonfly, Okavango Delta. DSLR, 100mm Macro Lens, f/5.6 @ 1/160, ISO 400***

As with all wildlife photography, patience is an essential aspect to macro. The tendency for insects to fly away just before you press the shutter can be frustrating, but occasionally a willing subject stays still just long enough for you to fire off a few shots. **JG**

▼ ***Spotted Bush Snake & Foam Nest Frog, Okavango Delta. SLR, 50mm Macro lens, Fuji Provia 100F***

Getting this close is rather unusual but these two were locked in battle and did not seem to mind my close proximity. There was a happy ending as the frog was too large for this non-venomous snake and after about half an hour it got away. **SS**

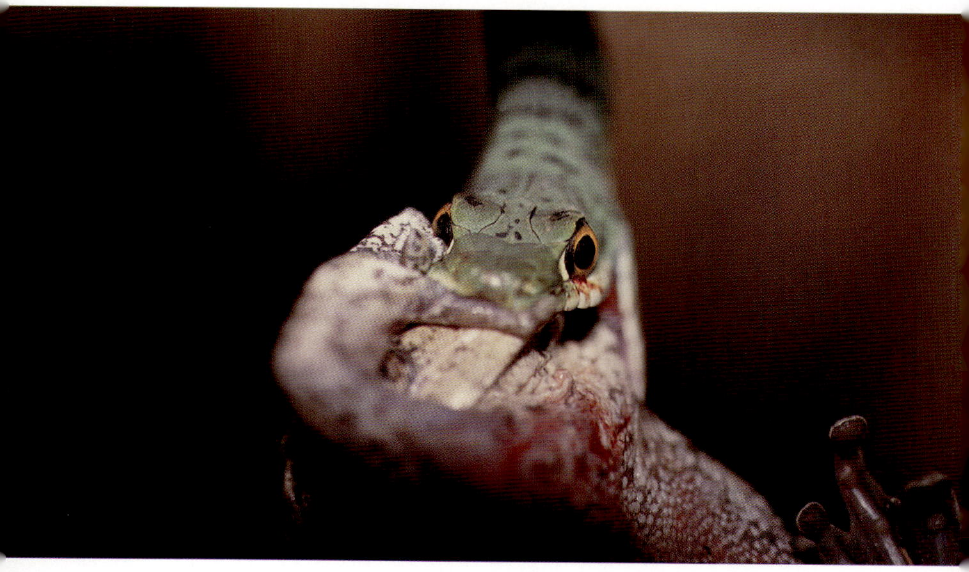

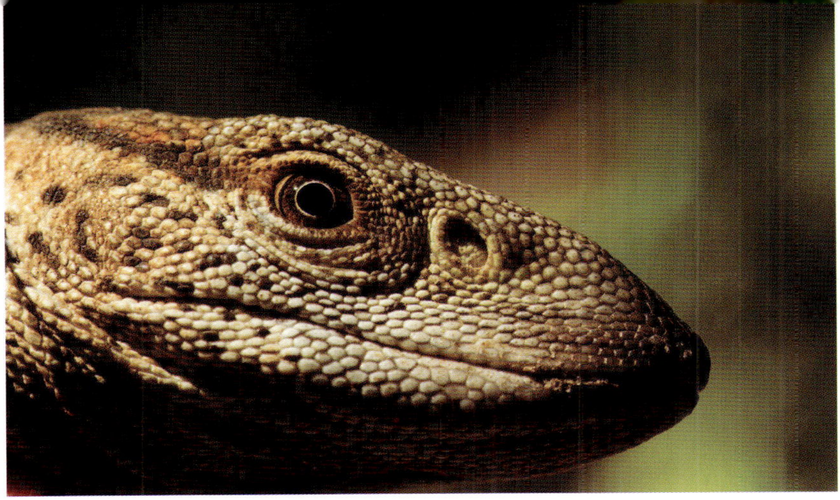

▲ ***Baby Rock Monitor, Maun. DSLR, 100mm Macro Lens, f/8 @ 1/250, ISO 100***

One advantage of living in Botswana is that sometimes the wildlife comes to you. I captured this image in my garden in Maun where a rock monitor had recently given birth. Although the young were moving around without their mother, their youthful inquisitiveness meant I could get much closer than would have been possible with an adult. **JG**

▼ ***Millipede, Makgadikgadi Pans. DSLR, 100mm Macro Lens, f/5 @ 1/60, ISO 200***

Often macro photography will involve lying on the ground to achieve optimum perspective, so get ready to get a bit dirty. Don't forget that compositional tools are equally important in macro as in normal photography – here the curve of the millipede's body leading out of the image is crucial to its appeal. **JG**

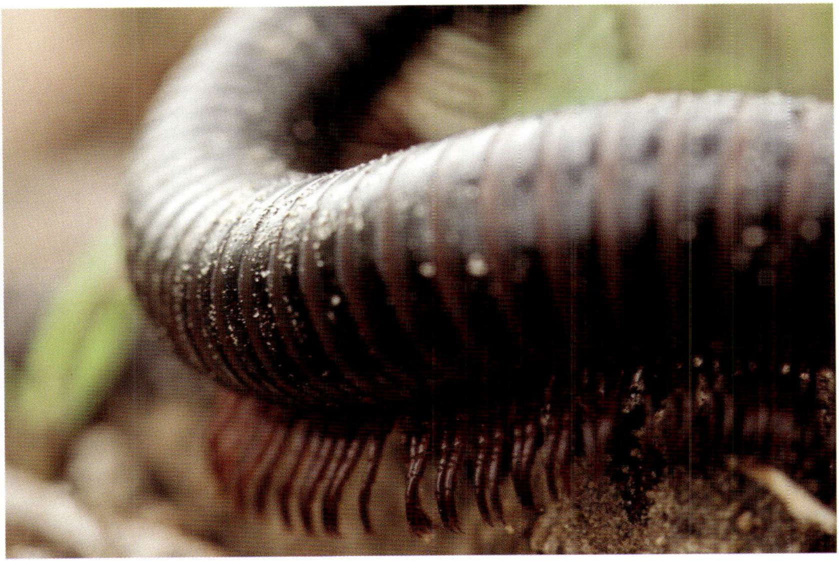

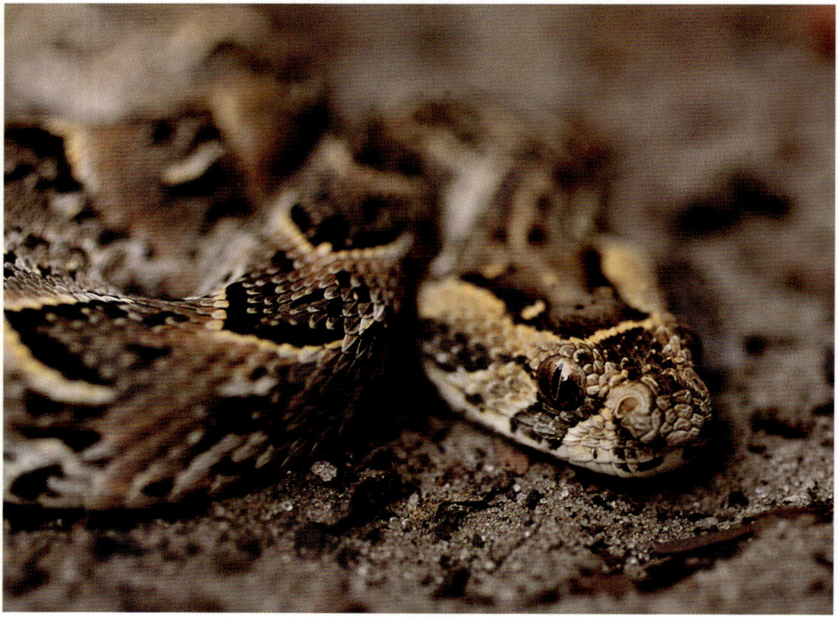

▲ ***Puff Adder, Okavango Delta. SLR, 50mm Macro Lens, Fuji Provia 100F***

Believe it or not, this puff adder is a mere 10-15 centimetres long, illustrating the magnification of a macro lens. Young puff adders' venom can be just as toxic as that of an adult and taking images such as these should be undertaken with extreme caution. **SS**

Focusing on the Little Things

An extremely shallow depth of field combined with short focal distances makes obtaining sharp focus the hardest element to macro photography. It is not normally possible to use focus lock and recompose the image because even adjusting the angle of the camera will change the distance to your subject thereby throwing it out of focus.

One solution is to first compose the image and then choose your focal point in the viewfinder without adjusting the camera's position. If your focal points do not line up with your subject, then switch to manual focus. A tripod will facilitate the process and help combat the exaggerated effect of camera shake caused by the short focal distances, simultaneously enabling a slower shutter speed.

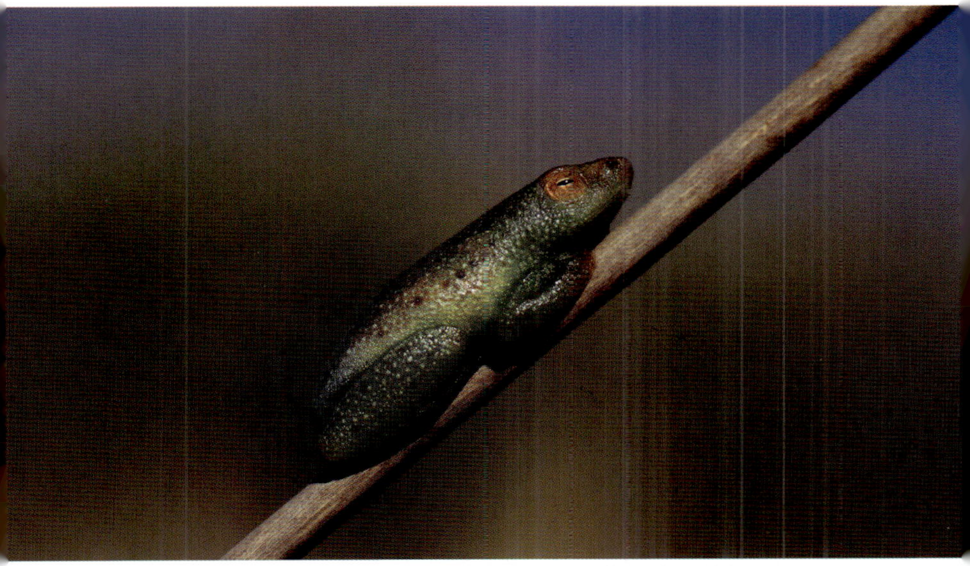

▲ ***Reed Frog, Okavango Delta. SLR, 50mm Macro Lens, Fuji Provia 100F***

You are likely to see reed frogs whilst out on a mokoro and I always take my macro lens on such excursions. These tiny frogs tend to remain obligingly still allowing you to get close to them. **SS**

▼ ***Jumping spider & Broad Scarlet Dragonfly, Okavango Delta. DSLR, 50mm Macro Lens, f/5 @ 1/160, ISO 200***

One of the joys of shooting macro images is the phenomenal amount of detail you can capture in an image. Luckily this jumping spider was so busy killing its dragonfly prey that I was able to get to within a few centimetres to take this shot. **SS**

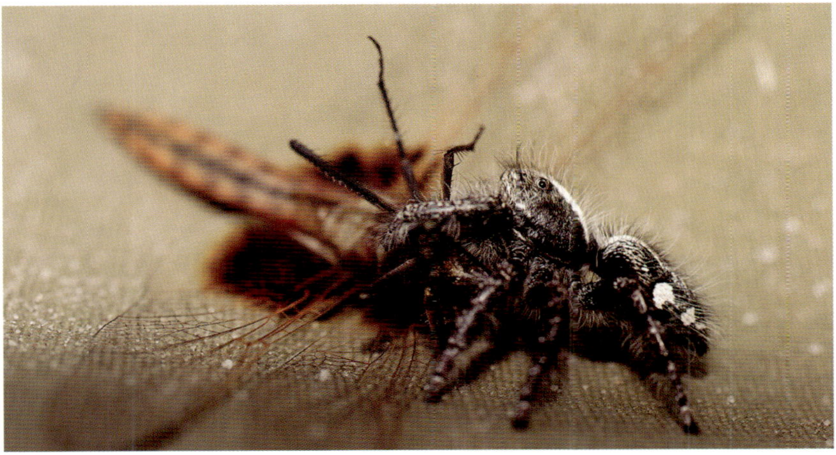

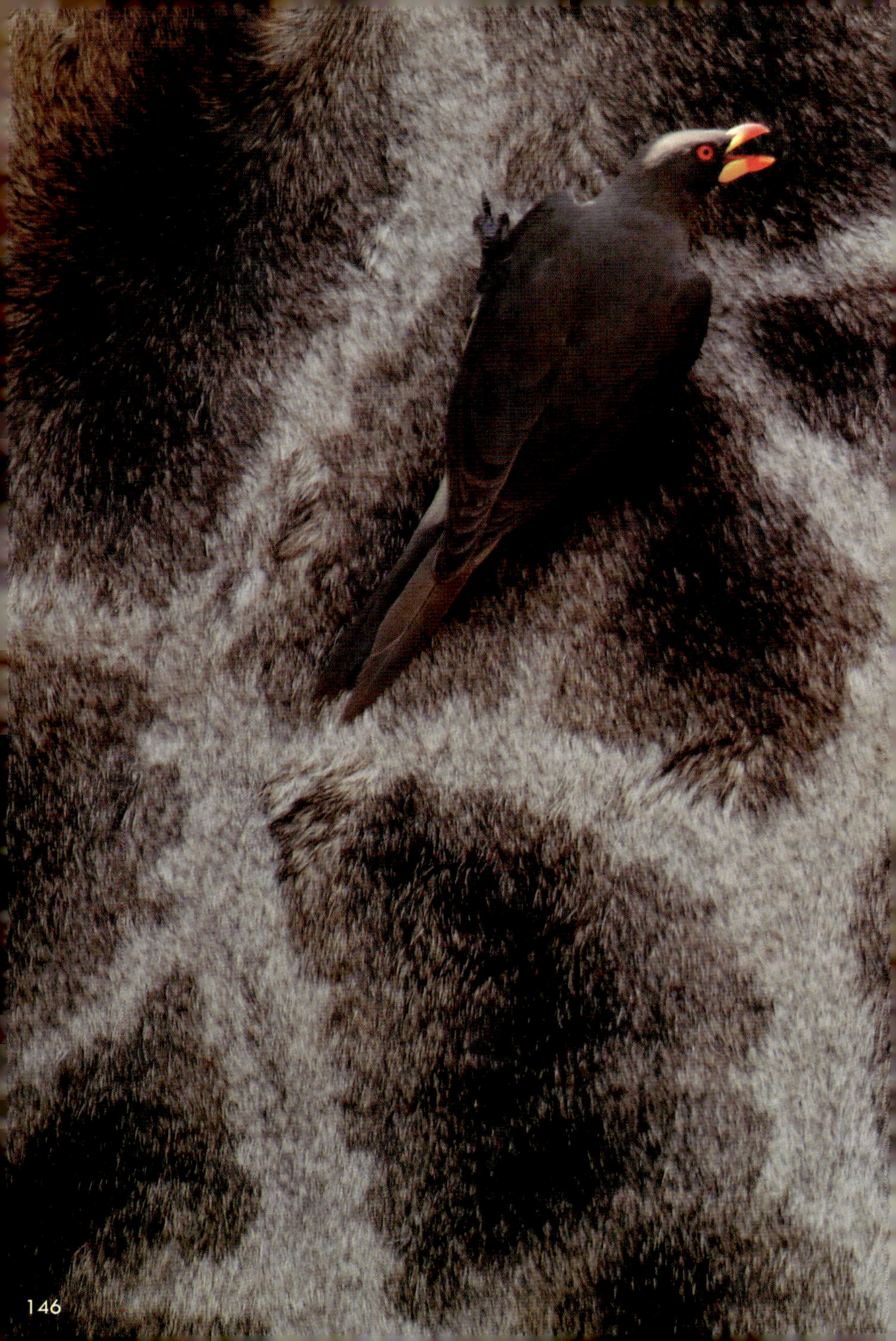

PATTERNS & TEXTURES
NATURE'S DESIGNS

"Simplicity is the ultimate form of sophistication."
Leonardo Da Vinci

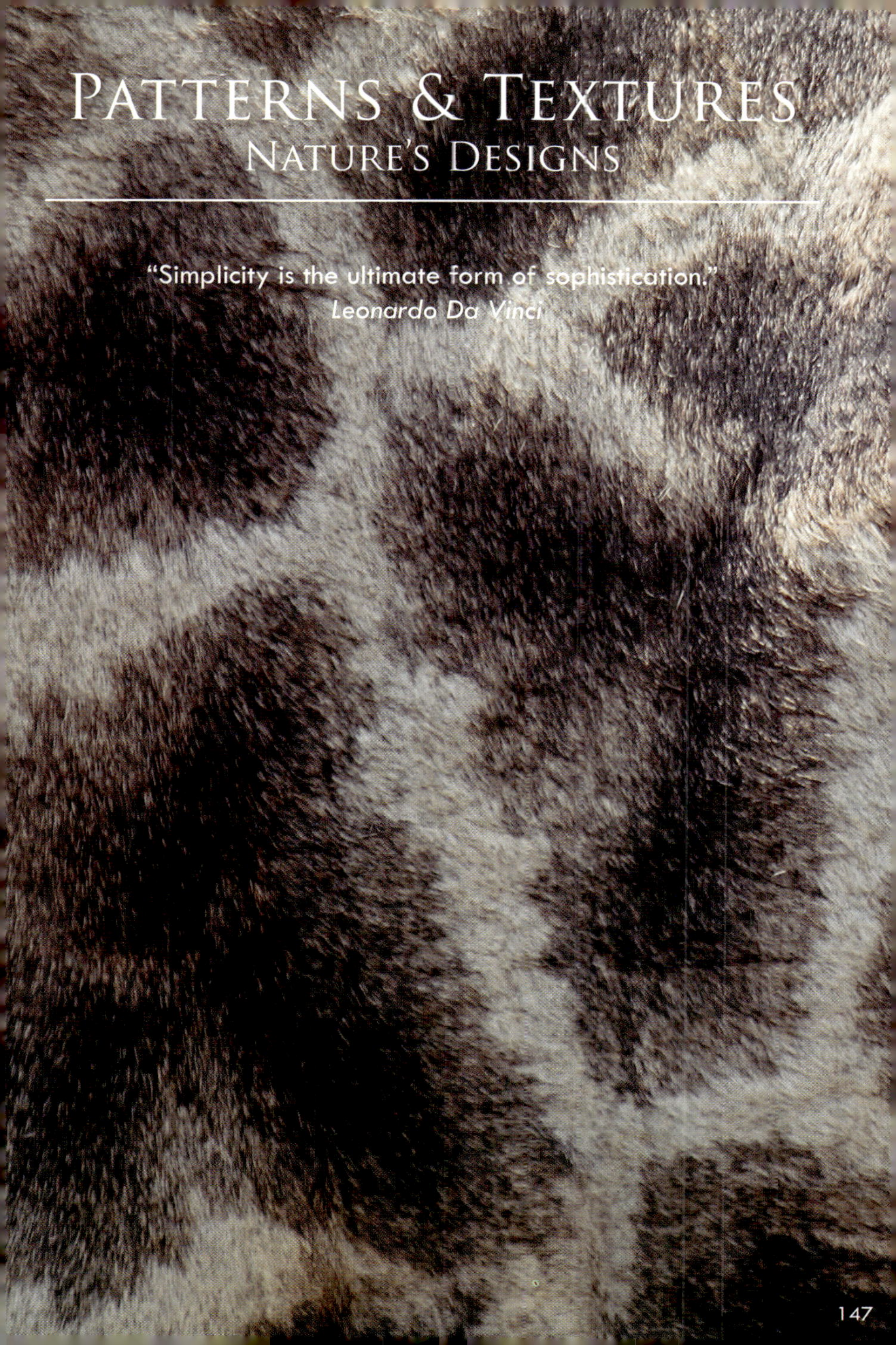

Patterns & Textures

Nature provides a tremendous array of textures and patterns to photograph. Abstract imagery makes the viewer think harder about the image and is an excellent way to present your subjects in an alternative guise. If you look a bit closer at the world around you, you will find many details that can be illustrated in a unique way.

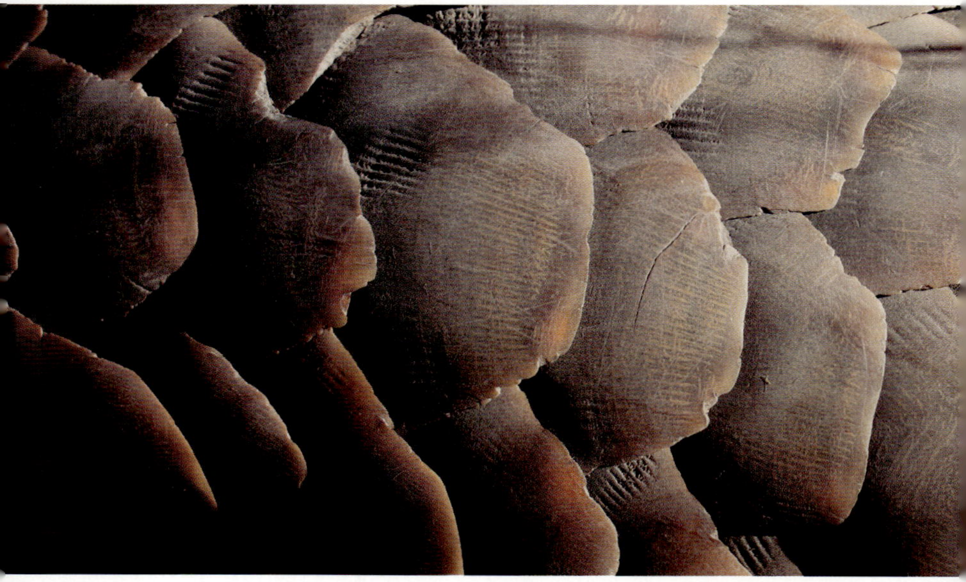

▲ ***Ground Pangolin, Okavango Delta. DSLR, 18-55mm Lens, f/8 @ 1/320, ISO 200***

The ground pangolin or scaly anteater's body is almost entirely covered with large brown overlapping scales. The serrated edges of these scales protect the animal from potential predators. **SS**

▶ ***Elephant Skin, Savuti, Chobe National Park. DSLR, 100-400mm Lens, f/5.6 @ 1/640, ISO 100***

Golden light is great for capturing skin textures. Not only are the colours softer, but the shadows formed by the low angle of the sun will also boost the contrast. Combined with the side lighting in this photograph, the result is that each individual wrinkle is accentuated. **JG**

◀ ***Southern Giraffe & Yellow-billed Oxpecker, Okavango Delta. DSLR, 100-400mm Lens, f/5.6 @ 1/250, ISO 200***

Whilst watching a herd of giraffe with oxpeckers, I thought it would be interesting to capture the bird with just the patterned fur of the giraffe. The position of the bird combined with the lines in the fur create a powerful composition. **SS**

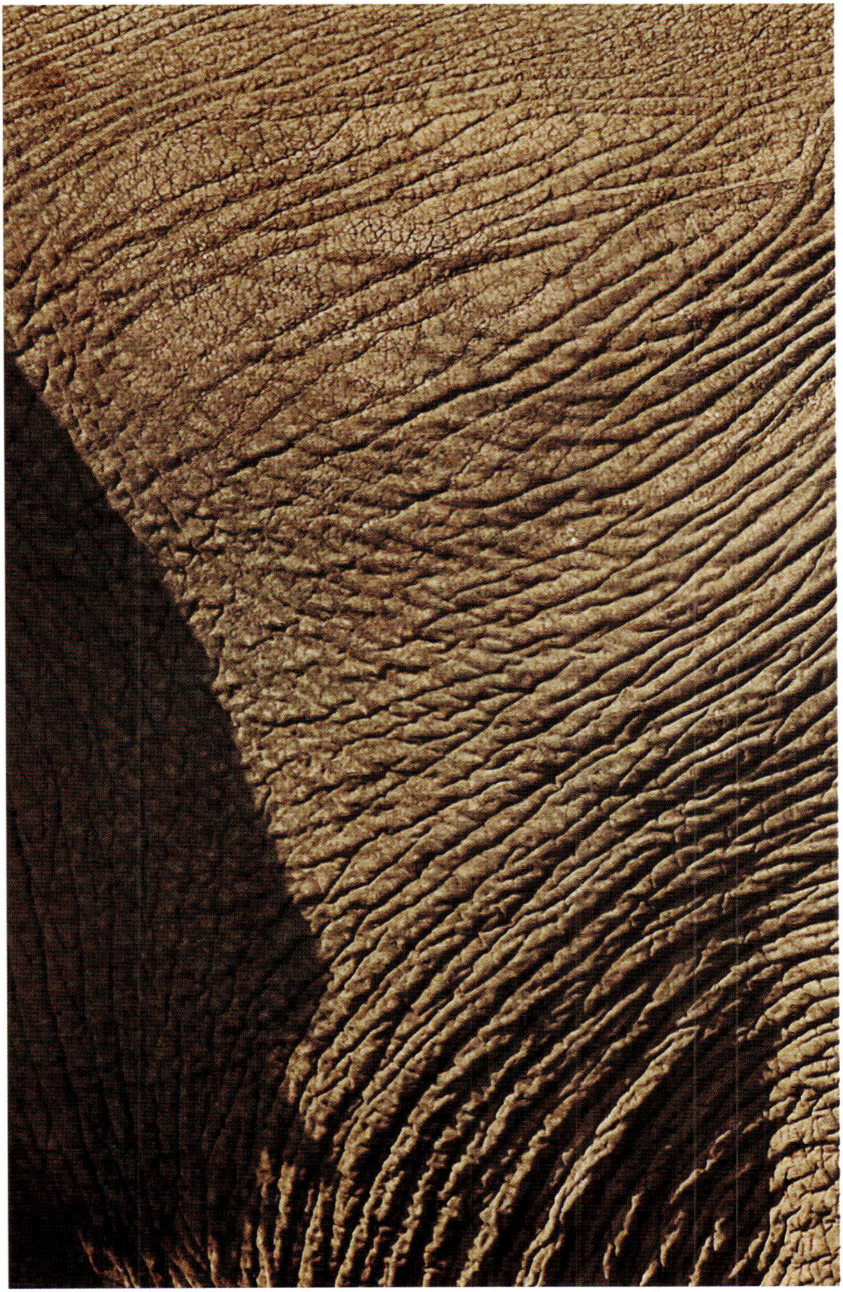

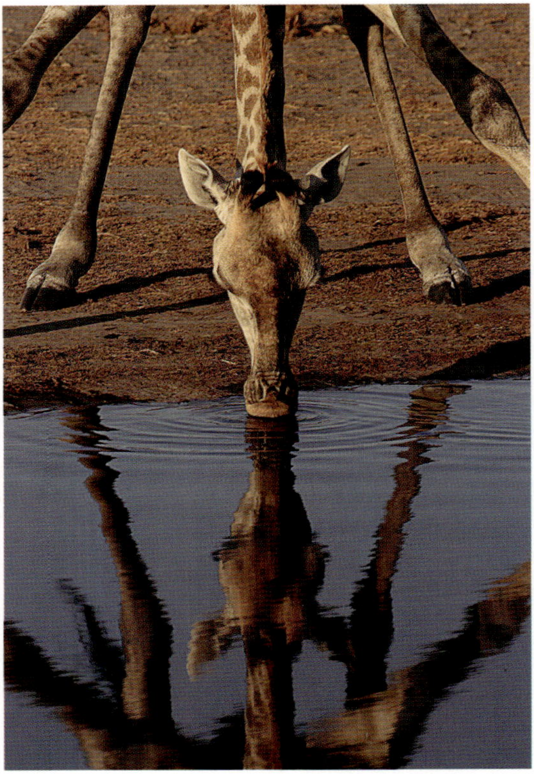

◀ ***Southern Giraffe, Savuti, Chobe National Park. DSLR, 100-400mm Lens, f/6.3 @ 1/320, ISO 100***

We had sat at this waterhole for over an hour before this individual arrived - yet another exercise in being patient. Before she bent down to drink, I had already envisaged how the pattern of her legs would combine with the reflected symmetry perfectly. **SS**

▼ ***Burchell's Zebra, Makgadikgadi Pans National Park. DSLR, 100-400mm Lens, f/5.6 @ 1/1600, ISO 100***

Zebras provide a host of pattern-related possibilities. Whether zooming in on a single individual for an abstract effect, or framing a number of animals, the combination of monochrome stripes aptly illustrate why a herd of zebra is known as a dazzle. By cutting out the background so that only the stripes are visible, you will maximise the allure of the final photograph. **JG**

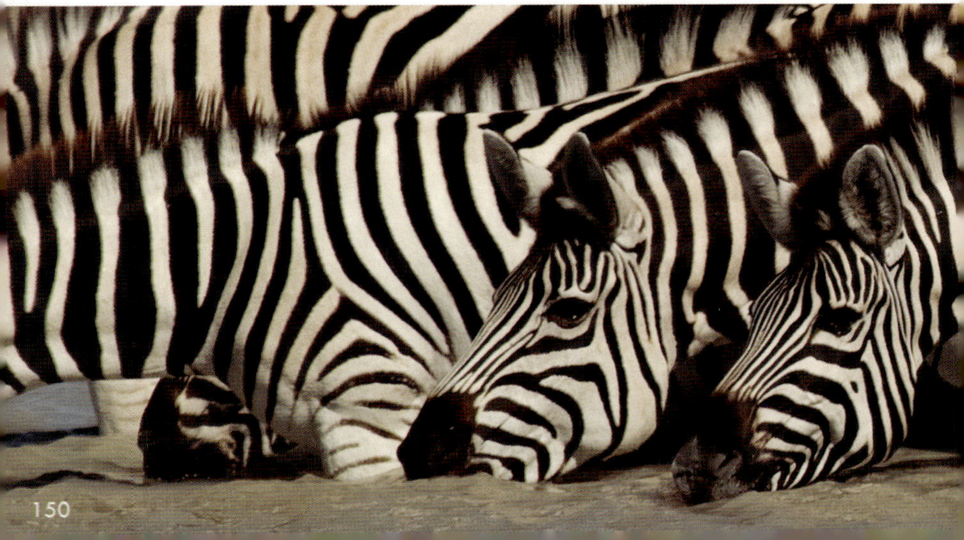

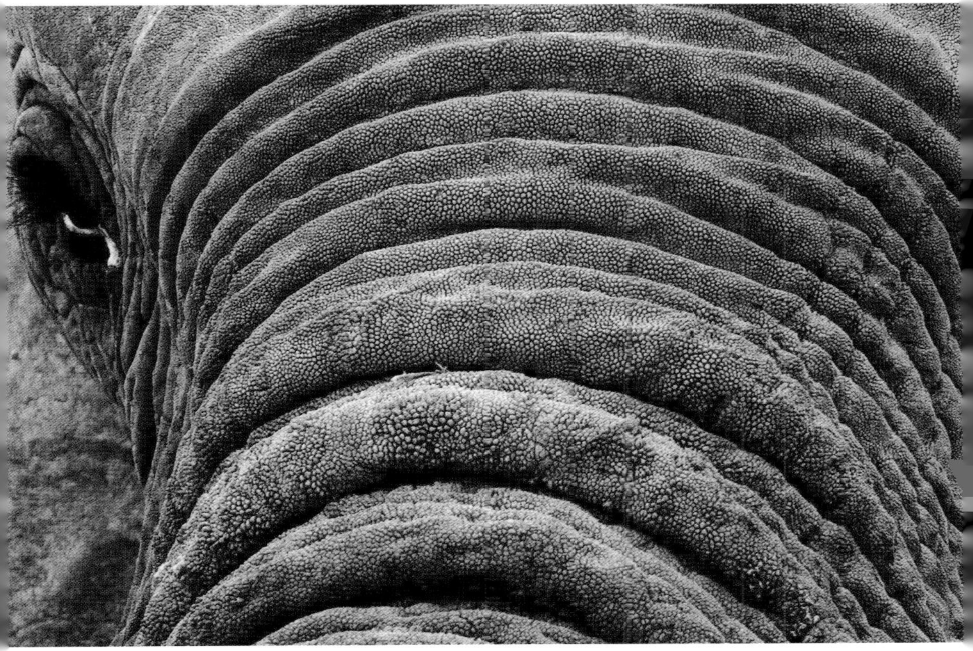

▲ *Elephant, Nxai Pan National Park. DSLR, 100-400mm Lens, f/5.6 @ 1/250, ISO 100*

As an alternative to the classic technique of focusing on the eye, choosing the elephant's skin as the primary subject creates a much more dramatic textural composition. By including the eye in the image, an interesting abstract becomes an unusual and emotive portrait. **JG**

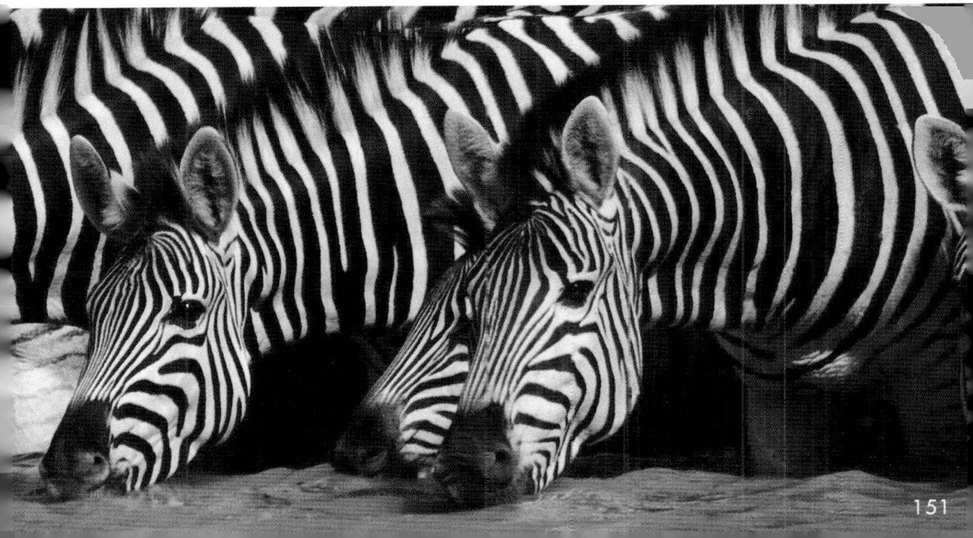

An Eye for Detail

It takes a different eye to pick out details in nature. When sitting close enough to a herd of animals, practice looking for potential images with your binoculars.

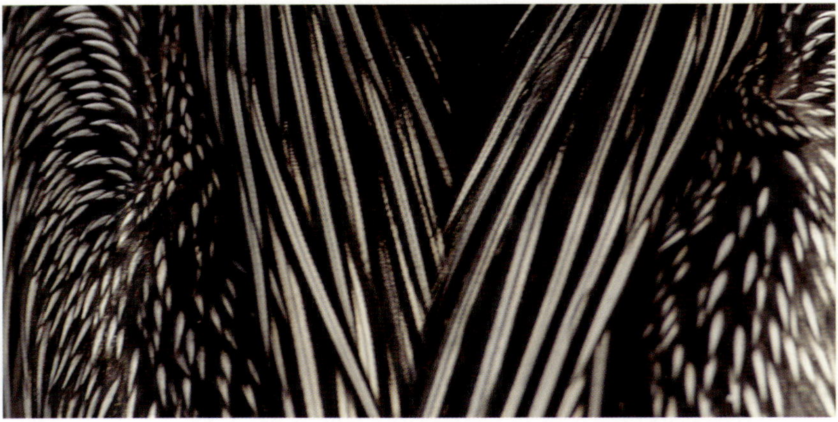

▲ ***African Darter, Okavango Delta. DSLR, 100-400mm Lens, f/6.3 @ 1/1250, ISO 100***

A detail shot of the striking feathers and textures of an African darter. **SS**

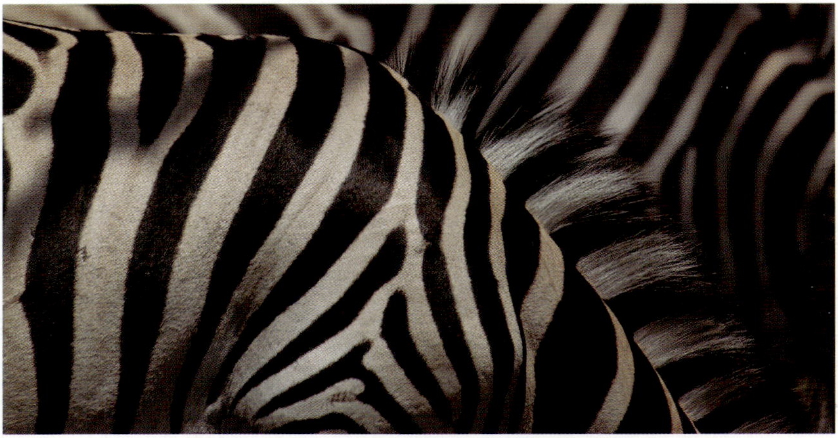

▲ ***Burchell's Zebra, Okavango Delta. DSLR, 100-400mm Lens, f/6.3 @ 1/1000, ISO 200***

This abstract image encapsulates the mesmerising effect of zebra stripes and also highlights the differences in texture between the animals' bodies and manes. A shallow depth of field adds the final touch. **SS**

▼ ***Leopard Tortoise, Okavango Delta. DSLR, 100-400mm Lens, f/5.6 @ 1/2000, ISO 1600***

This is a close-up image of the carapace or shell of a leopard tortoise that we found on the Khwai River. As one of the slower animals in the bush, you should have more time to try out a few different compositions. **SS**

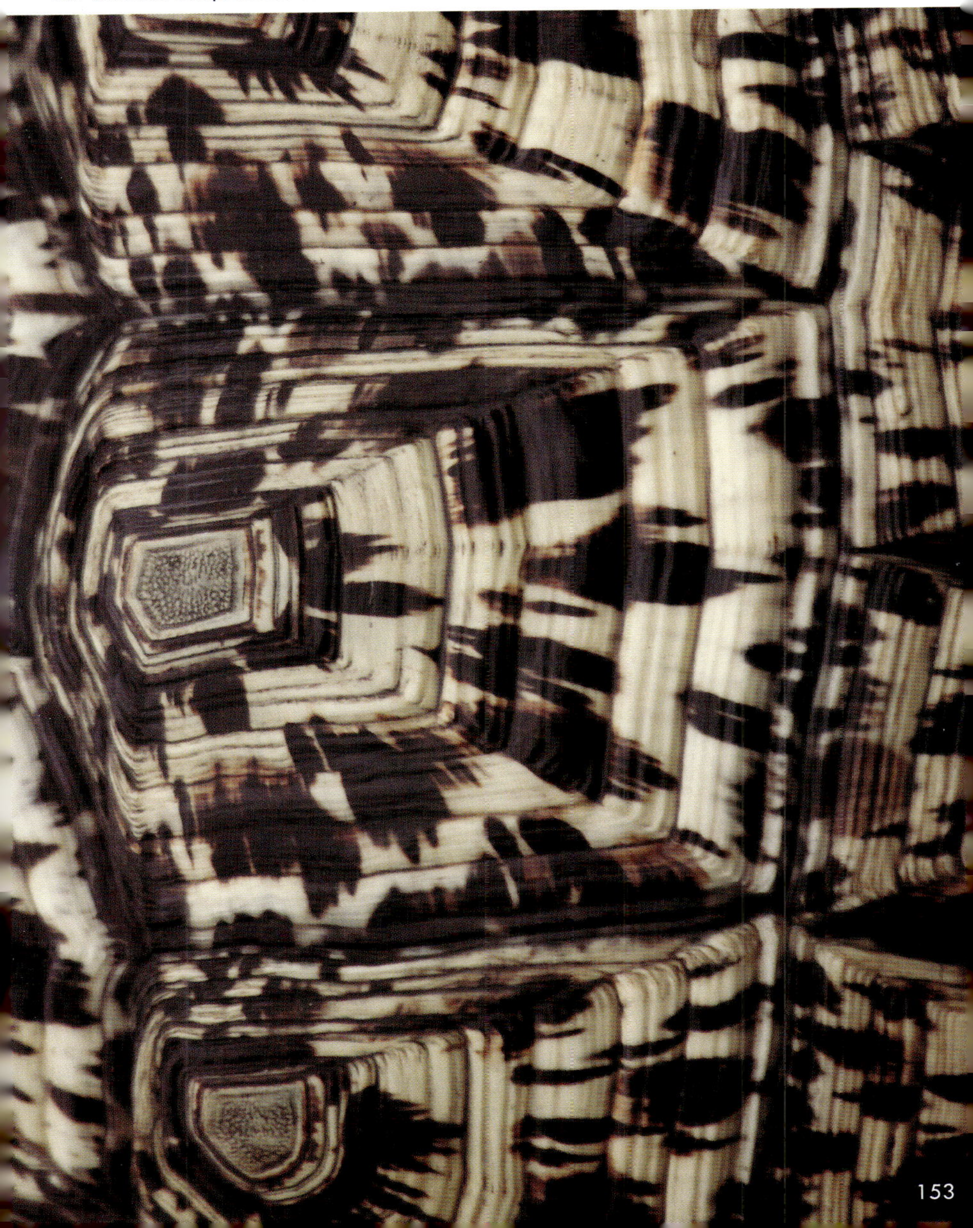

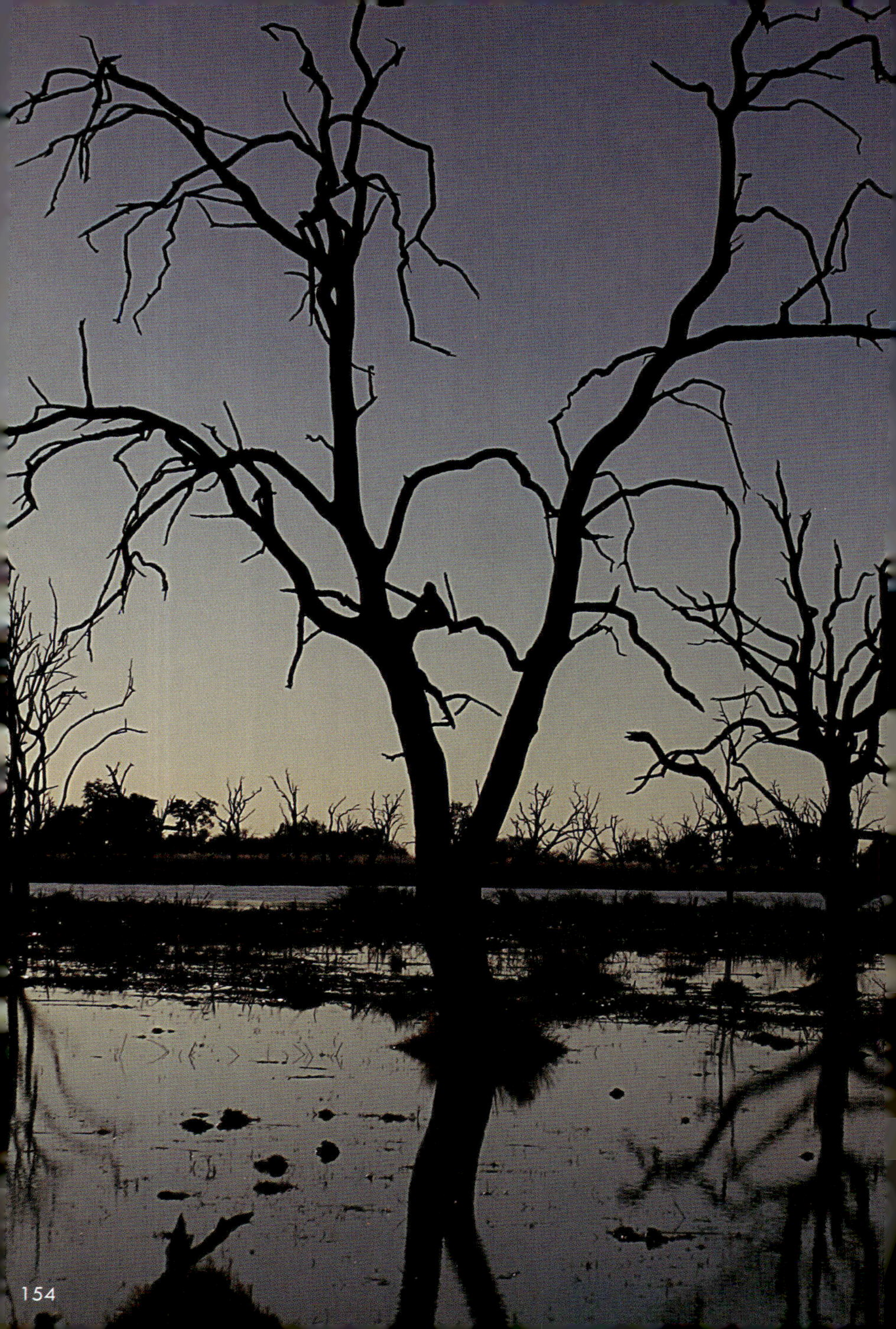

LANDSCAPES
THE SPACE BETWEEN

"Sometimes I do get to places just when God's ready to have somebody click the shutter." *Ansel Adams*

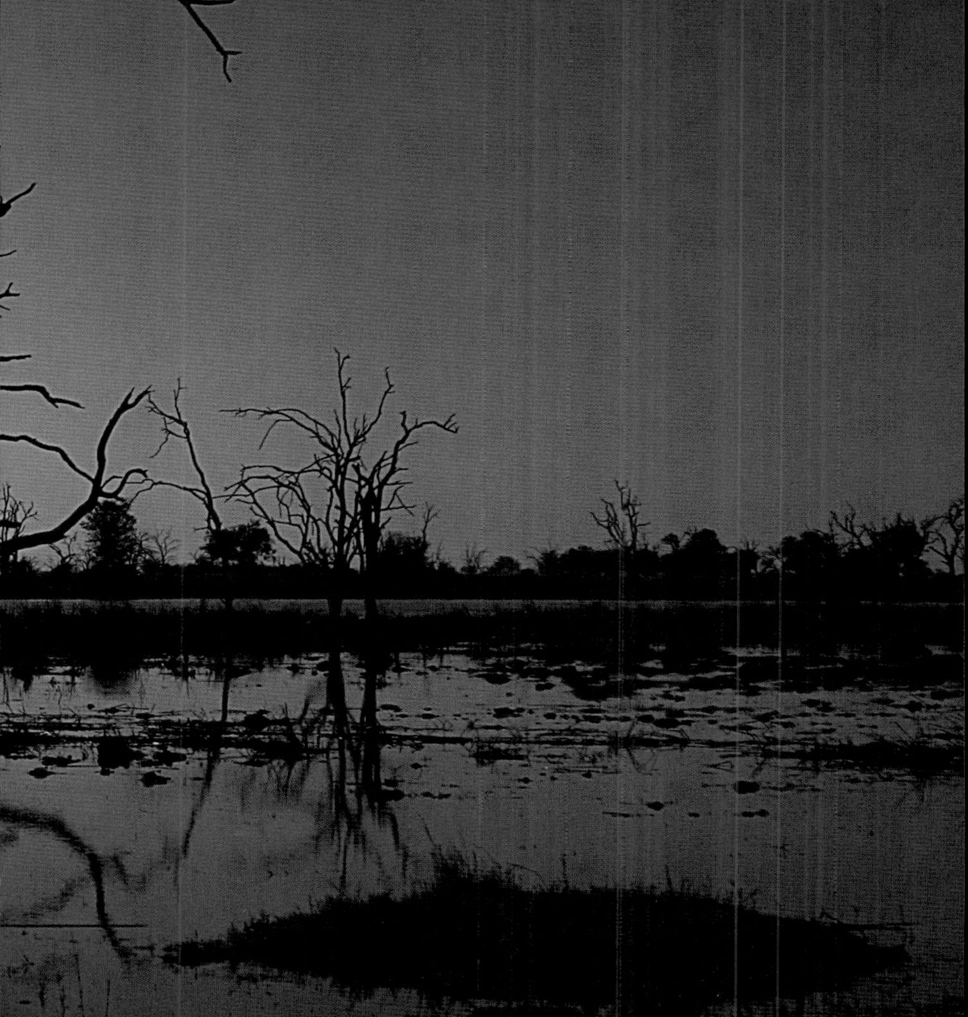

LANDSCAPES

Botswana is blessed with a habitat diversity that, when combined with good lighting, can create a stunning range of landscapes. Generally a wide-angle lens is most suitable as it allows you to include more of the scene and the rule of thirds will help you to achieve the best composition. Wherever you choose to position the horizon in the image, the most important thing is to make sure that it is level (using the focal points in the viewfinder will help).

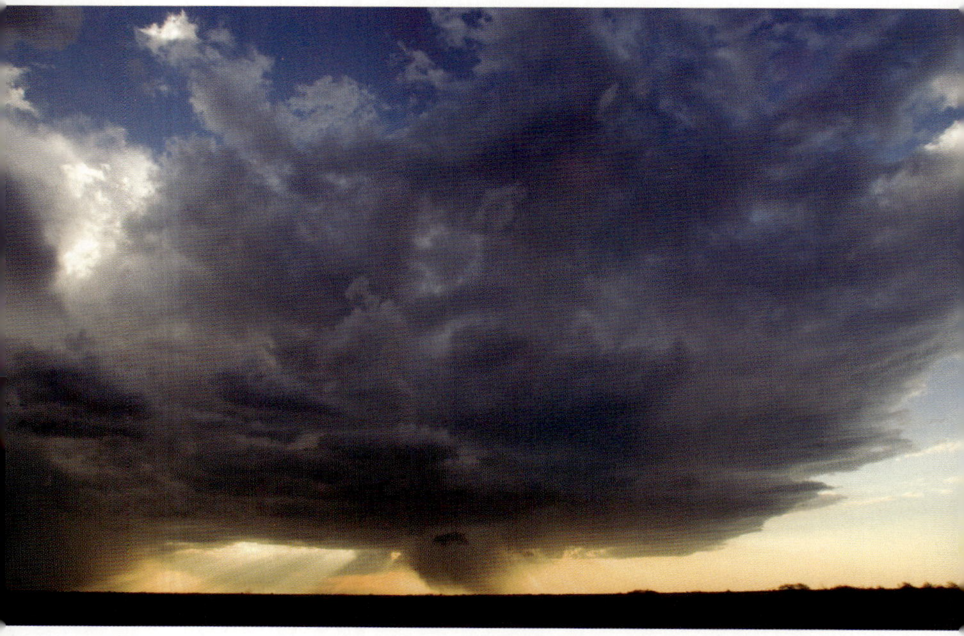

▲ ***Storm Clouds, Nxai Pan National Park. DSLR, 11-18mm Lens, f/18 @ 1/60, ISO 400***

As this storm was brewing, the poor light meant it was impossible to capture both the cloud formation and the landscape with the same exposure. Consequently, I had to stand on top of my car to avoid including the shapeless thick bushes in the foreground which would have detracted from the intensity of the sky. **JG**

▶ ***Boabab, Savuti, Chobe National Park. DSLR, 100-400mm Lens, f/5.6 @ 1/800, ISO 100***

Getting out early in the morning will allow you to find something interesting to photograph while the sun is still low in the sky. **SS**

◀ ***Dead Tree Island, Moremi Game Reserve. DSLR, 18-55mm Lens, f/5 @ 1/800, ISO 100***

Dead Tree Island in the Xakanaxa area is worth a visit just to witness and photograph the incredibly dramatic landscape of trees and water. This image was taken in the evening just after sunset. **SS**

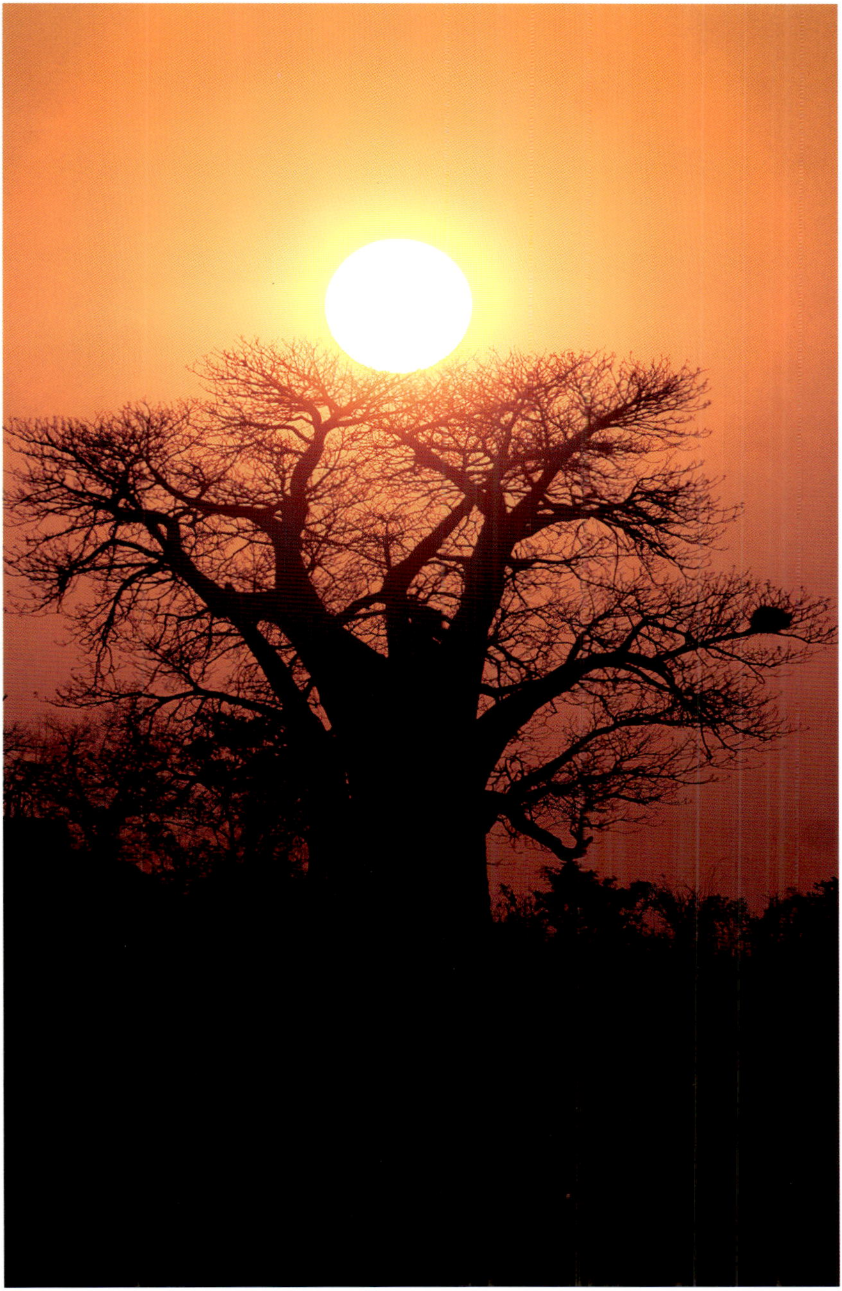

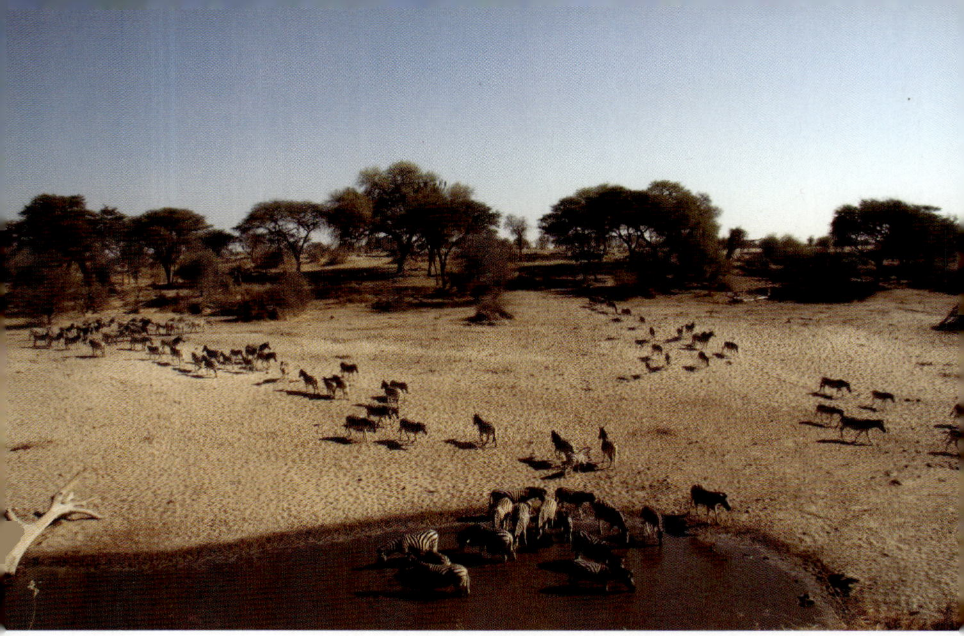

▲ ***Burchell's Zebra, Makgadikgadi Pans National Park. DSLR, 17-85mm Lens, f/18 @ 1/200, ISO 100***

Once in a while, the wildlife generously facilitates the photographer's compositional task. As this herd of zebra slowly meandered towards the waterhole, the natural lines they formed meant that all that was needed was to include the dead log in the foreground, so as to lead the eye into the picture. **JG**

BROADENING YOUR HORIZONS

A narrow aperture will maximise your depth of field resulting in a detail-packed image but be wary of using apertures much above f/18-f/22 as you will tend to lose some sharpness. The small aperture will enforce a slower shutter speed so whenever possible use a tripod. This will also allow you to shoot on 100 ISO for maximum quality.

Remember this is only a guideline - sometimes marginally reducing your depth of field by selecting a mid-range aperture (f/10 for example), can add extra emphasis to a specific subject whilst still maintaining a sense of its environment.

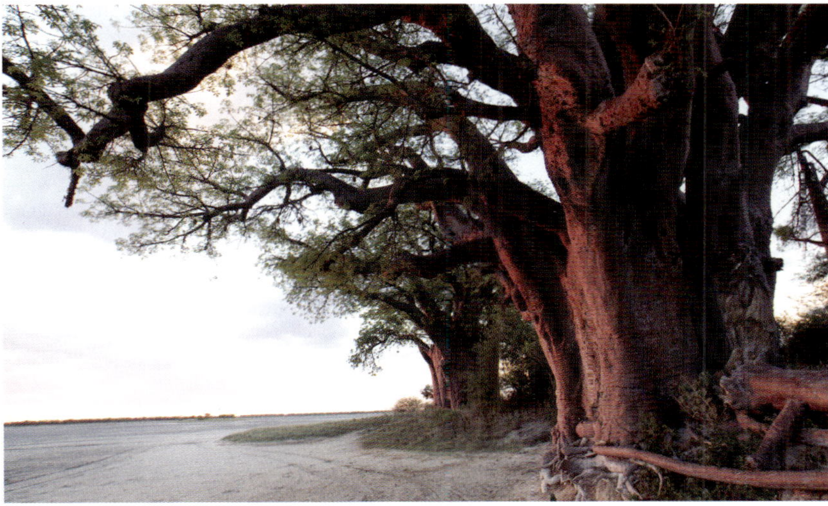

▲ ***Baines' Baobabs, Nxai Pan National Park. DSLR, 11-18mm Lens, f/8 @ 1/10, ISO 500***

Named after Thomas Baines who famously painted these seven majestic baobabs, I wanted to veer away from the conventional composition which includes all of the trees. I therefore moved to the other side of the pan and after a frustrating wait, the sun eventually broke through the clouds lighting up the bark in rich maroon tones. **JG**

▼ ***Springbok Horn, Central Kalahari Game Reserve. DSLR, 18-55mm Lens, f/4.5 @ 1/640, ISO 100***

Having found this springbok horn lying on one of the many pans in CKGR, I included it in the foreground to add to the drama of this desolate wilderness. **SS**

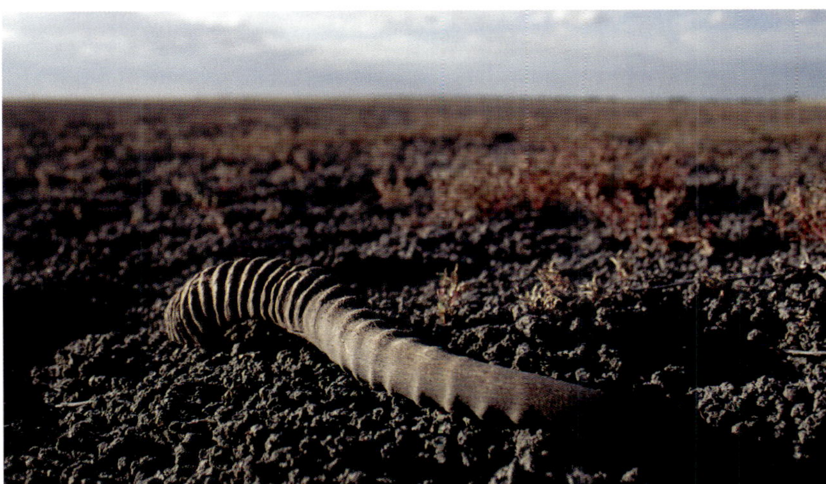

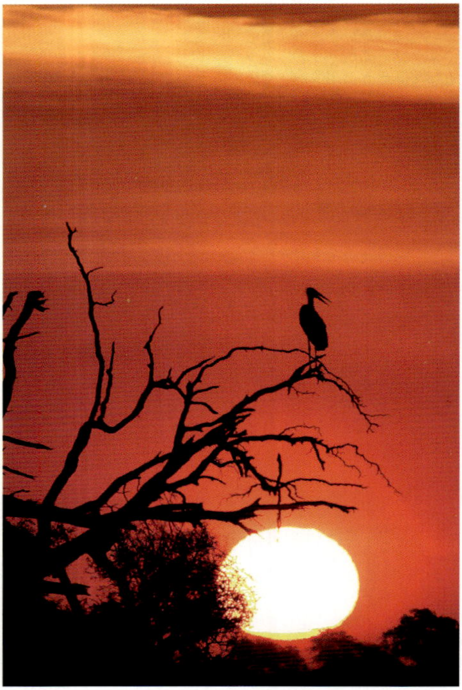

◀ ***Maribou Stork, Chobe National Park. DSLR, 100-400mm Lens, f/7.1 @ 1/400, ISO 100***

Botswana's wonderful big skies offer breathtaking vistas. Including an animal in a landscape will give the image more atmosphere. **SS**

▼ ***Springbok, Nxai Pan National Park. DSLR, 100-400mm Lens, f/13 @ 1/500, ISO 400***

If your subject matter is relatively far away, you can still take landscapes with a telephoto lens. As the sun broke through the clouds, the dappled rays lit up this herd and cast a shadow on the trees behind. This created an interesting split-lighting effect. **JG**

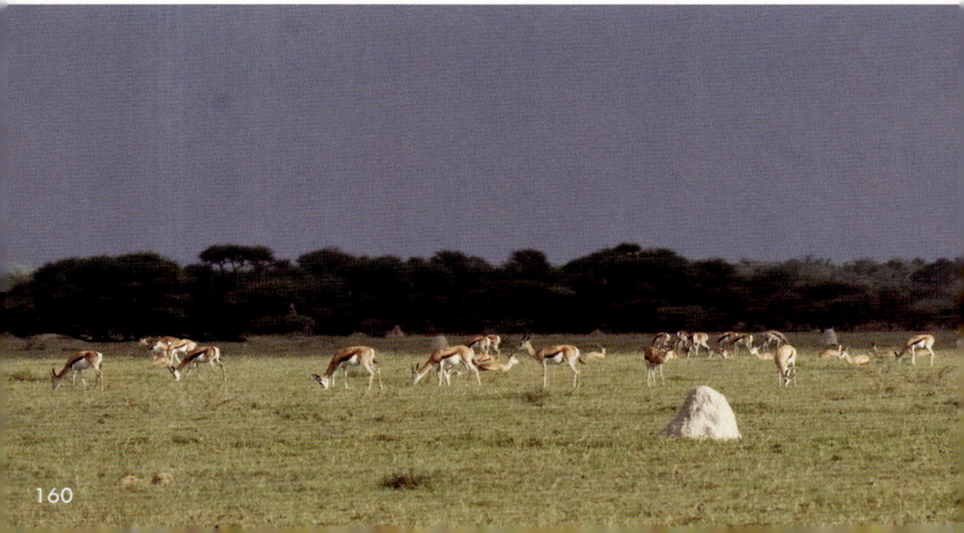

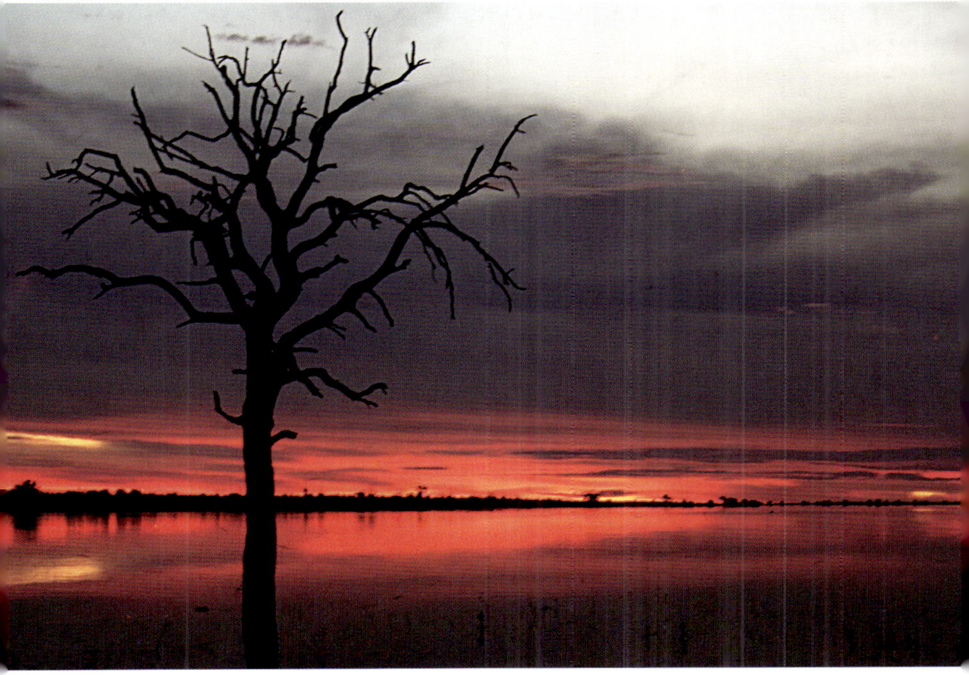

▲ ***Sunset, Chobe River. DSLR, 100-400mm Lens, f/5.6 @ 1/15, ISO 1600***

Using the rule of thirds both horizontally and vertically emphasises the stark beauty of this scene, while the vivid colours of the setting sun over the Chobe River in full flood provide the perfect backdrop. **SS**

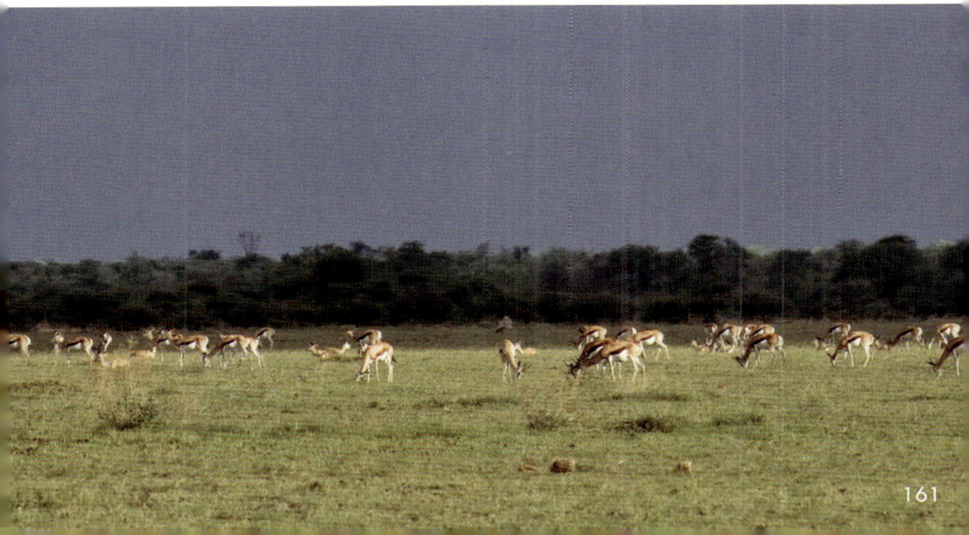

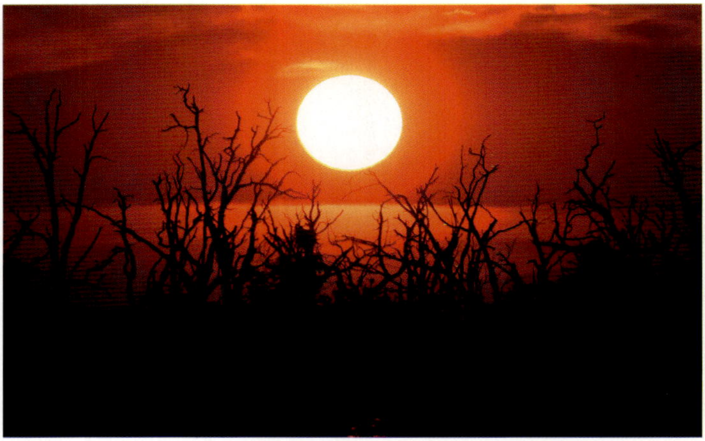

▲ ***Sunset, Okavango Delta. DSLR, 100-400mm Lens, f/5.6 @ 1/2000, ISO 200***

Most evenings in Botswana offer stunning sunsets. During the day I like to make a mental note of locations with good potential. The contrast of dead trees with a golden sunset makes for a winning combination. **SS**

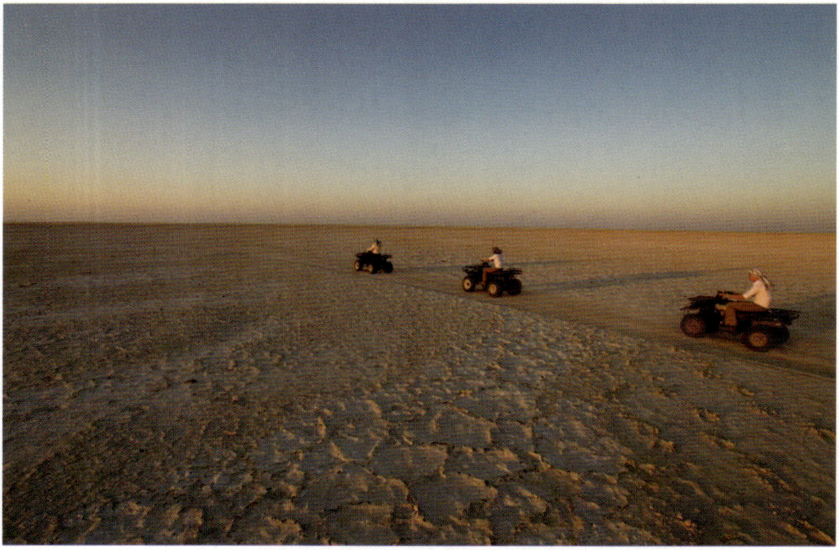

▲ ***Quad Bikes on the Makgadikgadi Pans. DSLR, 11-18mm Lens, f/7.1 @ 1/200, ISO 400***

Including people in this composition helps to illustrate the scale of the pans. Completely void of landmarks, it is remarkable that the early explorers succeeded in traversing them and they make a fascinating addition to any Botswana itinerary. **JG**

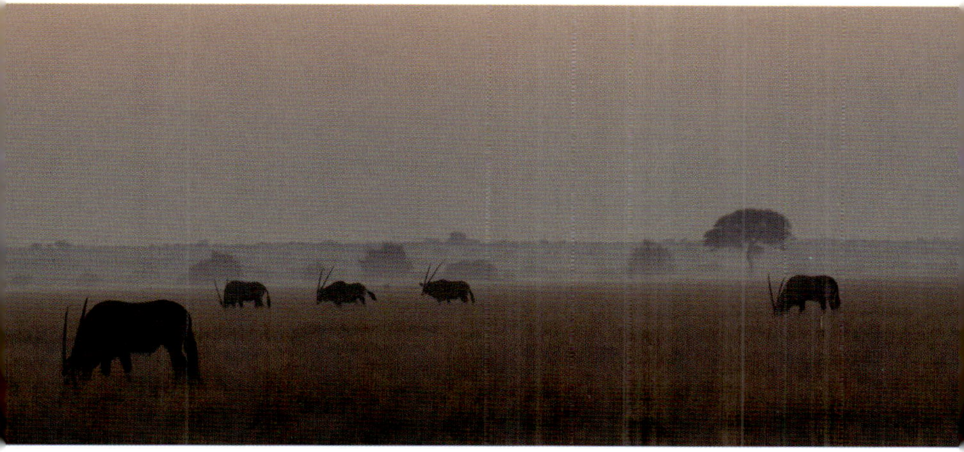

▲ Gemsbok, Central Kalahari Game Reserve. DSLR, 100-400mm Lens, f/11 @ 1/40, ISO 400

Winter mornings in the Kalahari can be surprisingly cold, shrouding the valleys in clouds of photogenic mist. By sunrise, most of this mist will have burned away so make the effort to get into the field before dawn. The foreground gemsbok adds vital depth to the scene. **JG**

▼ Storm on the Makgadikgadi Pans. DSLR, 17-85mm Lens, f/22 @ 1/80, ISO 100

Often capturing an impressive landscape is all about waiting for the best light. As this storm was threatening, I had only a couple of minutes to capture the amber hues of the setting sun reflected on the waterlogged pans before it disappeared completely. **JG**

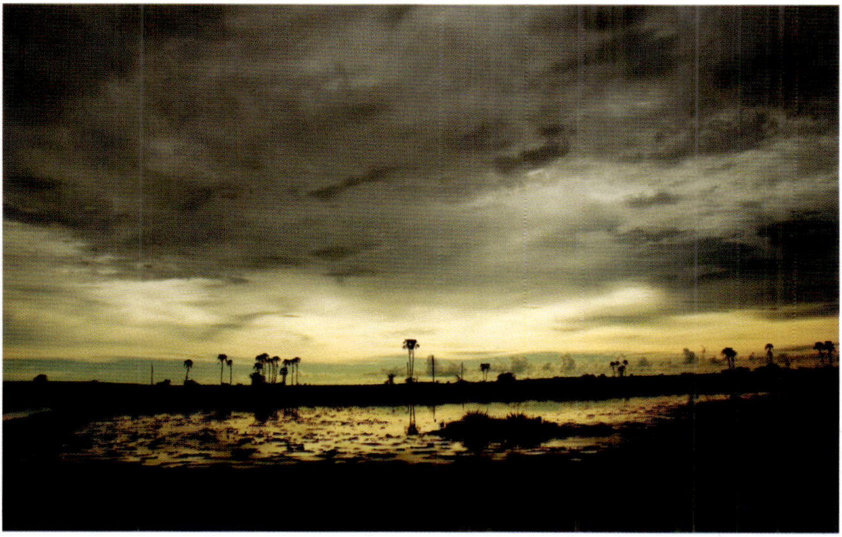

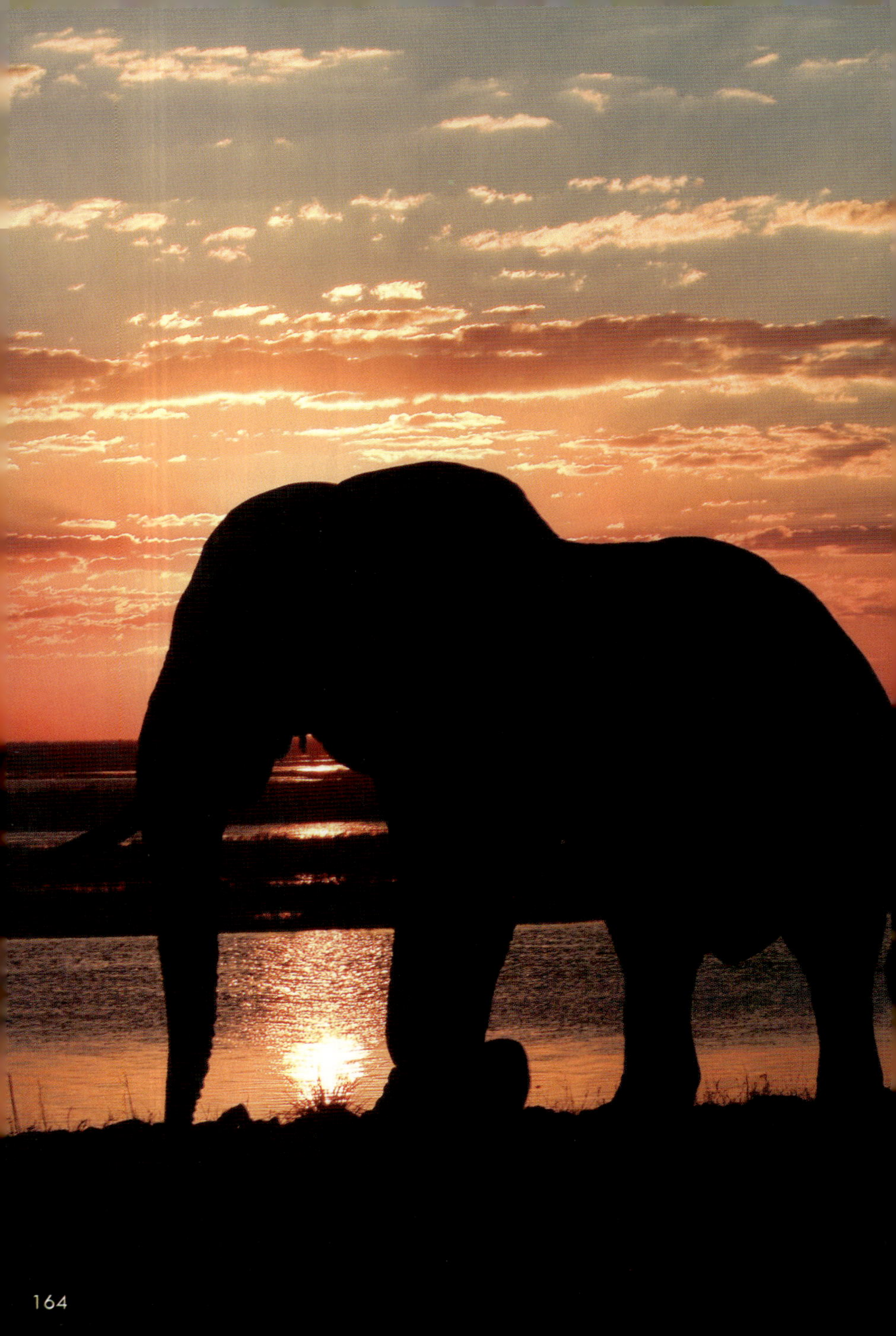

DUSK TILL DAWN
A SHOT IN THE DARK

"I believe a leaf of grass is no less the journey-work of the stars."
Walt Whitman

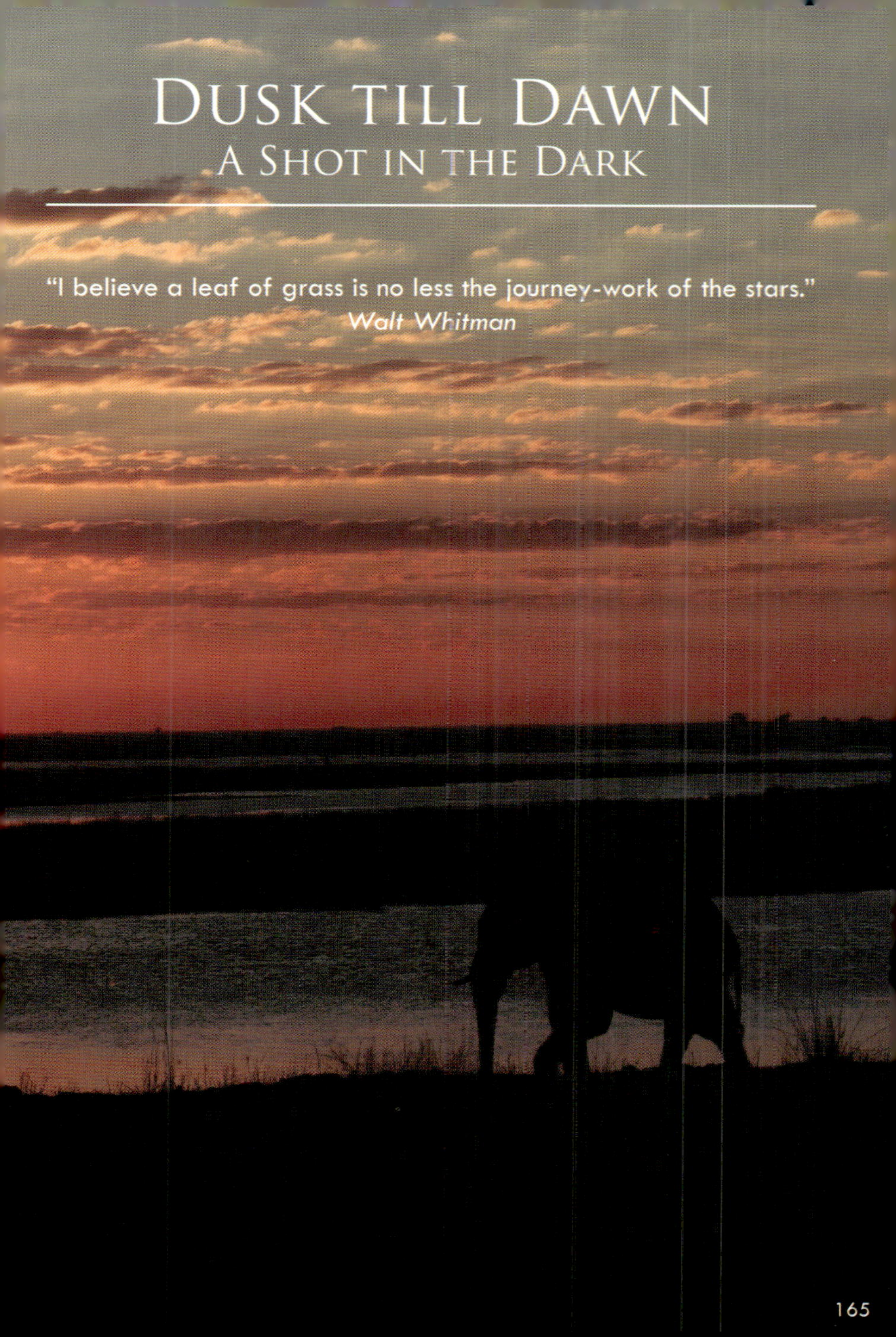

DUSK TILL DAWN

After the golden light has disappeared, there are still plenty of chances to broaden your photographic collection. From silhouettes and sparkling night skies to campfire scenes and the moon itself, this twilight period is full of opportunity. To create silhouettes, expose on a light part of the sky close to the sun (use spot metering and exposure lock). This saturates the reds whilst simultaneously darkening your subject. Review your images, adjust exposure compensation and reshoot if necessary.

◀ ***Elephant, Chobe River. DSLR, 18-55mm Lens, f/10 @ 1/250, ISO 200***

The setting sun silhouettes a bull elephant with a younger male walking behind him. The perspective of the two different sized animals gives one a sense of scale highlighted by the golden waters of the Chobe River. **SS**

▶ ***Sunset, Makgadikgadi Pans. DSLR, 17-85mm Lens, f/5.6 @ 1/30, ISO 400***

The tall palms of the Makgadikgadi towering above other low-lying vegetation make ideal subjects for sunsets. This classic shot epitomises the distinctive landscape. **JG**

▼ ***African Spoonbill, Okavango Delta. DSLR, 100-400mm Lens, f/5.6 @ 1/8000, ISO 200***

As the sun gets lower in the sky, golden light spreads out across the many rivers in the Delta. Watching this spoonbill during sundowners one evening, I waited until it passed through the brightest part of the image before taking the shot. **SS**

BAD VIBRATIONS

If you are using a tripod and don't have a remote switch then make use of your camera's self-timer. Stabilisation is critical in low light scenarios as you will certainly experience slow shutter speeds and any vibration on the camera could render the image useless.

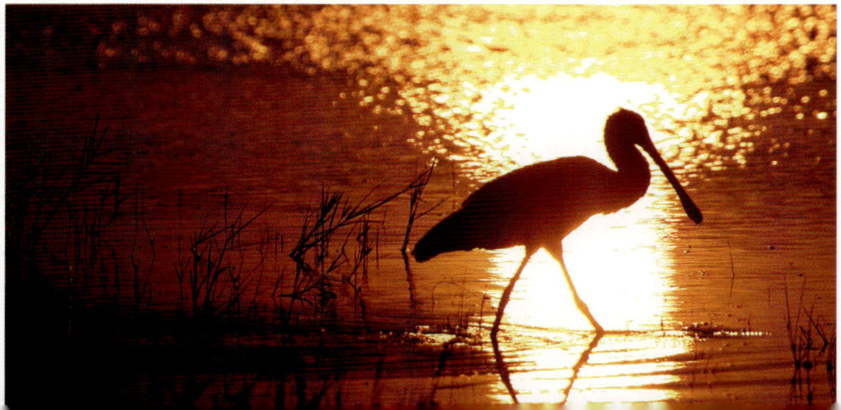

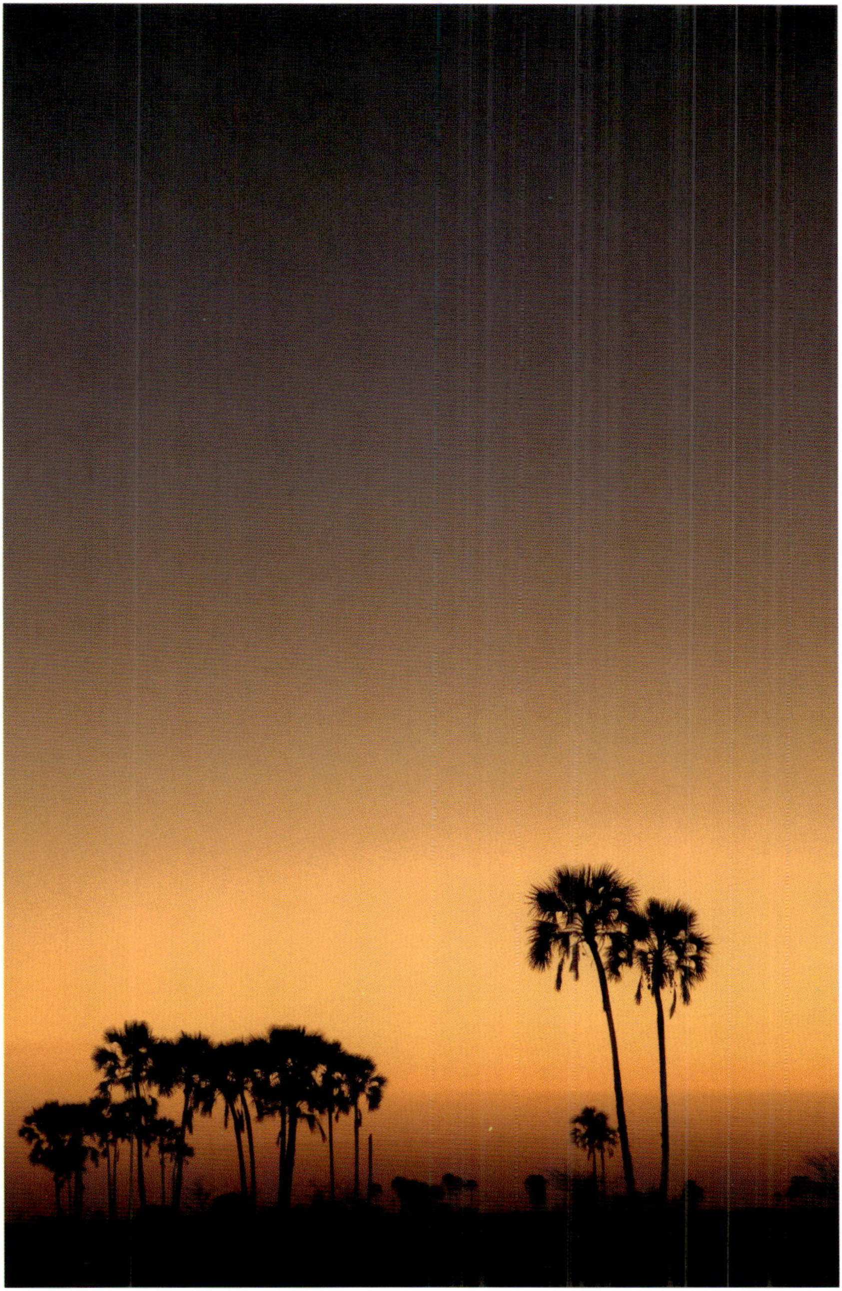

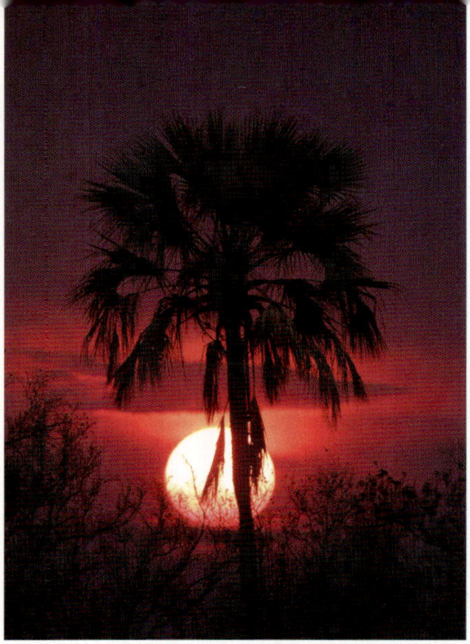

◀ ***Palm Sunset, Okavango Delta. DSLR, 100-400mm Lens, f/5.6 @ 1/160, ISO 200***

Day becomes night in the Okavango Delta. The real fan palm is widespread and will often feature in your imagery. To capture the sunset, I spot metered on the sky and locked the exposure. **SS**

▼ ***Brown Hyena at Sunset, Makgadikgadi Pans. DSLR, 17-85mm Lens, f/6.3 @ 1/100, ISO 400***

One of the most important aspects to capturing silhouettes is the angle of shot. To emphasise the shape of the animal, you will need to get down as low as possible - at least at eye-level and preferably below your subject. **JG**

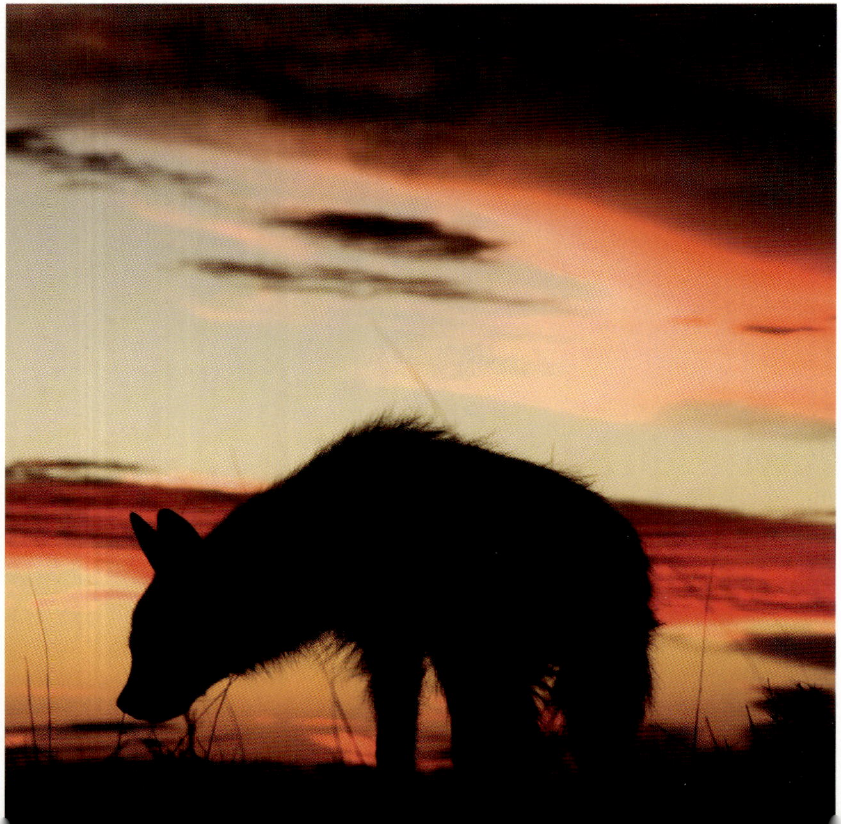

Shooting Stars

Requiring very slow shutter speeds, capturing star shots involves a tripod, remote switch and a lot of patience! You will have to switch to Bulb mode for shutter speeds longer than 30 seconds and, using manual focus, adjust the focusing ring until it lines up with the infinity symbol (∞). You may need to check this calibration by focusing on a distant point in daylight and marking the true infinity focal point on your lens. Use a wide aperture and a low ISO to minimise noise. To track the streaking movement of stars across the sky, you need to think in terms of hours for exposures and shoot in a southerly direction to capture a celestial arc. Don't forget to charge your battery beforehand!

▼ ***Moon & Spider, Okavango Delta. SLR, 100-400mm Lens, f/5.6 @ 30, Fuji Provia 100F***

A spider stands out against the rising full moon in the Delta. Images like this are rare to find and it was taken en route to my tent. (Always have your camera with you!) I had to quickly set up my tripod knowing that I would require a shutter speed of about 30 seconds. I also used the self-timer so that the camera was completely still when the image was exposed. **SS**

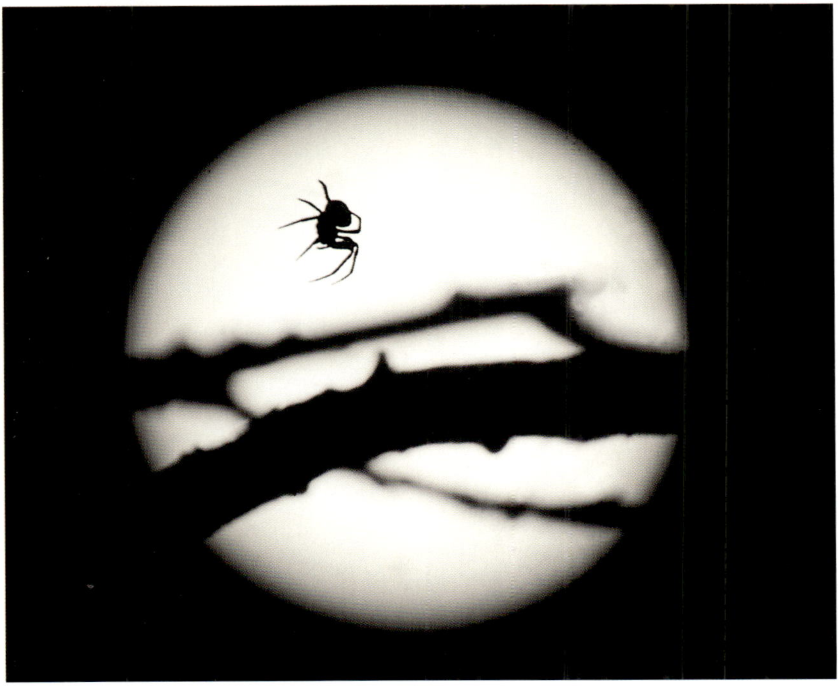

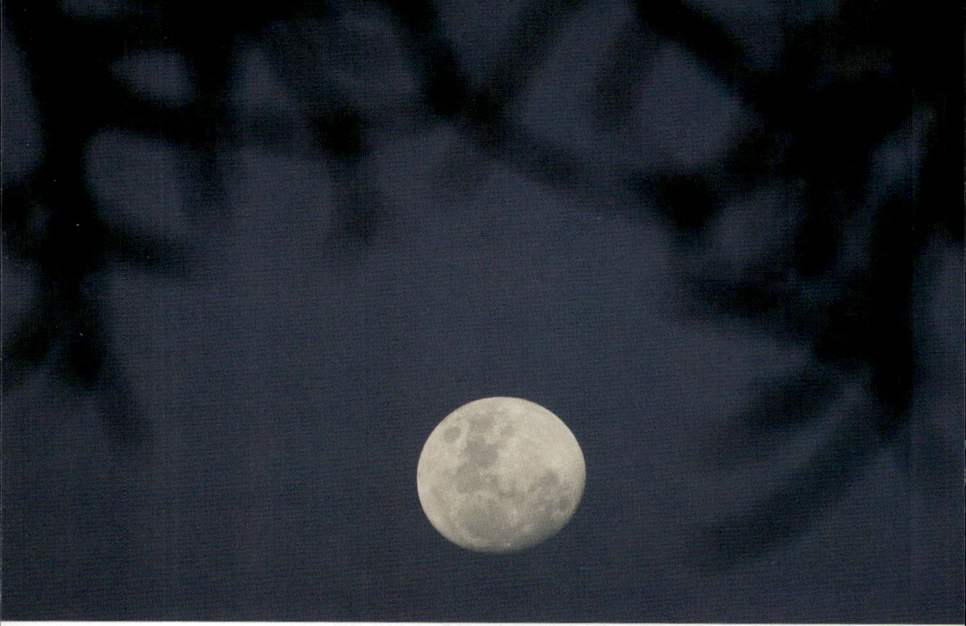

▲ ***Moon Rising, Makgadikgadi Pans, DSLR, 100-400mm Lens, f/5.6 @ 1/1000, ISO 200***

Taken a couple of days before full moon, the earlier rising time allowed me to capture the moon's full detail against a blue backdrop instead of the conventional black sky. Blurring the branches creates a natural frame. **JG**

▶ ***Trancedance, Makgadikgadi Pans. DSLR, 17-85mm Lens, f/4 @ 0.8, ISO 1600, Tripod***

A trancedance is an integral part of the Khoesian culture and is an incredibly mesmerising event. On this occasion, I was lucky enough to photograph on the pans where the lack of vegetation and natural moonlight created a stunning spectacle. **JG**

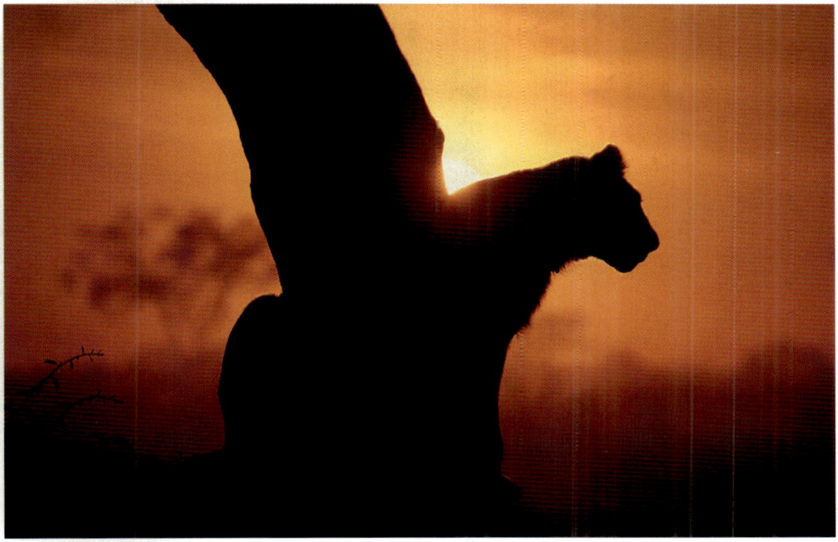

▲ ***Lion at Dawn, Savuti, Chobe National Park. SLR, 100-400mm Lens, Fuji Provia 100F***

Awoken early by lions calling, we skipped breakfast to get out early which was well worth the effort. A young lion had climbed a termite mound and the low angle of the sun (and the use of a bean bag) gave me this wonderful result. **SS**

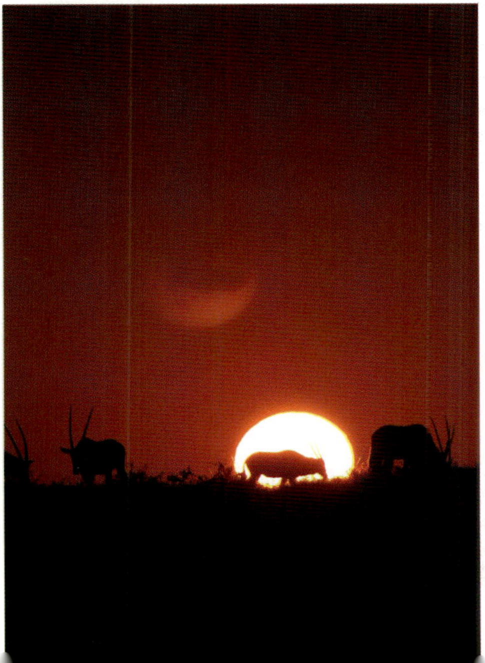

◀ ***Gemsbok at Dawn, Central Kalahari Game Reserve. DSLR, 100-400mm Lens, f/5.6 @ 1/800, ISO 100***

This is an all too rare example of a premeditated photograph that worked according to plan. While photographing a herd of gemsbok one evening, I noticed that a raised ridge in the east would give me the ideal angle for a sunrise silhouette the following morning. Fortunately, the next day the gemsbok positioned themselves perfectly. Even with a lens hood, sunspots are always a risk when you are shooting directly into the sun, but in this case the reflected gemsbok in the sunspot adds an extra dimension to the image. **JG**

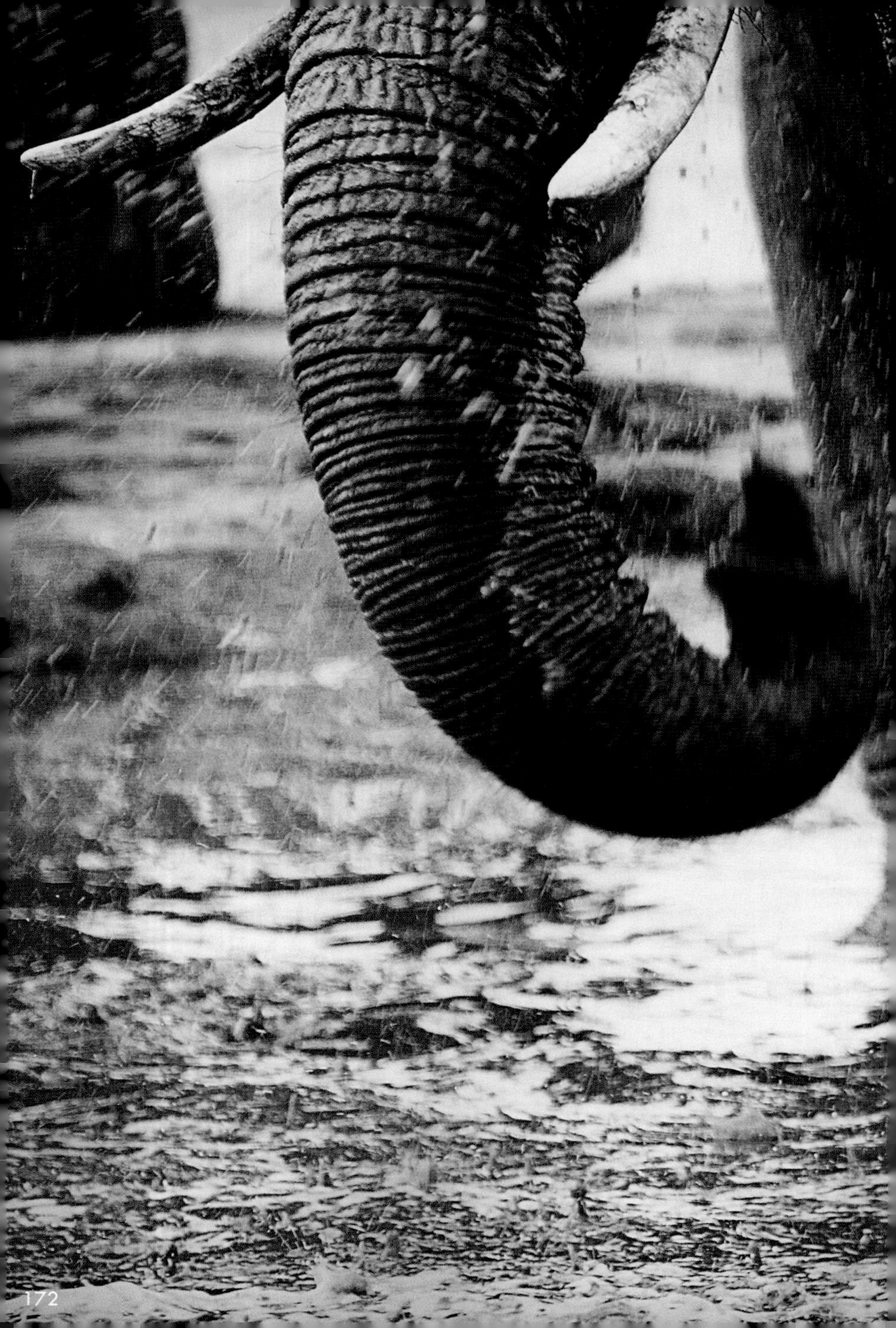

Black & White
A World of Contrast

"Manipulating shadows and tonality is like writing music or a poem." *Conrad Hall*

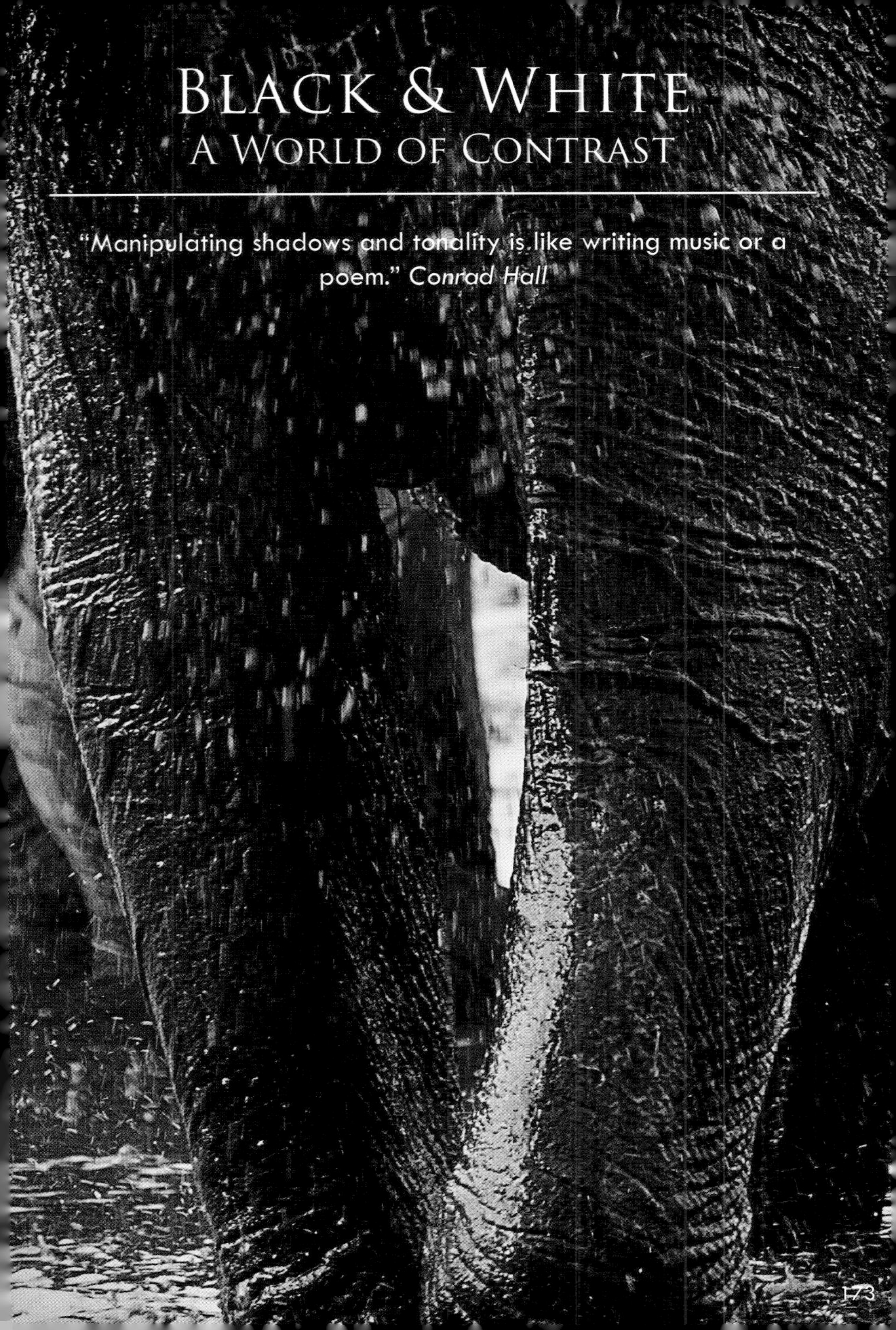

Black & White

Black and white photography requires you to think in terms of textures and tones rather than colours - the greater the tonal contrast, the stronger the final image. Soft lighting is also not a prerequisite. A photo shot under harsh or low lighting will often look much better when converted into black and white (either by shooting in monochrome or converting the image at a later stage). Furthermore, using sepia tones can inject a classic and timeless ambience to your images. More than anything, this medium opens up a wealth of creative opportunities so let your hair down and experiment.

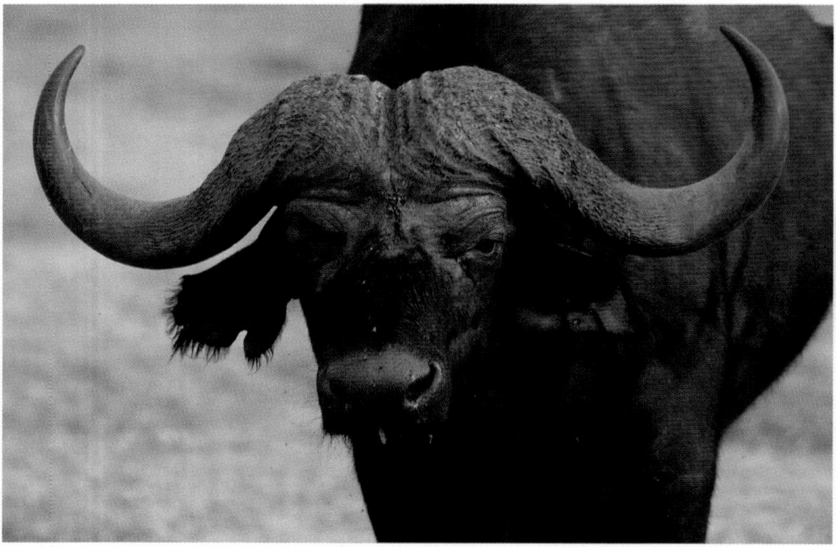

▲ ***Cape Buffalo, Chobe National Park. DSLR, 100-400mm Lens, f/6.3 @ 1/400, ISO 800***

The dark fur and texture of the horns of a buffalo are perfectly suited to black and white photography. Here, the side lighting casts dark shadows that add to the atmosphere. **SS**

▶ ***Bat-eared Fox, Central Kalahari Game Reserve. DSLR, 100-400mm Lens, f/5.6 @ 1/160, ISO 100***

When photographing in black and white, look out for the juxtaposition of light and dark tones as with the ears of this bat-eared fox. **JG**

◀ ***Elephant, Savuti, Chobe National Park. DSLR, 100-400mm Lens, f/5.6 @ 1/160, ISO 800***

A slower shutter speed blurs the motion of this bull at a water hole in Savuti. To create an effect like this your camera must remain absolutely still. **SS**

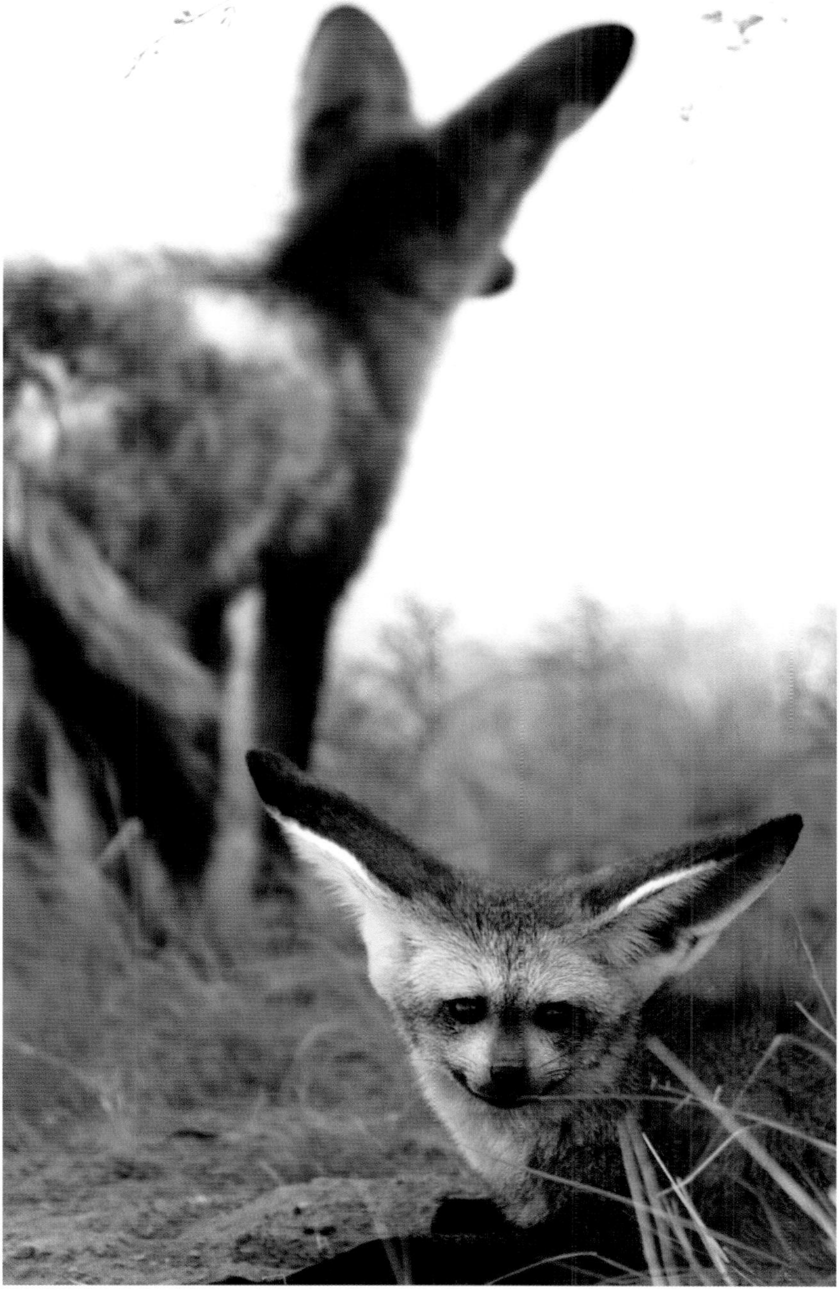

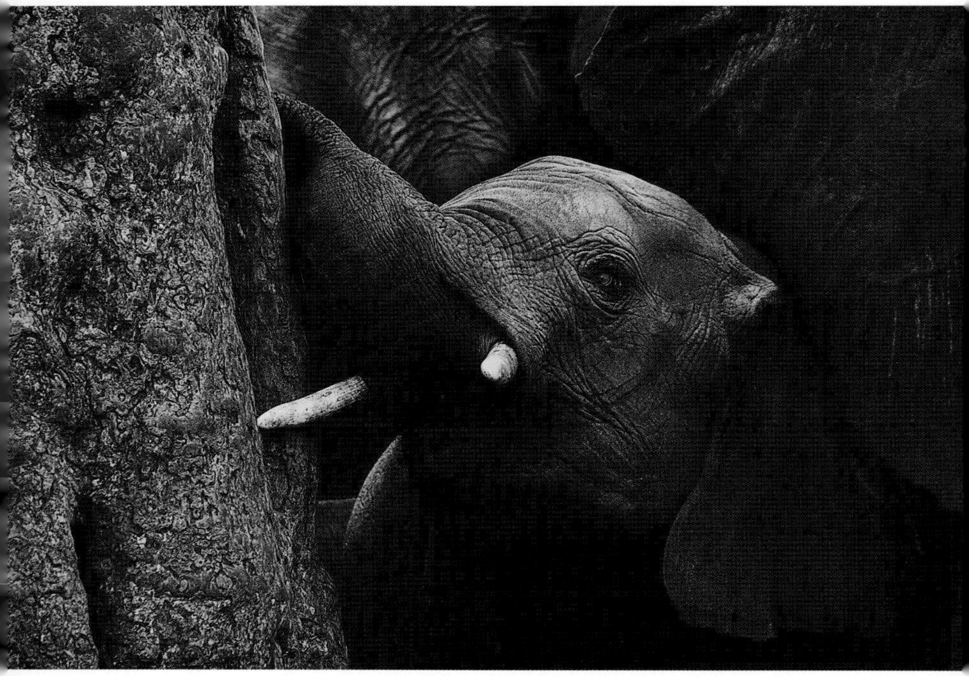

▲ ***Elephant, Chobe National Park. DSLR, 100-400mm Lens, f/6.3 @ 1/800, ISO 800***

This image captures the textural contrast between the elephant's skin and the bark of the tree. Converting to black and white highlights the life in the elephant's eye adding an additional allure. **SS**

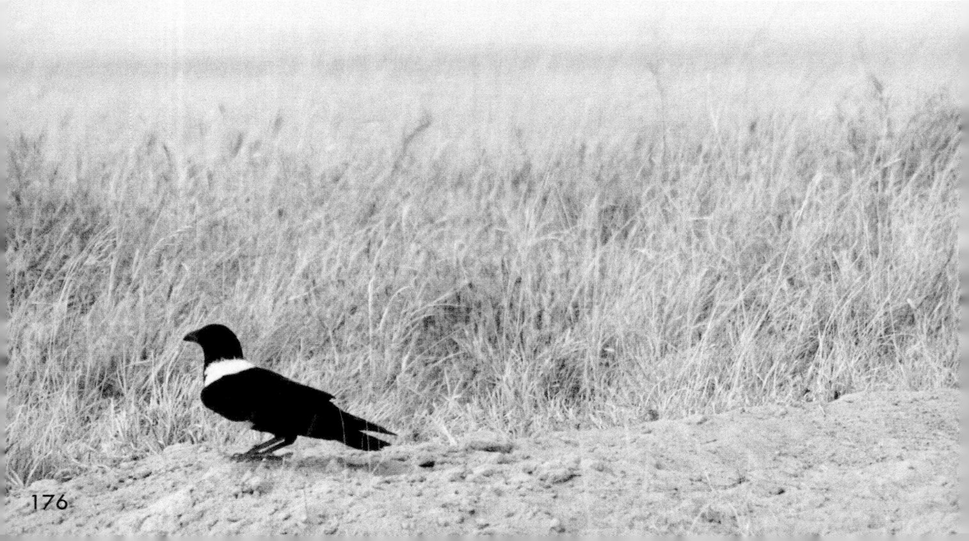

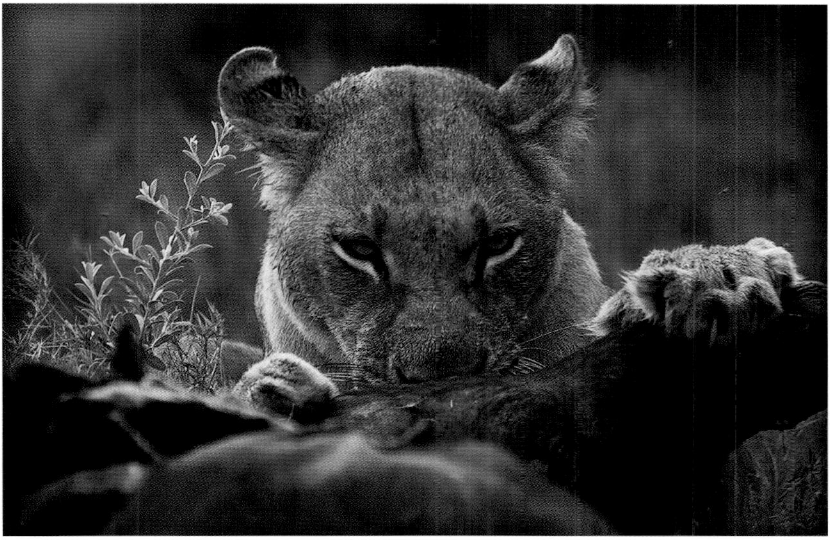

▲ ***Lioness, Okavango Delta. DSLR, 100-400mm Lens, f/5.6 @ 1/250, ISO 800***

Kill scenarios can be quite gory in colour but I found that this was softened in this black and white portrayal of a lioness eating a buffalo. **SS**

▼ ***Brown Hyena & Pied Crow, Makgadikgadi Pans. DSLR, 100-400mm Lens, f/5.6 @ 1/500, ISO 400***

Never turn down the rare opportunity to inject some humour into your photographs. **JG**

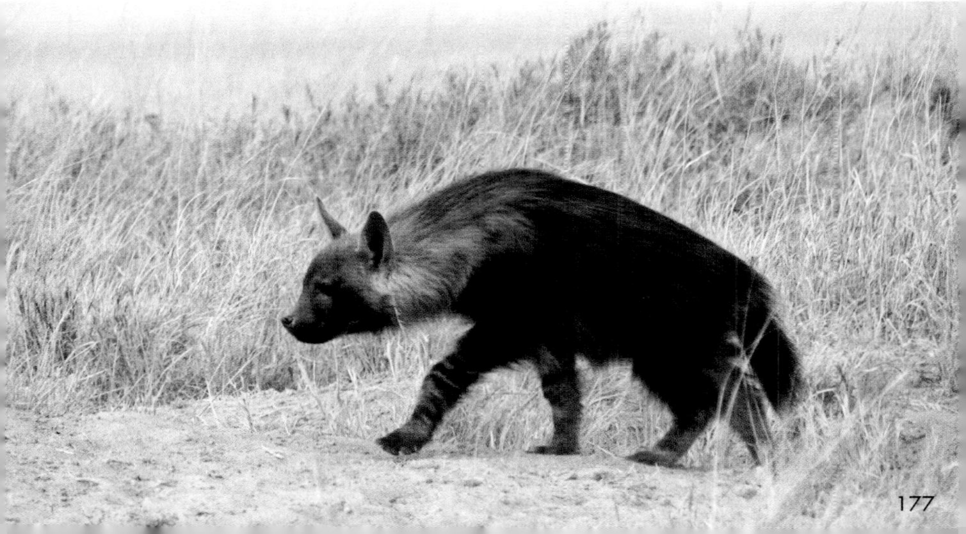

▶ ***Burchell's Zebra, Makgadikgadi Pans. DSLR, 100-400mm Lens, f/5.6 @ 1/8, ISO 160***

An illustration of how an ultra slow shutter speed can exaggerate the slow gait of an ambling zebra by using the panning technique. **JG**

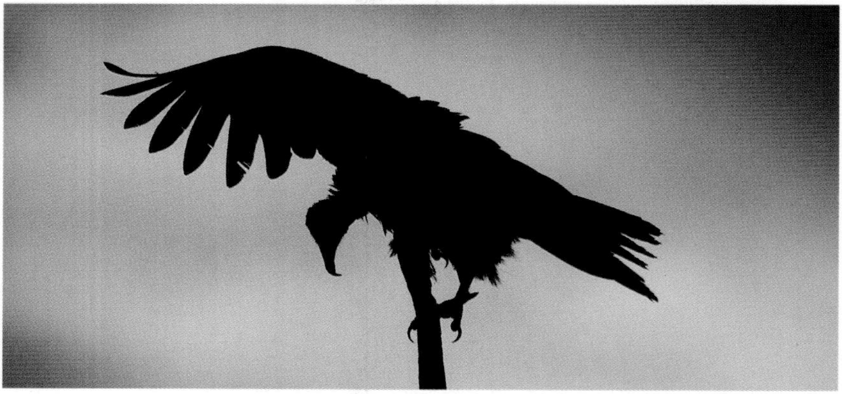

▲ ***Hooded Vulture, Okavango Delta. DSLR, 100-400mm Lens, f/5.6 @ 1/4000, ISO 800***

The atmospheric background behind this vulture sets the mood of the image. It also highlights the feather detail on the left wing. **SS**

▼ ***Black-backed Jackal, Central Kalahari Game Reserve. DSLR, 500mm Lens, f/4 @ 1/500, ISO 1000***

Shot just after a storm, the contrast caused by the jackal's sodden fur combined with the shallow depth of field made it perfect for converting into black and white. **JG**

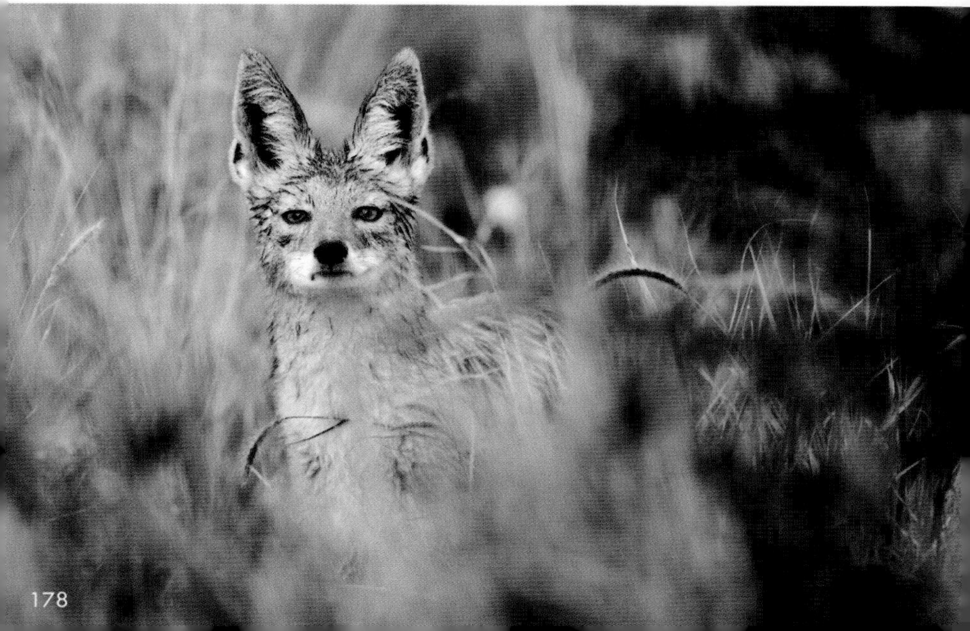

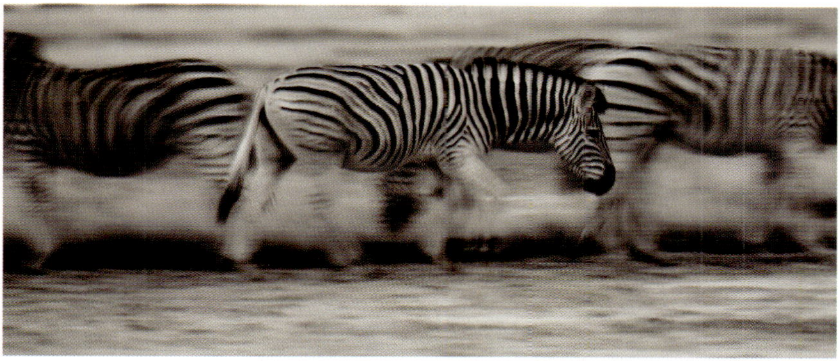

AGAINST THE GRAIN

High ISOs tend to increase grain or noise which reduces the quality of a colour photo but in black and white, this can actually add atmosphere to an image. Low light will often force you to increase your ISO to maintain a high shutter speed and the resulting grain may mean that black and white is your only viable option. However, you can also choose to increase your ISO in broad daylight to deliberately create that grainy effect.

▼ ***Red Lechwe, Okavango Delta. DSLR, 100-400mm Lens, f/5.6 @ 1/30, ISO 100***

When low light means that even raising your ISO does not allow for a fast enough shutter speed, try lowering the ISO back to 100 and combine with a slow shutter speed for a subtle panning effect. **JG**

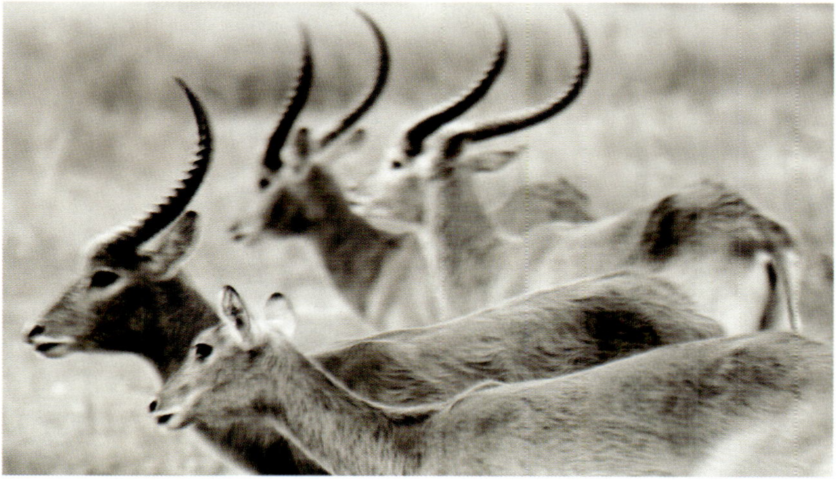

▶ ***Lion, Central Kalahari Game Reserve. DSLR, 500mm Lens, f/4 @ 1/200, ISO 12800***

With a monster ISO forced by the limited pre-dawn light, this image would have had too much grain to work in colour. But by shooting in RAW, I was later able to convert to sepia. **JG**

▼ ***Elephant, Savuti, Chobe National Park. DSLR, 100-400mm Lens, f/5.6 @ 1/1250, ISO 250***

With their smooth, white tusks and dark, wrinkled skin, elephants are perfect subjects for the textural and tonal world of black and white photography. **JG**

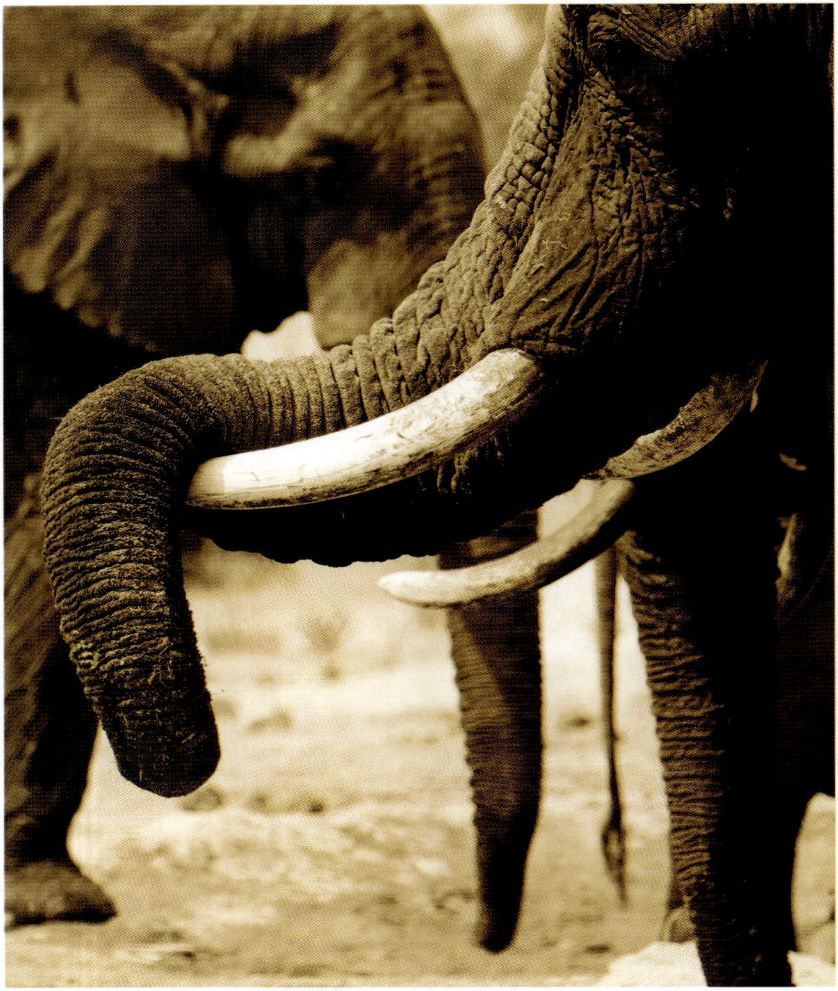

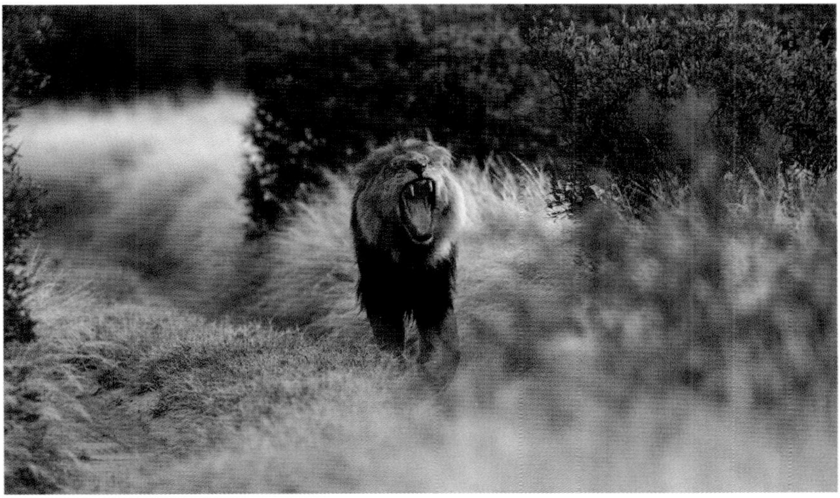

▼ *Lion, Central Kalahari Game Reserve. DSLR, 100-400mm Lens, f/5.6 @ 1/100, ISO 400*

Using a slower shutter speed than normal softened the lion's mane lending more atmosphere to this portrait. **JG**

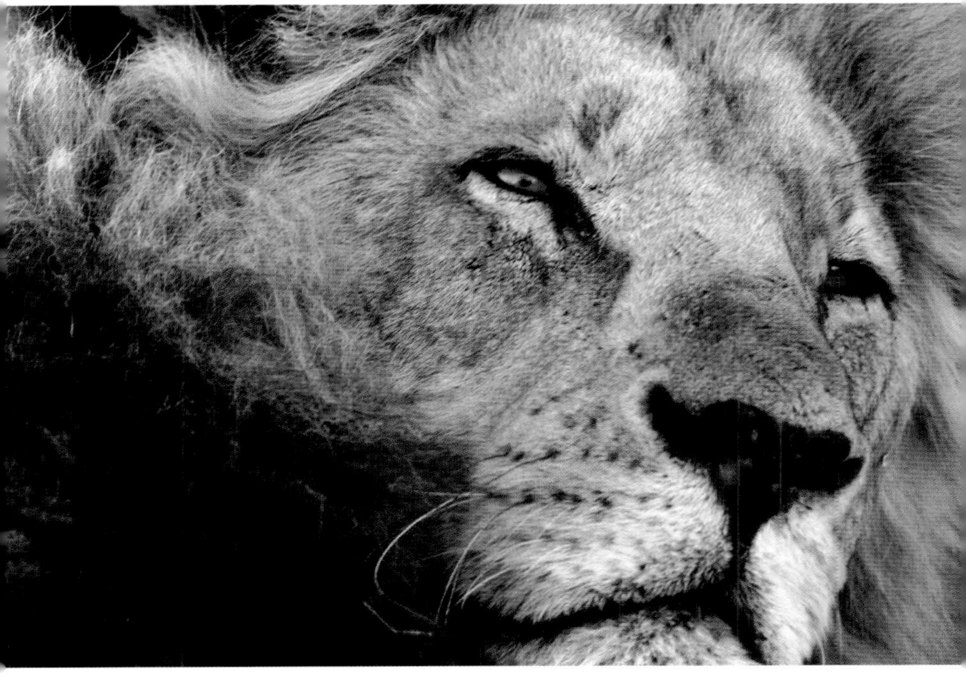

Post Production
Virtual Darkroom

If you are shooting in RAW, you will have to process your files once you get home. The power and complexity of today's editing software, such as Photoshop and Lightroom, mean that you could spend months learning all their tools and applications. Our personal view as wildlife photographers is that although necessary, digital processing should play a relatively minor role in producing your final image. However deep you decide to delve into post production, there is no substitute for capturing a correctly exposed and well-composed shot in the field. In this chapter we briefly touch on some basic techniques but recommend you read the books relevant to your specific software to learn more.

Converting from RAW

Depending on your make of camera, you will need the appropriate software to open and convert your RAW file. Two of the most useful editing tools in a RAW converter are the ability to make minor changes to exposure (check the histogram first) and to adjust the white balance (to correct colour casts).

Editing Tips

Levels and Curves are used to boost contrast and increase tonal range, as not every image histogram will contain both very dark and very light tones. The Levels dialogue box can be used to specify the location of 100% black and 100% white as well as the mid-point of the range. By adjusting these points, you can broaden the tonal range thereby giving it more depth, but be careful not to overdo it and clip shadows or highlights. The Curves tool has a similar effect but gives you more control, allowing you to adjust any point on the tonal spectrum. These two devices are probably the most important (and sometimes the only required) steps in the editing process.

Sharpening will not fix an out of focus image, but it can help to clarify detail. There are a whole host of methods, but oversharpening can create halos around your subject and create an unnatural effect. Often sharpening only a selected area is preferable, the eyes being an obvious example.

Cropping can either be used to create a more interesting composition by eliminating elements of the picture, or to magnify your subject. In both scenarios your cropped image will contain fewer pixels (reducing the potential printing size) unless you tell the computer to maintain the original pixel count by 'resampling'. This effectively creates extra pixels by 'guessing' their colour. Although the deterioration in image quality will become more apparent the greater the crop, resampling works surprisingly well.

Taking the Next Step

It is very difficult to forge a professional career solely from wildlife photography, but with persistence it is possible to make money from your photographs. Try entering competitions or submitting images to magazines (writing an article to go with your photographs will greatly improve your prospects). If you are serious, then you will need to start filing your images. Use keywords to define the species and location so that you can easily find a specific photo when required. Most importantly, be disciplined about deleting - a photograph that is not sharp should almost always be discarded, irrespective of the subject. Always back up your files in at least one place and keep your RAW originals as you may need them for competitions or if you decide to re-edit at a later date.

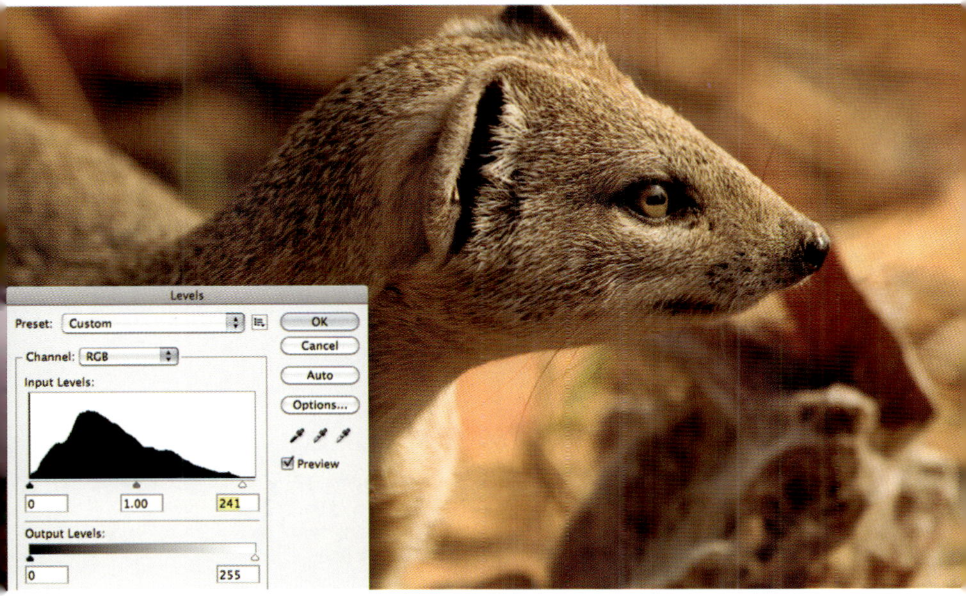

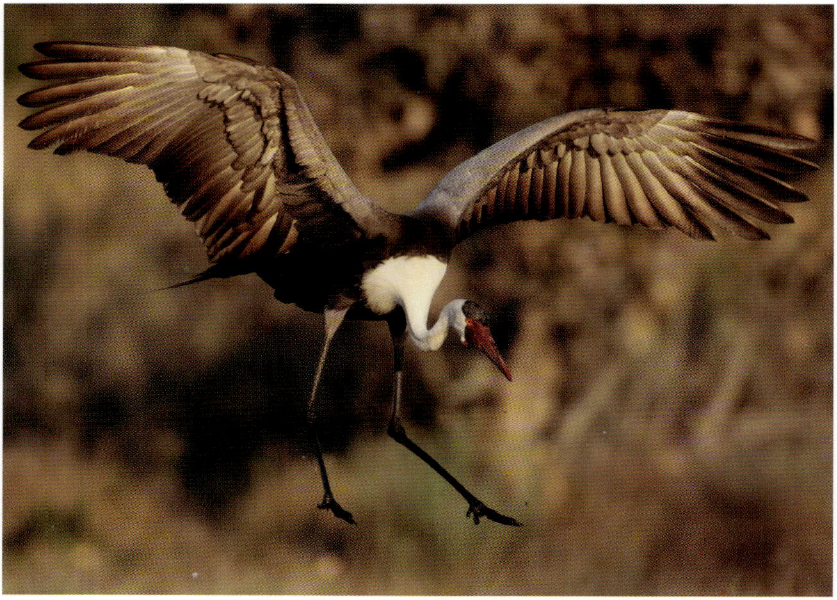

▲ ***Wattled Crane, Okavango Delta. DSLR, 500mm Lens, f/4 @ 1/1250, ISO 200. SS***
IUCN Red List status: Vulnerable. Population trend: decreasing.

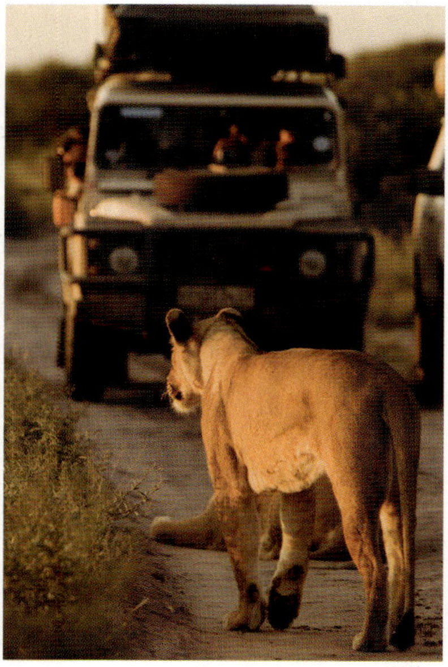

◀ ***Lioness & Tourists, Central Kalahari Game Reserve. DSLR, 100-400mm Lens, f/5.6 @ 1/320, ISO 400. JG***
IUCN Red List status: Vulnerable.
Population trend: decreasing.
World human population estimate (2010): 6,815,100,000 (source: United Nations).

▶ ***African Wild Dog, Okavango Delta. DSLR, 100-400mm Lens, f/9 @ 1/100, ISO 200. SS***
IUCN Red List status: Endangered. Population trend: decreasing.

Ethics of Wildlife Photography
Stepping Lightly

Travelling on safari will certainly mean that you will have an impact on the environment in some way. No wildlife image is worth taking if it means that you will disturb the animal's natural behaviour. Please take the utmost care to be respectful to both the wildlife and the people who work to protect the wilderness.

The Parks and Game Reserves have a set of rules that should be carefully read through and adhered to. Show consideration for your fellow travellers by being thoughtful of their view at a sighting and keep talking and movement to an absolute minimum.

Botswana also has many active research projects and there may be times when you will encounter researchers in the bush. Their vehicles are clearly marked and should not be followed. If you see a collared animal, be aware that it is contributing to the understanding and conservation of these animals. Common sense should prevail so as to maximise the enjoyment of your stay in Botswana.

For more information on endangered species visit:
www.iucnredlist.org & www.birdlifebotswana.org.bw

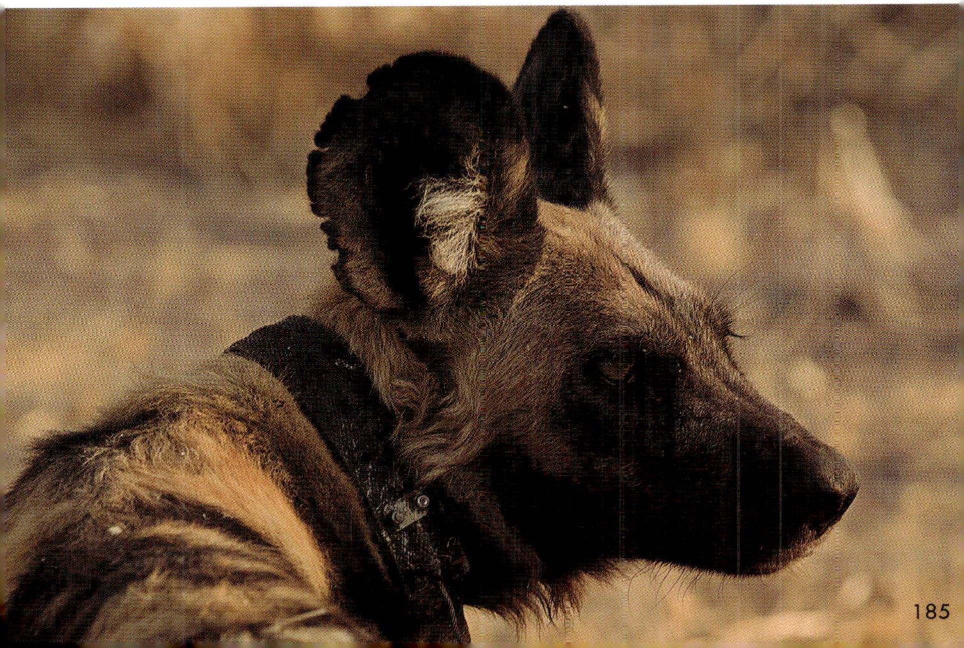

GLOSSARY

AI Servo - See Continuous focus
Aperture - The hole in the lens through which light passes before it hits the camera sensor, denoted by a f-number.
Aperture Priority Automatic Exposure - The photographer selects the aperture and the camera calculates the appropriate shutter speed to expose correctly.
AEB (Auto Exposure Bracketing) - Takes a series of images at different exposures.

Buffer - Temporary storage space in a digital camera where a sequence of shots taken in rapid succession can be held before transfer to a memory card.

Centre-circle metering - See Partial metering
Centre-weighted metering - Averaging the metering across the scene but giving more weight to the objects in the centre of the viewfinder.
Clipping - Losing detail in the lightest or darkest areas of your image due to incorrect exposure or processing.
Continuous drive mode - A mode where the camera takes repeated exposures while the shutter button is depressed.
Continuous focus - A mode where the camera continually refocuses on the focal point, eliminating the option to focus-lock and recompose.

Depth of field - The distance in front of and behind the point of focus in a photograph in which the objects remain in acceptably sharp focus.
DSLR (Digital Single Lens Reflex) - A camera where you look through the lens and the viewfinder gives an accurate representation of focus and composition.

Evaluative metering - A default metering system, by which the camera uses a database to determine how to meter the scene.
Exposure - The quantity of light reaching the camera sensor as determined by shutter speed and lens aperture.
Exposure compensation - Instructing the camera to adjust the aperture or shutter speed to lighten or darken the image by a specified amount.
Exposure lock - Locking the exposure, allowing you to recompose the image without any subsequent changes to aperture or shutter speed.
Extender - A lens attachment used to increase the focal length.

Fill-in flash - Using flash to 'fill-in' shadows during daylight.
Flash exposure compensation - Instructing the camera to increase or decrease the brightness of the flash fired overriding the internal metering.
Focal length - The distance between the optical centre of the lens and the focal point. It is used to describe the magnification of the lens.
Focal plane - The plane perpendicular to the axis of the lens passing through the focal point. Effectively contains all the points that are in focus.

Focal point - The precise point of focus in a photograph.
Focus lock - Locking the focus on a subject, allowing you to recompose the image before taking the picture.

Histogram - A graph displaying the distribution of tones in an image.

ISO (International Standards Organisation) - Refers to the sensitivity of film or the sensor to light. A higher ISO produces a correct exposure with less light.

Lens hood - A device used to block the light to prevent glare and lens flare.

Manual Exposure - The photographer selects both aperture and shutter speed, using the in-built light meter to ensure correct exposure.
Matrix metering - See Evaluative metering
Metering - The method by which the camera calculates the exposure of a scene.

Panning - Tracking the subject during exposure using a slow shutter speed to create a blurred, streaked background but maintaining a sharp subject.
Partial/Centre-circle metering - Similar to spot metering, but using a slightly larger area.
Pattern metering - See Evaluative metering
Polarising filter - Reduces the amount of light entering the lens, saturating blues and greens, and reducing reflections.
Prime lens - A lens with a fixed focal length.
Program Automatic Exposure - The camera selects both aperture and shutter speed to ensure correct exposure.

RAW - This is the maximum file size available on your camera based on the number of pixels. The file acts as a "negative" and records all the shooting information.
Remote switch - A wireless or cabled device allowing you to take a picture without having to press the shutter button, useful for long exposures.

Shutter Priority Automatic Exposure - The photographer selects the shutter speed and the camera calculates the appropriate aperture to ensure correct exposure.
Shutter speed - The length of time the shutter is open during exposure.
Spot metering - Metering on a small area at the centre of the viewfinder.

TTL - A metering system that evaluates exposure from the light passing Through The Lens. For external flashes, this effectively automates flash exposures.

White balance - A digital control used to calibrate colours under unnatural lighting.

Zoom lens - A lens with a variable focal length.

INDEX

About the Authors

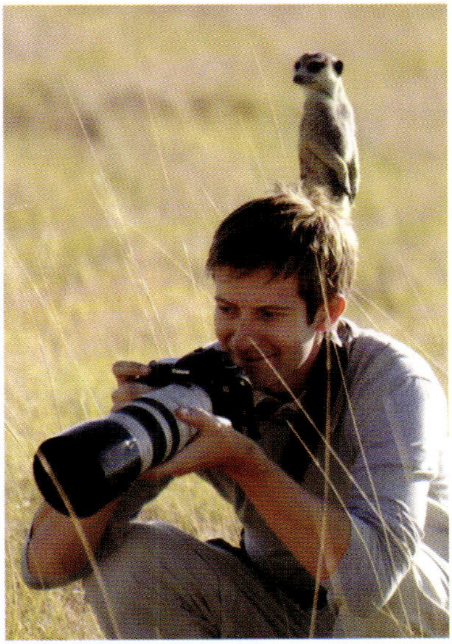

▲ ***James Gifford***

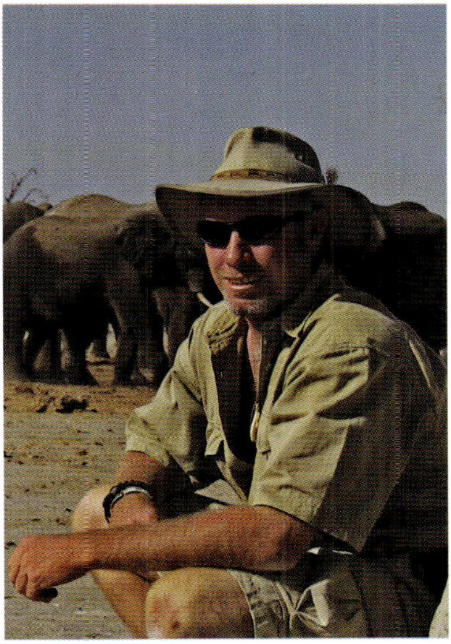

▲ ***Steven Stockhall***

James was brought up in the UK and now lives in Maun. Having moved to Botswana, he initially worked in the safari industry before devoting himself to photography and writing full-time. His articles and photographs have appeared in numerous magazines including CNN Traveller, Africa Geographic and Travel Africa. He recently advanced to the semi-finals of the 2010 Africa Photographic Awards.
www.jamesgifford.co.uk

Steven was born in Zimbabwe and raised in Cape Town, South Africa. With numerous years of experience in Botswana working as a photographic guide, he aims to highlight the plight of diminishing wildlife around the world through photography. He is also the author of the book "Earth|Ark Botswana - a Photographic Safari through northern Botswana" and contributes regularly to Air Botswana's inflight magazine - Peolwane - and Discover Botswana.
www.earthark botswana.com

Special thanks to Rebecca Lee for her fastidious proof reading, Dr. Sallie Burrough for contributing a short history of Botswana and to Dino for her enthusiasm, support and fine food.

This book is about sharing both the natural world and the joy of photography with people.

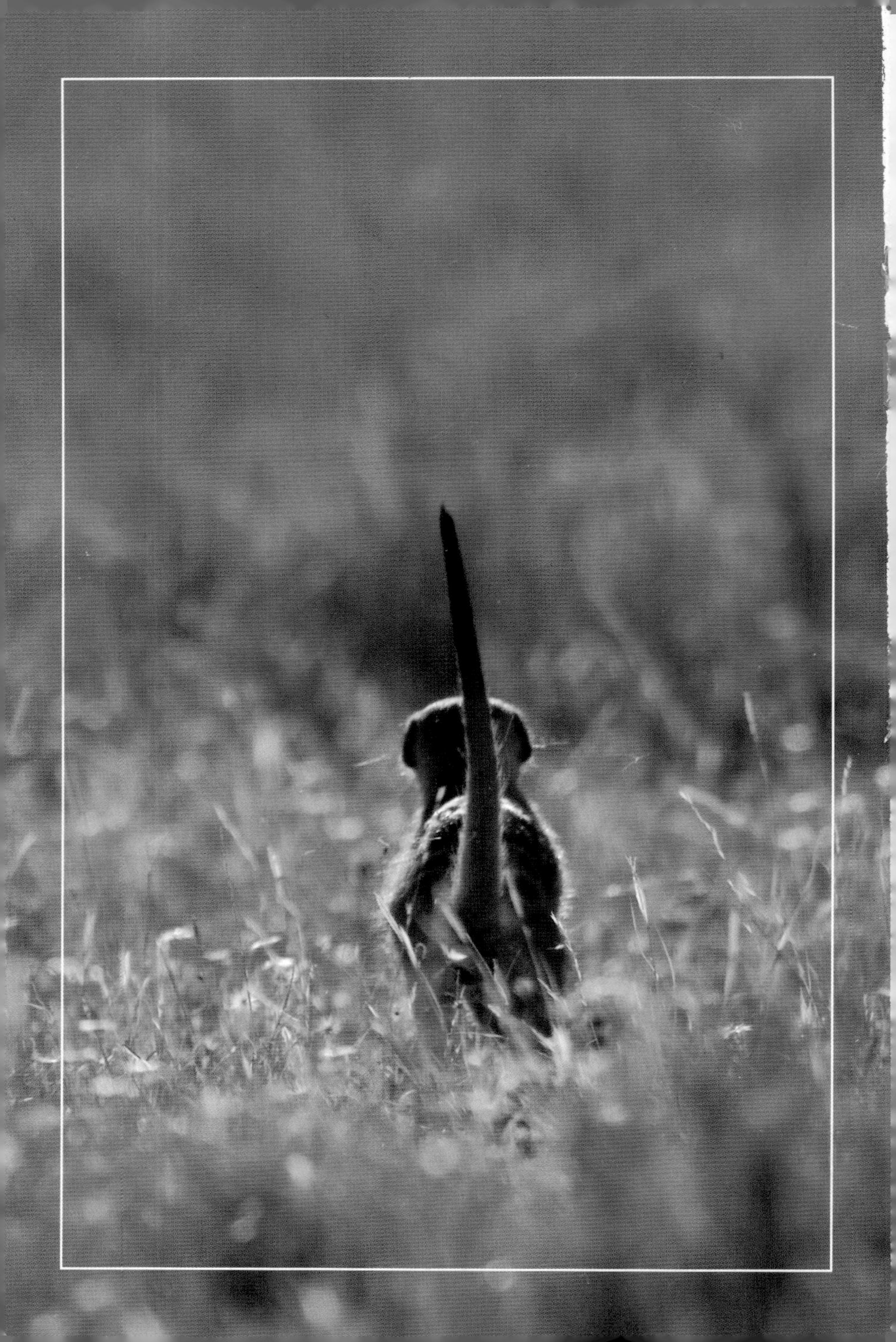